James Baldwin to Kenneth Clark, 1963

"It is entirely up to the American people whether or not they are going to face and deal with and embrace the stranger whom they maligned so long. What white people have to do is try to find out in their own hearts why it was necessary to have a nigger in the first place."

BLACK AMERICA

Accommodation and Confrontation in the Twentieth Century

Edited with an Introduction by Richard Resh

University of Missouri, St. Louis

D. C. Heath and Company

A Division of Raytheon Education Company, Lexington, Massachusetts

For Linda

Library of Congress Card Number: 69—119318

Preface

This volume grew out of my preparations for a course in black history. Unlike other books of readings, this one does not cover the entire field of Negro history. Rather, it is limited to the twentieth-century period in the belief that many undergraduates are coming to prefer greater depth in their reading. Finally, I have included both primary and secondary sources to demonstrate that Negro history is one of the richest areas of the American past for both student and teacher.

The book would not have been possible without the cooperation of the library staffs at Washington University, the State Historical Society of Wisconsin, and the University of Missouri, St. Louis. Thanks are also due to Mr. Regan Kenyon for his frequent and helpful assistance.

Richard W. Resh
University of Missouri-St. Louis

CONTENTS

1 PROGRESSIVISM, SELF-HELP, AND WORLD WAR I

2 THE TWENTIES AND THE NEW NEGRO

3 DEPRESSION, NEW DEAL, AND WORLD WAR II

4 THE MODERN PERIOD: FROM SIT-IN TO SOUL

Acknowledgment is gratefully made to the following photographers for illustrations appearing in this volume: page x Nicholas Welsh; page 40 Anna Kaufman; page 59 Anna Kaufman; page 88 Dwayne Bey; page 119 Eileen Ahrenholz; page 127 Anna Kaufman; page 154 Nicholas Welsh; page 196 Dwayne Bey; page 243 Nicholas Welsh.

BLACK AMERICA

Introduction

In the spring of 1847, while visiting England, Frederick Douglass spoke fervently about the nation which had enslaved so many of his fellow blacks. "The fact is, the whole system—the whole network of American Society—in one great falsehood."[1] Douglass' words reverberated into the twentieth century as many Negroes continued to indict a society which had freed them in name only. For such contemporary critics as James Baldwin and Stokeley Carmichael, American society and its institutions have not only failed but may not be worth saving. The white man's historical record, they charge, consists of evasions, postponements, and brutal repressions. The black man must use his own devices—however apocalypical—to confront America with its failure to solve the racial problem. As Douglass warned in 1857: "Those who enslave, rob, and torment their cooks, may well expect to find death in their dinner-pots."[2]

Voices of accommodation have challenged the advocates of confrontation. Beginning with the teachings of Booker T. Washington through the exhortations of Dr. Martin Luther King, Jr., many American Negroes have insisted upon the possibility of racial progress. There has been, to be sure, an urgency in their voices; they feared a racial holocaust. But basically their views were those of optimistic men who believed that persistent action within the power structure would secure meaningful gains for the Negro. Typical of this faith were the remarks of Washington as he addressed the National Education Association in St. Louis in 1904: "There should be no disguising the fact that these are anxious days of my race, and serious effort is ahead; but never for a moment do I doubt our ultimate triumph. Freedom can never be given. It must be purchased."[3]

Washington committed himself to the concept of self-help. The black man must begin his struggle at the bottom of the economic ladder and slowly—always with white guidance—bring himself up. Not all Negroes approved of this concept. W. E. B. DuBois, the brilliant sociologist, suggested in *The Souls of Black Folk* (1903) that Washing-

[1] From "Report of Proceedings at the Soiree Given to Frederick Douglass, London Tavern, March 30, 1847" in Benjamin Quarles, ed., *Frederick Douglass* (Prentice-Hall, 1968), 35.

[2] From "Two Speeches by Frederick Douglass . . . On The Dred Scott Decision" in *ibid.,* 66.

[3] "Address Delivered at the Forty-Third Annual Meeting of the National Educational Association Held At St. Louis, Missouri . . . 1904" in E. Davidson Washington, ed., *Selected Speeches of Booker T. Washington* (Doubleday, Doran and Co., 1932), 144.

ton's emphasis upon thrift, patience, and industrial training neglected the larger issues of the right to vote, civic equality, and the education of youth according to ability. For the most part, however, the majority of Negro leaders shared the Tuskegee president's optimism, and the founding of three important organizations in the early years of the twentieth century was evidence that many believed in the possibility and desirability of progress through accommodation.

The first sign of this reform optimism appeared in 1906 with the creation of the Committee for Improving the Industrial Condition of the Negro in New York. The purpose of CIINC was to broaden employment opportunities for the city's Negroes. Although the organization drew heavily upon the ranks of city Progressive leaders, the major impetus came from its founder, Dr. William Lewis Bulkley, the first Negro principal in the New York City school system. Born into slavery in South Carolina, Bulkley earned a doctorate in ancient languages and literature from Syracuse University and came to support DuBois' demand for full Negro equality. At the same time, he emphasized the importance of technical training for Negro youth and established an employment bureau in the CIINC to locate and help create jobs. In 1911 the organization merged with two other groups to form the National League on Urban Conditions Among Negroes, better known as the National Urban League.

The second important Negro organization of the twentieth century, the Urban League illustrated the importance of what Alexis de Tocqueville called voluntary associations. With branches in major urban areas, the League assisted the migrant Negro, often from the South, to adjust to an industrial, urban environment by directing him to jobs and lodging. It also developed a program for the training of youth for social work and established fellowships to support students while studying at the School of Philanthropy in New York. "The Urban League," declared Executive Secretary Eugene K. Jones in 1923, "feels that the Negro, as a group, must be brought up to a higher social plane so that he can accept his rightful place in society as his opportunities come. His leaders must be trained and given a chance to gain wider experience with his fellows." The League's motto was "Not Alms, but Opportunity," and its official journal became known as *Opportunity* and was edited by Charles S. Johnson, director of the League's Department of Research and Investigations.

The National Association for the Advancement of Colored People became the third important voice of Negro accommodation in the early years of the twentieth century. It grew out of the impatience of younger Negroes with the older leadership and out of a widespread revulsion against lynchings, whose numbers had remained alarmingly high since the late nineteenth century. In 1905, DuBois and a group of like minded dissidents met in Niagara Falls, Canada, to draw up a crisply worded platform which blamed white America for the nation's racial problems. The Niagara Movement met again in such symbolic places as Harper's Ferry, Boston, and Oberlin, and although split by factionalism it provided a base of support for a new organization demanding fuller citizenship for the Negro.

Lynch law—which the dissidents pointed to as the most savage example of racism—continued to claim black lives even while Washington insisted that Negroes did not want social equality. In the decade after 1889, the average number of lynchings per year was 187.5; in the following decade, 92.5. But the decline was hardly cause for optimism. The proportion of lynchings taking place in the South increased from 82 percent to 92 percent in the two decades. And the proportion of white victims declined from 32.4 percent to 11.4 percent.[4] But lynching, while becoming increasingly a Southern and racial phenomenon, was not limited to one section of the country. In Springfield, Illinois, the home of Abraham Lincoln, a race riot in August, 1908, claimed the lives of two Negroes and four white men. The alleged leaders of the mob went unpunished, but for some white Progressives the time had come for remedial action.

The bulk of Progressives were either hostile or indifferent to the Negro. Neither Theodore Roosevelt's *The New Nationalism* (1910) or Woodrow Wilson's *The New Freedom* (1913), both collections of major campaign speeches, mentioned the Negro. But the Springfield riot did arouse the sensibilities of reformers like Mary White Ovington, a social worker, and Oswald Garrison Villard, publisher of the New York *Evening Post*. In 1909, following a call by Villard, a National Negro Conference was held in New York which led to the formation in the following months of the National Association for the Advancement of Colored People. Although most of the members of the Niagara Movement joined the NAACP, all the chief officials were at first white. The exception was DuBois, who became director of publicity and editor of the group's journal, the *Crisis,* whose first issue appeared in November, 1910. By 1914 the Association had 6000 members in fifty branches, and DuBois labeled it "the new abolition society."[5]

The CIINC, the Urban League, and the NAACP somewhat eased the transition to urban life. Ever since the 1880's, demographers had noted a change in the direction and volume of Negro migration. The movement was clearly from the South to northern cities, and the impetus lay in the promise of economic prosperity. Many firms sent recruiters to southern areas and paid transportation costs of those

[4] The figures are from C. Vann Woodward, *Origins of the New South* (Louisiana State University Press, 1951), 351–352.

[5] *Crisis,* VII (December, 1913), 88.

who moved to New York, Philadelphia, and Chicago. From 1910 to 1920, over half a million Negroes left the South for northern areas, and for many of the young and unskilled the adjustment would be a hard one. The Reverend Adam Clayton Powell, Sr., recognized this fact and in 1923 urged young migrants to take advantage of the informal educational facilities offered by his Abyssinian Baptist Church in Harlem.

World War I increased Negro migration to the cities and added to his problems. War industries suffered from a lack of workers because of high draft calls and the cessation of European immigration. For the first time, many Negroes found full time employment. The war seemed to offer other opportunities for achievement: the black man would rally to President Woodrow Wilson's cause and prove that colored citizens were Americans in every sense of the word. After some doubts, DuBois used his influence in the editorial pages of the *Crisis* to support America's entry into the conflict in his famous editorial entitled "Close Ranks." Of over two million Negroes who registered under the Selective Service Act, 367,000 were called into service. Although they served with distinction in many cases, they did so in segregated units and were frequently the objects of villification and derision from their white comrades.

The home front was hardly more charitable. On July 2, 1917, a race riot in East St. Louis claimed the lives of nearly two hundred Negroes and destroyed almost half a million dollars worth of property. Returning Negro soldiers in 1919 encountered a revival of the Ku Klux Klan, the scarcity of jobs due to demobilization, and a series of over twenty brutal race riots that ranged from Longview, Texas, to Washington, D.C. Perhaps most significant was the riot in Chicago involving the deaths of twenty-three Negroes and fifteen whites. Many observers noted a ready willingness on the part of blacks to retaliate when attacked, and a Negro editor in New York bade good-by to Uncle Tom. "The Old Negro and his futile methods must go. . . . His abject crawling and pleading have availed the Cause nothing. . . . The New Negro now takes the helm."[6]

The statement reflected more than melodrama. It was a dramatic assertion on the part of many colored Americans that they viewed their race with pride, not apology. From the early 1920's through the mid-1930's, Negro writers, artists, and musicians proclaimed that their history and culture held vital, pulsating themes worthy of exploitation. For many intellectuals the center of this creative ferment was Harlem. As James Weldon Johnson wrote in 1925: "In the make-up of New York, Harlem is not merely a Negro colony or community, it is a city within a city, the greatest Negro city in the world.

[6] Robert T. Kerlin, ed., *The Voice of the Negro,* 1919 (E. P. Dutton, 1920), 25.

. . . There is nothing just like it in any city in the country. . . ."[7] Some of the literature of the Harlem Renaissance failed to rise above a crude level of social protest. But much of it—especially the work of Claude McKay and Langston Hughes—reflected considerable artistic detachment.

The Great Depression dissipated much of the optimism of the Harlem Renaissance. Once again the Negro found himself extremely vulnerable. "The reason why the Depression didn't have the impact on the Negroes that it had on the whites," remarked the acerbic George S. Schuyler, "was that the Negro had been in the Depression all the time."[8] With the recovery of white America as its first priority, the New Deal was not overly concerned with the Negro. The National Recovery Administration provided for a minimum wage scale and the abolition of child labor under the age of eighteen, but few Negroes were represented at code hearings. In addition, government cost of living differentials discriminated against the unskilled groups in which most blacks were to be found. The Agricultural Adjustment Administration paid out a great deal in subsidies, but little of it went into the black tenant farmer's pocket. Similarly, many Negroes were not covered under the Social Security Act.

Despite these considerable omissions, Negroes made some gains under the New Deal. For the first time the federal government admitted qualified Negroes in larger numbers into various governmental departments. Robert L. Vann, editor of the influential *Pittsburgh Courier,* served as Special Assistant to the Attorney General, while William H. Hastie, Dean of the Howard University Law School, became Assistant Solicitor in the Department of the Interior, where he was joined for a time by Robert C. Weaver. The founder and president of Bethune-Cookman College, Mrs. Mary McLeod Bethune, was active as the Director of the Division of Negro Affairs of the National Youth Administration. Altogether the NYA enrolled 64,000 young blacks in the student-work program. The agency with the best record of enrolling Negroes was the Civilian Conservation Corps, which during its existence from 1933–1942 placed some 200,000 youths in segregated camps established by the agency.[9]

World War II eased the country out of the Depression but once again the Negro found his position a decidedly inferior one. Few could question his patriotism. "From 1619 to the present day," editorialized the *Pittsburgh Courier* on December 13, 1941, "we've worked to make America ours. . . . And now that OUR country is at war, for-

[7] James Weldon Johnson, "Harlem: The Cultural Capital," in Alain Locke, ed., *The New Negro: An Interpretation* (Albert and Charles Boni, 1925), 301–302.

[8] Quoted in Gilbert Osofsky, *Harlem: The Making of a Ghetto* (Harper and Row, 1963), 149.

[9] The figures are from John Hope Franklin, *From Slavery to Freedom* (Alfred Knopf, 1967), 536.

gotten are the differences under which we have labored. Buried deep in the recesses of our minds are the injustices to which we have been subjected." But injustices continued in the form of Jim Crow regiments and harassments from white officers. The popular image of the Negro serviceman was one of a jitterbugging and crapshooting individual who was unreliable in combat. On the home front, race riots broke out in 1943 in Harlem and Detroit. A young lawyer for the NAACP, Thurgood Marshall, investigated the Detroit riot and concluded that the police contributed to the violence by encouraging the white mob and by refusing to protect Negro citizens and their property. In the future, others would repeat the charge that the police bear a share of the blame for civil disorders.

The postwar years intensified the American Negro's demand for full equality. Having won the battle over military segregation in 1947, leaders turned to the problem of education and voting. In 1954 the Supreme Court struck down the principle of separate but equal school facilities. But the deep South remained intransigent and thwarted integration through violence and evasions. In 1957 Congress passed a civil rights act—the first since 1875—which authorized the federal government to bring civil suit in instances where any person was denied or threatened in his right to vote. The bill also created a U.S. Commission on Civil Rights, an agency empowered to investigate allegations of the denial of the right to vote. The real revolution in the Negro's thrust for equality would not come until the 1960's and it would leave the nation, black and white, confused and bitter.

It is always difficult to date the origins of a revolution, and what has been called The Negro Revolution is no exception. Certainly the actions of four students from the Negro Agricultural and Technical College in Greensboro, North Carolina, on February 1, 1960, introduced a new word into the public vocabulary. The students entered a white-owned variety store, sat down at the lunch counter and ordered coffee, and when refused service remained seated until the store closed. Throughout the early sixties, the sit-in became a dramatic weapon in the struggle for equal accommodations. Southern lunch counters began to serve their customers on an integrated basis, but the violence which accompanied the victory showed just how difficult the coming struggle would become.

Sit-ins were accompanied by Freedom Riders. In May, 1961, the Congress of Racial Equality—founded by James Farmer in 1942—sent a young group of activists into the deep South to test the legality of segregation in interstate transportation. Brutally attacked by a mob in Montgomery while the police looked on, the Freedom Riders finally secured the protection of federal officers somewhat reluctantly dispatched by Attorney General Robert Kennedy. Finally, the Interstate

Commerce Commission ruled that passengers on interstate carriers must be seated without regard to race. Another small victory had been won.

Many of the activists in the 1960's were new to the civil rights movement. They were young and tough. To them habitual patience was a vice, not a virtue; they had a disrespect for authority and proudly bore the title of agitator. Their chief weapon, however, was civil disobedience. Many of these young people—"the new abolitionists" as they came to be called—found a home in the Student Non-Violent Coordinating Committee, an organization founded to aid the southern Negro in his struggle to gain the vote. Despite the Civil Rights Acts of 1957, 1960, and 1964, the Commission on Civil Rights found that Negroes insisting upon exercising their voting rights "continue to be harassed,shot at, and subjected to economic reprisals."[10]

In large part, SNCC was a student revolution, perhaps the first of its kind in American history. Its biracial membership drew from Negro colleges in the South, the Ivy League universities, large state universities, and from scores of lesser known institutions. Student apathy of the 1950's had changed to a feeling of commitment in the 1960's. The Negro's cause helped politicize a generation of young whites, which was a reversal from previous reform movements in which whites and the goals of the white community had played the dominant role.

SNCC, in its earlier stages at least, believed in working with the white community, but the existence of other organizations that do not believe in cooperation worry many Americans. Black nationalists question whether Negroes really want or should want integration. The most vocal exponents of this view include Elijah Muhammad and the late Malcolm X, who have insisted that the white man's duplicity makes it imperative that the blacks look to themselves for salvation. The white man is anathema because through oppression and discrimination he taught the black man to despise himself. Self-hatred, the black nationalists declare, produces the high incidence of crime, alcoholism, and drug addiction among the Negro community. It creates apathy and helps keep the colored man poor and ignorant. And worst of all, self-hatred leads to the idealization of everything white and the deprecation of everything black. The "white devil," in short, has created the "nigger."

Black muslims argue that separation is the answer. Their interpretations of Mohammedism call for highly disciplined, self-sacrificing followers to patronize muslim-owned establishments and to purge

[10] U.S. Commission on Civil Rights, *Political Participation: A Study of the Participation by Negroes in the Electoral and Political Process in 10 Southern States Since Passage of the Voting Rights Act of 1965* (Government Printing Office, 1968), 115.

themselves of white values and institutions. Nonetheless, muslim grocery stores offer "Shabazz Saving Stamps" and their newspapers carry advice-to-the-love-lorn columns, suggesting that white culture has a tenacious way of hanging on. The appeal of separatism, however, is not limited to the muslims. It is recently found in the slogan of Black Power.

In 1966, the new chairman of SNCC, Stokeley Carmichael, insisted that Negroes must think in terms of "Black Power" to combat the repressive forces of "white power." Carmichael and his followers have not merely advocated the election of black politicians to office; city hall machines could too easily corrupt them. Black Power means that Negroes must have an effective share in the *total* power—especially economic—of society, and this means black control of ghetto schools, businesses, and political machines. To charges that such views represent racism in reverse, Carmichael replies: "The black people of this country have not lynched whites, bombed their churches, murdered their children, and manipulated laws and institutions to maintain oppression."[11]

The Negro Revolution of the 1960's is characterized by growing militancy and youth. Moreover, it has become apparent that the problem of race relations is not limited to the South. While important, the right to be served at a lunch counter and the right to vote have not brought full equality to the Negro. The "long, hot summer" of 1964 demonstrated that the northern ghetto could and would violently explode. In mid-July, the killing of a Negro teenager by an off-duty policeman in New York city led to rioting and looting in Harlem and Bedford-Stuyvesant. Similar outbreaks occurred in Jersey City, Philadelphia, and Chicago, and observers noted that large numbers of unemployed youths were conspicuous among the rioters.

There was more of the same the following summer. The Watts area of Los Angeles erupted after the arrest of a young Negro charged with reckless driving. Cries of "Burn, Whitey, Burn" were heard at the height of the violence which claimed 34 lives and millions of dollars worth of property damage. With depressing regularity, the disorders continued, and from the white community there came cries of "Law and Order." In a two-week period of July, 1967, Newark and then Detroit ignited into scenes of extraordinary violence. The Presidential Commission charged with investigating the causes for the riots reported that "Our nation is moving toward two societies, one black, one white—separate and unequal" and called for "the realization of common opportunities for all within a single society."[12]

[11] Stokeley Carmichael and Charles V. Hamilton, *Black Power: The Politics of Liberation in America* (Vintage Edition, 1967), 47.

[12] *Report of the National Advisory Commission on Civil Disorders* (Bantam Edition, 1968), 1.

A CBS television poll in September, 1968, suggests that the majority of Negroes interviewed reject separatism and violence. Roy Wilkins of the NAACP and Whitney Young of the Urban League command the allegiance of many black Americans. Missing from the poll was the name of Dr. Martin Luther King, Jr., the victim of an assassin's bullet in April, 1968. Dr. King enjoyed his greatest successes in the 1950's and early 1960's. In Montgomery and Selma he dramatized the Negro's cause in a poignant way, and his doctrine of nonviolence was a comfort to white Americans. But his death may have marked the passing of an era: for many, nonviolence is an impotent weapon in a violent society. "People are trapped in history," novelist James Baldwin once observed, "and history is trapped in them."[13] If Baldwin's remark is correct, then King's dream will become a nightmare for all Americans—white and black.

[13] James Baldwin, *Notes of a Native Son* (Bantam Edition, 1964), 138.

1

Progressivism, Self-Help, And World War I

Gilbert Osofsky □ Progressivism and the Negro: New York, 1900–1915

In the last few years, younger scholars have examined Negro history in terms of institutions and their impact upon the black community. Professor Gilbert Osofsky, of the University of Illinois at Chicago, has explored the structure of the New York Negro community in *Harlem: The Making of A Ghetto*. In this essay, he describes the attempts of New York Negroes and Progressives to organize the black community into agencies of self-help.

From the 1890s through the First World War there was a significant migration of southern Negroes to northern cities. It was the migration of Negroes in these years, in fact, which laid the foundation for the development of large, segregated Negro communities in New York City, Chicago and Philadelphia. As the Negro populations of these areas increased rapidly, the dominant reaction of the majority of white Northerners was one of heightened racial hostility. There was an overall hardening in patterns of social and residential segregation, and occasional outbreaks of racial violence, in every city to which Negroes came in large numbers. "One of the striking developments of very recent years," wrote one northern commentator in 1906, "is the recrudescence of prejudice against people of African descent. . . ."

The emergence of racial violence and antagonism, and the increas-

From Gilbert Osofsky, "Progressivism and the Negro: New York, 1900–1915," *American Quarterly*, Vol. XVI, No. 2, part 1 (Summer 1964), pp. 153–168.

ing number of varied social problems brought on by Negro migration, created a need for reform in the North in the early twentieth century. The movement for social and economic reform in northern cities, a vital part of the national Progressive movement, was deeply concerned with the welfare of the Negro people. In the years preceding World War I there was a revitalization of interest in Negro life among Progressives in every major northern city. These reformers, were, in the words of a Negro businessman, the "doers" not the "talkers" of American society.

The white people involved in this movement were primarily social workers and urban reformers who had established settlement houses or tried in other ways to improve living conditions in the industrial and tenement-house areas of northern cities. They also established settlement houses for Negroes in the North—many of them branches of parent organizations founded for immigrants in the 1890s. In the first decade of the twentieth century Progressives organized the Frederick Douglass Center in Chicago, the Robert Gould Shaw House in Boston, the Eighth Ward Settlement in Philadelphia, the Stillman House and two Lincoln Settlements in New York. Frances Bartholomew, Carl Kelsey and R. R. Wright Jr., in Philadelphia; Isabel Eaton in Boston; Celia Parker Woolley, Sophinisba Breckinridge and Louise DeKoven Bowen in Chicago; Mary White Ovington, Victoria Earle Matthews and William Lewis Bulkley in New York City were all actively engaged in social work among Negroes. Perceptive studies of Negro society were undertaken as well in these years. In typical Progressive fashion, volumes of facts and statistics were gathered in order to learn how best to improve living conditions. "We must not forget," wrote W. E. B. DuBois in 1903, "that most Americans answer all queries regarding the Negro a *priori,* and that the least that human courtesy can do is to listen to evidence." Between 1899 and 1915 such works as DuBois' *Philadelphia Negro* (1899), Ray Stannard Baker's *Following the Color Line* (1908), R. R. Wright Jr.'s *The Negro in Pennsylvania* (1908), Mary White Ovington's *Half A Man: The Status of the Negro in New York* (1911), George Edmund Haynes' *The Negro at Work in New York City* (1912), Louise DeKoven Bowen's *The Colored People of Chicago* (1913), Frank U. Quillin's *The Color Line in Ohio* (1913), William A. Crossland's *Industrial Conditions Among Negroes in St. Louis* (1914), John Daniel's *In Freedom's Birthplace: A History of the Boston Negro* (1914) and Frances Blascoer's *Colored School Children in New York* (1915) were published. Numerous articles on Negro life also appeared in contemporary periodicals. In 1909–11 the first national Negro defense and improvement societies were founded —the NAACP and the National League on Urban Conditions Among Negroes. Both were founded in New York City. The general movement to improve the status of the Negro in the North in the first decade of the twentieth century was led by persons, Negro and white, who responded in a positive manner to the same problems that produced increased alienation among the majority of Northerners.

Concern for the welfare of Negroes among the white people of New York City had traditionally been associated with religious groups, and more particularly with the Society of Friends. Quakers were leading abolitionists in New York and played an important part in founding free schools for Negro children. After the Civil War, the only white organization that continued its works among the city's Negroes was the New York Colored Mission. There were a few Negro churches in these years, however, that gave some assistance "to needy persons who find themselves in the great city without a home for a few days."

The "Friends' Mission," as some contemporaries called it (more vituperative observers named it the "Nigger school"), was founded primarily as a religious institution which did missionary work among Negroes and offered them "Christian Fellowship." It distributed religious tracts, temperance literature and Bibles by the thousands to New York's Negro population. Prior to its incorporation in 1871, the society had been called the "African Sabbath School Association." When it was incorporated it conceived of its task basically as a religious one: "To conduct in the City of New York a Sabbath School for Religious Instruction," and hold "Social, Religious Meetings." Whatever practical assistance the organization would give Negroes was to be secondary to its religious obligation. The City Mission and Tract Society contributed enough money to the Colored Mission to permit it to purchase a building of its own in the Tenderloin, the midtown area of Manhattan in which the majority of the city's Negroes then lived. "Inasmuch as ye have done it unto one of the least of these my brethren, ye have done it unto me," was the motto of the organization.

In reality, however, as the Negro population of Manhattan increased, slightly in the 1870s and 1880s, more rapidly in the 1890s, the Colored Mission was slowly transformed into a social service agency. It conducted an employment bureau, provided temporary housing and inexpensive meals for migrants (a "Sunday bowl of soup and slice of bread"), opened a small "infant school" which cared for and fed Negro children for five cents a day, and bought glasses for Negroes who wanted to learn how to read (most wished to read the Bible). Destitution was so widespread in the depression winter of 1893–94 that the Colored Mission distributed tons of coal and barrels of food to Negro families—flour, corn meal, oatmeal, hominy, rice, bread, beans, pork, milk. "The records of those months are so sad that one shrinks from recurring to them," wrote the society's missionary. "No fire, no food, dispossession impending, illness, death . . . confronted us." Between the Civil War and the 1890s, with this one modest exception, there were no organizations in New York City concerned with the welfare of Negroes. By 1915 there were more than a dozen.

Increasing interest in Negro life emerged in the 1890s and the first decade of the twentieth century among white and Negro reformers. The movement was widespread and involved some people who disagreed with one another on the overall methods of improving the position of the Negro in American society. Some were avid supporters of the gradualism of Booker T. Washington, others were followers of W. E. B. DuBois. Whatever theoretic differences may have existed among them, there was basic agreement on the need for solid, practical reforms which would immediately improve the generally harsh lives of Negroes in the city. Reformers were primarily concerned with finding jobs and decent homes for Negro migrants, opening playgrounds for Negro children, breaking down the color barrier in employment opportunities, improving health and sanitary conditions in the Tenderloin, San Juan Hill and Harlem (two other areas of Negro concentration), protecting Negro domestics from the exploitation of employment agents.

The first organization that this new spirit of social welfare produced was the White Rose Industrial Association. The "White Rose Working Girls' Home" (as the sign which hung over its door read) was founded in 1897. Its organizer was a Negro, Mrs. Victoria Earle Matthews.

Mrs. Matthews was the youngest daughter of a Georgia slave. She was born into slavery herself just one month after the Civil War began, but came to New York with her mother and family in the 1870s. When she arrived in the city Victoria was young enough to attend the Negro public schools, and after graduation she became a writer. Her stories and articles were published in white and Negro journals. She thought of herself as an emancipated woman, founded a Negro protest and women's rights society in the city (the "Women's Loyal Union of New York and Brooklyn"), and delivered lectures on "The Awakening of the Afro-American Woman." When she learned of the "unscrupulous employment agents who deceive the unsuspecting girls desiring to come North," Mrs. Matthews decided to "check the evil." She established a home which provided lodgings and meals for women until they were able to find work. The society kept agents at piers in Norfolk as well as New York City to answer questions, escort women to their places of employment or, instead, to the White Rose Home. Aside from this, its major function, Mrs. Matthews and her fellow workers extended their activity to the general Negro population of New York City. The White Rose Home became a settlement house as well as a temporary lodging place for migrants. The classes that were presented there in domestic training and "race history," the library of books on Negro life, and the facilities for recreation were all open to the public as well as to residents of the home. The Home continued its work among Negroes even after Mrs. Matthews' death in 1907, and finally moved to larger quarters in Harlem in 1918.

The same fear of exploitation of Negro women by "intelligence agents" that motivated Victoria Earle Matthews led to the founding of an organization which attempted to do on a national scale what the White Rose Home did for Negro migrants who came to New York City. The initiator of this movement was the white reformer Frances A. Kellor. She also spent a good part of her early crusading career attacking the corruptions of private employment bureaus. In 1903, sponsored by the Woman's Municipal League of New York, she was given the responsibility of collecting as much data on the problem as a thorough investigation could produce. She gathered information from 732 private employment agencies, published her findings in 1904 in *Out of Work: A Study of Employment Agencies* and bombarded municipal officials with the information she had uncovered. Her criticisms and prodding resulted in the creation of the Office of Commissioner of Licenses in New York City, and were also influential in establishing the first state-controlled employment bureau in New York in 1911.

The underlying concern that seemed to motivate Frances A. Kellor and other municipal reformers in this area was not only that many employment agents were dishonest and treated their clients in a shoddy manner, but that many agencies were used as guises which subtly tried to draw women into the arms of "the alluring procuresses of the city." Some Negro women were given jobs as maids and cooks in what Miss Kellor called "sporting houses." "They are often threatened until they accept positions in questionable places and are frequently sent out without knowing the character of their destination," she wrote in *Out of Work*. The recruiting of women for "immoral purposes" by "intelligence agents" was the first point the Commissioner of Licenses listed in a memorandum which explained why the office had been created. "The southern states, especially Virginia and Georgia, are honey-combed with the slick agents of these employment bureaus," Miss Kellor said in 1905. ". . . good wages, easy work . . . and good times, are promised. . . . To them, going to Philadelphia or to New York seems like going to Heaven, where the streets will be paved with gold, all will be music and flowers!"

The disparity between image and reality led Miss Kellor to establish a society for the protection of Negro women—the National League for the Protection of Colored Women. The League had offices in New York

City and Philadelphia and agents in many southern port cities. It distributed literature to southern Negro pastors and schools urging them to "educate the women on these conditions." Like the White Rose Home, and sometimes in conjunction with it, the League stationed its workers at the major depots within the city and offered general fellowship and advice to country strangers who came to town for the first time: "It is the aim of the League to furnish helpful information to colored girls who are intending to come North, to protect them during the journey . . . and to find work or friends or homes for them" when they arrive. The National League for the Protection of Colored Women continued this work until 1911 when it became one of three Negro reform agencies which consolidated into the National League on Urban Conditions Among Negroes.

Victoria Earle Matthews and Frances A. Kellor were reformers who concentrated primarily on a single problem—the exploitation of Negro domestic workers. The first prominent New Yorker to fully devote her energy to improving all aspects of Negro life in New York City, and eventually in the entire nation, was Mary White Ovington.

Miss Ovington's background was similar to that of many other urban reformers of her generation. She grew up in comfort and gentility, the daughter of a well-to-do New York merchant. Her home in an exclusive section of Brooklyn was geographically not too distant from the working-class districts, but it was as separate from them in spirit as two distinct worlds could have been: "In my youth," she recalled in an autobiographical sketch, "no place was more remote than the section of the city in which persons of different caste lived."

The patrician's daughter had the typical education of a young woman of refinement. As a child she studied exclusively in private schools, and when she was ready for college, Miss Ovington was sent to Radcliffe. After her graduation the family expected her to take her proper place in society—"what we called 'going into society,'" she said. But the quiet, secure and stable world into which Miss Ovington was born seemed too remote in the America of the 1880s and 1890s. Industrialization had created major social problems on a scale unequaled in the previous history of the nation. It had created slums, and the immigrants who lived in them often experienced poverty, distress, illness and a sense of hopelessness which was difficult to overlook: "I found out about conditions in my own city of which I was utterly ignorant," she remembered.

Miss Ovington's reaction to these new conditions, similar to the responses of other Progressives, was positive and optimistic. Involvement in a movement for social reform also gave added meaning and fulfillment to her own life. There was, she recalled, a "fervor for settlement work in the nineties, for learning working class conditions by living among the workers and sharing to some small extent in their lives. . . . The desire for such knowledge was in the air—hope was in the air." In 1896 Miss Ovington opened a settlement house "among white working-class people" in Greenpoint, Brooklyn. Her five-room home grew into a forty-room settlement in the seven years she remained there. "That I should later work for the Negro never entered my mind," she wrote.

Her first awareness of the seriousness of Negro conditions in the city came at a lecture given by Booker T. Washington. The "Social Reform Club," of which she was a member, invited Washington to speak before it. He apparently described in detail many of the restrictions on Negro equality in New York City and Miss Ovington was shocked to hear about them: "To my amazement I learned that there was a Negro problem in my city. I had honestly never thought of it before." She decided at that time to find out more about these conditions and, from 1904 till her death in 1951, devoted her life to trying to improve them.

Although Washington's descriptions may have appeared new and shocking to her as an adult, Mary White Ovington had heard similar stories as a child. The Ovington family had originally come from New England. William Lloyd Garrison had been a friend of her grandmother's. Miss Ovington was born in 1865 and grew up when memories of the Great Rebellion were very much alive. She listened attentively to her grandmother's tales of abolitionism, the Underground Railroad, anti-abolitionist rioting in Boston, and the preaching of Garrison's close friend and follower, the Rev. Samuel J. May. She was taught to despise Daniel Webster and Henry Clay for compromising on the slavery issue. When Frederick Douglass came to speak at Plymouth Congregational Church, Miss Ovington went to see one of her idols. "I was," she wrote, "a sympathetic listener." Garrison "was my childhood's greatest hero."

Mary White Ovington's parents were abolitionists too. Her father told her that he severed connections with Plymouth Congregational Church because Henry Ward Beecher dealt with a missionary association which had contact with a slaveholder. He joined a Unitarian congregation (and his daughter continued in this religion) led by an abolitionist "of the strictest brand." "Ours was an abolition family," she recalled.

The Ovington family, similar to other supporters of abolitionism, lost contact with Negro life after the Civil War. Slavery had been the great evil and it was destroyed. The Thirteenth, Fourteenth and Fifteenth Amendments were passed and Negroes were legally made equal American citizens. It seemed to them that there was nothing left to be done: "Slavery was ended," she said. "That was the great point."

Booker T. Washington reawakened Miss Ovington's interest in the Negro people. She decided to open a settlement house for Negroes in New York City and asked Mary Kingsbury Simkovitch of Greenwich House for advice. They both decided that the first thing to be done was to gather as much specific information as possible on Negroes in New York City. Miss Ovington was made a Fellow of Greenwich House in 1904 and began the studies which led to the publication of *Half A Man* seven years later.

The difficulties Negroes faced in finding decent and inexpensive living accommodations impressed her as a most important problem. Henry Phipps, steel magnate and philanthropist, had previously constructed model tenement houses for immigrants in the city. The City and Suburban Homes Company managed them and Phipps accepted the modest profit of 4 per cent on his investment. Miss Ovington and Phipps had a mutual friend, John E. Milholland, whom she went to see. Milholland was convinced of the need for the project and he, in turn, persuaded Phipps to construct a model tenement for the Negroes of San Juan Hill. When the Tuskegee Apartments were completed on West 63rd Street in 1907 they seemed an incongruity in the neighborhood. This fireproof, steam-heated, roof-gardened, six-story house stood out against the older rundown tenements on the West Side. (The Phipps apartment houses have survived a half-century of construction and can still be seen today.) Miss Ovington also hoped that Phipps would support a settlement house for Negroes in the building and decided to live there herself: "I hoped by quietly renting on my own account, to persuade him to add social work."

She moved into the Tuskegee Apartments, the only white person in the entire house, in January 1908. There she gathered information for her book, became a close friend of the Rev. Dr. George H. Sims of Union Baptist Church on the block, attended his services occasionally, and read "Peter Rabbit" and other stories to the Negro youngsters who knocked at her door. (She later published stories for Negro children.) Miss Ovington lived on West 63rd Street for eight months, but was unable to get the philanthropist to support a Negro settlement house there. In September 1908, as is well known, she read an article in *The Independent* which diverted her attention to broader Negro problems and changed the course of her life. William English Walling's "The Race War in the North" attacked the growing racial antipathy and apathy that were developing in the North and called for a revival of "the spirit of the abolitionists. . . ." Miss Ovington responded to this appeal and called a small meeting of her friends to discuss what could be done to counteract this burgeoning racism. A National

Negro Conference met in 1909 at the Henry Street Settlement House. The NAACP was born of the National Negro Committee that was established at this conference, and Mary White Ovington spent the rest of her career working within this organization.

Although her main energies were channeled into the NAACP (she was called "Mother of the New Emancipation"), Miss Ovington continued to be active in social work among New York Negroes. She was an executive of the Committee for Improving the Industrial Condition of the Negro in New York City, chairman of its "Neighborhood Work" subcommittee, president and main fund-raiser of the Lincoln Settlement which she helped found for Negroes in Brooklyn, and organizer of the West End Workers' Association which was active among the Negroes of San Juan Hill. The Negro woman who was her private secretary from 1905 till her death remembers Miss Ovington as a person who was totally dedicated to the struggle for Negro rights and honestly devoid of any racial prejudice. "No white woman's life in America has been colored more by the clash of color and race," editorialized a Negro newspaper. "That the sincerity of my friendship has never been doubted," wrote Miss Ovington when she resigned as Chairman of the Board of Directors of the NAACP, "has been my greatest joy."

The reforming zeal that was evident in Mary White Ovington reached a high point in 1906 when the Committee for Improving the Industrial Condition of the Negro in New York (CIICN) was founded. The primary motivation that led to the organization of the CIICN was the desire to broaden employment opportunities for the city's Negroes. Its members, supporters, directors and subcommittee chairmen were the most important reformers in New York City in the Progressive era. Many of them were later active in the NAACP and other areas of municipal reform. The CIICN was interracial in structure and was composed of social workers, philanthropists, educators, clergymen, writers, publishers, physicians, supporters of Hampton and Tuskegee, businessmen. The founder of the CIICN was a Negro principal in the New York City school system, Dr. William Lewis Bulkley. Bulkley was motivated to organize this Committee, he said in 1906, after seeing Negro students leaving his school "to open-doors, run bells or hustle hash for the rest" of their lives.

Dr. Bulkley was the leading Negro educator in New York City in the early twentieth century. He was a bright, idealistic and ambitious man who had risen from the slavery into which he was born in South Carolina in 1861 to earn a doctorate in ancient languages and literature from Syracuse University. As a boy he attended the local log cabin school and finally graduated from Claflin University, in his home state, in 1882. He came north to continue his studies at Wesleyan University in Connecticut and at Syracuse. In 1893, after completing his master's degree, he earned the Ph.D.

For a time, Dr. Bulkley was a professor of Latin and Greek at Claflin University. During his student days, however, he had taken a variety of odd jobs to support himself. At different times he worked as a janitor, a steward, a cook and a salesman. To save the little money he did earn in this way he scrimped wherever he could. His meals often consisted of oatmeal and water; he washed and darned his own clothing, and pressed his socks and handkerchiefs between the pages of his books of under the mattresses on which he slept. William Lewis Bulkley, in the language of his day, achieved "Success Under Difficulties." The "Slave Boy Now a Professor" was "A Noble Example of the Triumph of Perseverance."

Bulkley thought of himself as a Southerner who had been driven from his home by racism: "There is not one of us who would not gladly go back home if we did not know that every right dear to any full man has been ruthlessly torn from our grasp," he said in 1909. He longed to share the "soul-refreshings that only a [southern] Negro revival can give." Dr. Bulkley came to New York City in the 1890s and was appointed seventh grade teacher in a lower Manhattan public school. In 1899 he became principal of P.S. 80 on West 41st Street in the Tenderloin. This school, in the heart of the Negro district, had formerly been an all-Negro institution which was made a ward school as a result of the city's integration policy which went into effect in 1884. In 1909, despite protest meetings and petitions of the teachers in P. S. 125, Bulkley was appointed the first Negro principal of a predominantly white school in city history.

William Lewis Bulkley insisted that Negroes be given full equality in American society immediately. He supported the demands made by W. E. B. DuBois along these lines, and became a founder of the NAACP. During his summer vacations he was a temporary expatriate who lived in Switzerland and France with his wife and children. His family sometimes remained there when he returned to resume his duties in the fall. On retiring from the New York City school system in 1923 he left the country and established a private school in Nice. He died there in 1934. That a supporter of DuBois should have founded an organization that tried to find practical, industrial employment for the Negroes of the city seemed the height of inconsistency to Booker T. Washington's supporters. "You will see that this opponent of industrial education is not practicing what he preaches," wrote one of them. "This is inconsistency with a vengeance." White social workers, like Mary White Ovington, Jane Addams and Julia Richman, on the other hand, thought highly of Bulkley's work.

Bulkley was a pragmatist who met conditions in the city as he saw them and tried to improve them as best he could. One of the first things he did after becoming principal of P. S. 80, for example, was to open a kindergarten class to relieve the working mothers of the neighborhood. In 1903 Bulkley established an evening school in the building which specialized in classes offering industrial and commercial training to its students. Some of the most diligent students in the school were elderly Negro men and women, some in their seventies and eighties, who had no opportunity for education as young people, and now wanted to learn to read and write. Bulkley invited friends and associates to visit the school. On one occasion, when members of the Board of Education made an inspection tour, they stated "that it was the most successful evening school that ever was established in New York. . . ."

The idea for a permanent industrial organization to assist Negroes in New York City had apparently originated with William H. Baldwin. Baldwin, president of the Long Island Railroad and philanthropist, was one of Booker T. Washington's key financial supporters. It was Dr. Bulkley, however, who initiated the movement which led to the creation of the CIICN.

Since 1902 Bulkley had agitated for the need of an organization to do on a broad scale what he had attempted to do as an individual at his school: "With an Afro-American population in New York increasing yearly at a very great, I had almost said alarming rate," he said in one speech, "it behooves every thoughtful man and woman in this city to stop long enough to think what it may mean to us and to them."

Early in 1906 the Negro educator initiated a series of local meetings to discuss the subject. He, Mary White Ovington and others lectured these gatherings on the harsh facts of life that each Negro in New York City was forced to experience. Finally, in May 1906, at a meeting of some sixty Negro and white New Yorkers, Bulkley's hope became reality. The CIICN was founded and issued a public statement on its goals. "Here at home," the report maintained, "conditions are piling up which must be met . . . at once." The Committee would endeavor to provide equal "economic opportunities" for all citizens: "A square deal in the matter of getting a livelihood is held to be fundamental." William Jay Schieffelin, philanthropist, urban reformer, heir to the Jay family abolitionist tradition, and president of the Board of Trustees of the Armstrong Association, was appointed chairman. Schieffelin immediately began to contact his friends to mobilize support for the new organization. With "seventy thousand Negroes in New York," he wrote in one letter, "we ought to feel a responsibility concerning them."

The CIICN was divided into subcommittees, each headed by an

eminent specialist in a particular area of work—"Employment," "Neighborhood Work," "Craftsmen," "Publication," "Trade Schools," "Social Centers," "Legal Affairs," "Public Meetings." Negro streets in the city were canvassed to gather information on social problems which seemed most pressing. Regular public meetings were held in Negro churches to stimulate interest in the Committee's work and provide a sounding board for local discontent. An employment bureau was established to locate and help create jobs for Negroes. The names of skilled Negro workers were collected and these craftsmen were organized into small trade units. Such associations were created for dressmakers, printers, mechanics, waiters, carpenters. A slight dent was made in the policies of racial restriction normally adhered to by unions when, under prodding from the CIICN, the Grand United Brotherhood of Carpenters and Joiners of America issued a charter to a Negro local in the city. Jobs were found for plumbers, construction workers, painters, bricklayers, masons, decorators. Subway companies were contacted and asked to hire Negro motormen. The subcommittee on Trade Schools, headed by a New York City school superintendent, collected a thousand names on a petition for new night schools in the Negro districts. Two more evening schools were created primarily for Negroes in these years. The City and Suburban Homes Company was encouraged to build additional model tenements for Negroes.

The CIICN also cooperated with the other Negro reform agencies in the city. In 1908, for example, it began to send people to the docks to assist Frances A. Kellor's organization with the always increasing numbers of migrants who came to town. When the Committee on Urban Conditions Among Negroes was established in New York in 1910, the CIICN sent spokesmen to the new organization to map out lines of cooperation with it. The problems which emerged from Negro migration grew more complex each year. It was obviously wasteful to have a number of separate bodies which defined their spheres as particular aspects of what was one broad and interrelated problem. In 1911 a general agreement for consolidation was reached among the CIICN, the National League for the Protection of Colored Women and the Committee on Urban Conditions Among Negroes. All three organizations merged into a new and stronger society which is still operating today, the National League on Urban Conditions Among Negroes (National Urban League).

The founding of the two most prominent national Negro organizations, the NAACP and the National Urban League was, therefore, a culmination and fulfillment of individual local reforming efforts that had begun in the North in the first decade of the twentieth century.

The serious revitalization of concern in the Negro people that this demonstrated was evident in New York City in a variety of other ways as well. Spontaneously, each year brought to life some new Negro welfare institution. Two settlement houses, one of which was a branch of the Henry Street Settlement, were founded for Negroes in 1904 and in 1907. In 1911 they consolidated into one large unit, the Lincoln Settlement House. Lillian D. Wald sent Negro nurses into the Tenderloin, San Juan Hill and Harlem to help these communities with their medical problems. A Negro Music School Settlement, numerous free nurseries and kindergartens, homes for delinquent girls and two new Negro Y's were established. The NAACP opened an office in Harlem to provide help for Negroes who were discriminated against in any way. The National Urban League organized a housing bureau which tried to clean up the streets of Negro areas and locate clean, respectable and inexpensive homes for Negro families. Tuberculosis was an ever-present disease among Negroes and the New York City Board of Health conducted special evening classes for colored people on its prevention. Some migrants, fresh from the country, were given rudimentary lessons in the use of modern sanitary and plumbing devices. Playgrounds and summer camps were opened for Negro children. A Negro Fresh Air Committee was established in 1905.

When the new century began the prevailing attitude toward the Negro in New York City was one of hostility and increasing alienation. As far as the majority of the population was concerned, this continued to be the dominant reaction of the city to the Negro people. The racial antagonism of the majority made necessary the creation of segregated communities like Harlem. A sense of renewed promise and hopefulness among Negroes, however, was born of the important reform movements that were established to cope with the problems which resulted from the settlement of southern Negroes in New York City. In 1900 Booker T. Washington and W. E. B. DuBois would have agreed that the Progressive movement seemed to overlook the Negro. Ten years later, both recognized a new "awakening" of interest in Negro life. This general reform movement was, in the words of a Negro New Yorker, "a veritable godsend to the colored people."

Seth M. Scheiner □ President Theodore Roosevelt and the Negro, 1901–1908

Historians have portrayed Theodore Roosevelt as the focal point of the Progressive era. Roosevelt, unlike many of his followers, found himself forced to deal with racial problems. In October, 1901, the president invited Booker T. Washington to the White House for a conference, and the incident touched off a furor in the southern press. The luncheon is cited by scholars as an example of the president's broadmindedness, but it is forgotten that the Negro educator never received another invitation and that Roosevelt himself admitted his action was an error. In this essay, Professor Seth Scheiner, of Temple University, examines Roosevelt's dealings with the Negro community during his two administrations. Professor Scheiner is the author of *Negro Mecca: A History of The Negro in New York City, 1865–1920.*

In the period 1901–1908 the question of Negro rights was a major national issue. All areas of government—national, state, and local—were involved in the uproar. Political campaigners, both North and South, debated the Negro question. President Theodore Roosevelt could not avoid the ramifications of this problem.

The question of Negro rights brought the President into conflict with all areas of the population. At different times, Roosevelt was opposed by southerners and northerners, Negroes and whites, liberals and conservatives, moderates and extremists. No thorough examina-

From Seth M. Scheiner, "President Theodore Roosevelt and the Negro," *Journal of Negro History,* XLVII (July 1962), pp. 169–182. Reprinted by permission of the *Journal of Negro History.*

tion has been made of Theodore Roosevelt's Negro policy. Many historians have used a few facts to make broad generalizations without examining carefully Roosevelt's statements and actions.

Mark Sullivan claimed that whenever a Negro appointee was attacked the President remained firm. Others have criticized Roosevelt for raising the race issue, rather than letting it remain dormant. Some state that T. R.'s actions were a cause of the Negro-southern conflict which arose at the turn of the century. Almost all of these writers, however, have overlooked the other factors that brought the Negro issue to the forefront of the national scene. Another school of thought divides Roosevelt's policy into two phases: a pro-Negro first term and an anti-Negro second term. This hypothesis oversimplifies Roosevelt's position. Nor does the contention that the President acted solely for political reasons explain Roosevelt's policy. Though this view contains a large degree of validity, it does not devote adequate space to its philosophical basis.

Theodore Roosevelt believed that the English-speaking peoples were the superior race. He argued that the United States' policy towards the Philippines was in "the interest of civilization." We are marching along "the path of wise and proper treatment of weaker by stronger race," he contended. It is the duty of the English-speaking peoples, with their high form of civilization, to spread "lasting benefit" to the weaker races. Roosevelt distinguished between stronger and weaker racial groups; the Negro he placed in the latter category.

Roosevelt believed that the Negro—as a group—was inferior to the white race. It is not clear if he made this distinction for sociological or physiological reasons. In his writings, Roosevelt did not distinguish between the two; in fact, both environmental and physical explanations overlap.

Negro troops were condemned by Roosevelt for cowardice during the Spanish-American War. He blamed the Negro's lack of fighting spirit on his birth. To his novelist friend, Owen Wister, he wrote: "I entirely agree with you that as a race and in the mass they are altogether inferior to the whites." This view, despite Roosevelt's public utterances and actions, was constant throughout his career.

The Booker T. Washington Dinner was the first incident that involved President Roosevelt in the question of Negro rights. In October, 1901, T. R. invited the Negro educator to the White House for a conference. At the last minute, T. R. extended a dinner invitation to his Negro guest. Washington accepted the President's hospitality. Within a few days the southern press angrily learned of the meal. The New Orleans *Times Democrat* wrote: "When Mr. Roosevelt sits down to dinner with a negro he declares that the negro is the social equal of the white man." The New Orleans *Daily States* called it a "studied insult to the South." Josephus Daniels, a Virginia editor and later Woodrow Wilson's Secretary of the Navy, wrote: "It is not a precedent that will encourage southern men to join hands with Mr. Roosevelt." Though condemnation was louder by far, Roosevelt also received some praise. Henry Cabot Lodge wrote that T. R. was "utterly right" and the South must "learn and broaden."

Roosevelt was dismayed by the reaction to the Washington Dinner. He stated that he would not judge a man by his color and would invite Washington to dinner as often as he pleased. But T. R. never asked the Negro educator to dinner again, and—in later years—admitted it "was a mistake."

In the course of the period 1901–1904, a series of incidents occurred that brought the question of Negro rights to the foreground. Certain of these incidents, however, have been mentioned rarely by historians. Too often, many students of this subject rely upon the Washington Dinner, Dr. William Crum's appointment, and the forced resignation of a Negro postmistress in Indianola, Mississippi for their conclusions. To present and examine only these incidents would lead to superficial and erroneous conclusions. To understand Roosevelt's policy, every incident in this period concerning the Negro must be examined.

Throughout his years in the White House, Roosevelt used Booker T. Washington as a political referee for patronage. The President used political referees to avoid reliance on state party organizations, for, on the whole, these Republican bodies were allied with T. R.'s Republican opponent, Mark Hanna. In 1901, Roosevelt made two appointments on the advice of Booker Washington—a Negro as a Justice of the Peace in the District of Columbia and ex-Governor T. G. Jones, of Alabama, as a United States District Judge for the Alabama area. Republicans regarded Jones, a Democrat, as moderate on the Negro question. Roosevelt wished to placate many Negroes and, at the same time, deliver a blow to the Hanna organization with the Jones appointment. Neither of these selections aroused protests, but it was not to be long before clouds collided and thunder emerged.

In mid-1902, Roosevelt was involved in a conflict with the Republican "lily whites." The "lily whites" wished to remove the odor of "Black Republicanism" from their party in the South. They proceeded to eliminate Negroes from state delegations and held conventions in hotels that would not cater to Negroes. Another factor, that clouded the picture also, was that Mark Hanna controlled "lily white" delegations in certain southern states and, in others, Negro delegations. Consistent anti-lily white or pro-Negro policies would complicate Republican politics. If one followed the former position, he would ostracize state organizations that adhered to a pro-Negro policy. The question, therefore, remained whether a national political figure could take an unequivocal stand on Negro rights. Roosevelt found this a knotty problem.

The President's first action was in Alabama, where he refused to reappoint a "lily white" District Attorney. Instead he selected a Democrat, Thomas R. Roellas. Roosevelt used two men, James S. Clarkson, former surveyor of the Port of New York, an expert on the spoils system, and Henry C. Payne, the Postmaster-General, as his political advisers. Clarkson and Payne believed that T. R. should oppose the "lily whites" and follow a pro-Negro policy. Roosevelt denied a *New York Times* report that these men influenced his decisions, or that his appointments were political; he called the article "malicious" and "scandalous." The President's contention does not agree with the facts, for Roosevelt instructed Clarkson to undermine the position of the Hanna "lily whites" in Alabama. T. R. alleged that he opposed a segregated party in the South, but later events indicate that more than altruism influenced his decision.

Before the ramifications of the Roellas incident had cleared, another intraparty battle occurred. This conflict involved "lily whites" of North Carolina. Roosevelt wished to reappoint Samuel Vick, a Negro, as Postmaster of Wilson, North Carolina. Republican Senator Jeter Pritchard of North Carolina, however, issued an immediate protest, calling Vick a disloyal Republican. At first, Roosevelt refused to back down on Vick's appointment, but he finally surrendered to Pritchard's demands. T. R. withdrew his support of Vick and appointed Pritchard's "lily white" selection, turning his back on Clarkson who had advocated an anti-"lily white" policy. An indication of the Rough Rider's deviation from the Clarkson philosophy was evident by December, 1902, when he appointed a "lily white" Collector of Customs at New Bern, North Carolina. On March 24, 1903, T. R. retreated further—he dropped Vick and appointed another "lily white." The "lily whites," at least in North Carolina, received the backing of the President. It appears that Roosevelt had turned from the views of Clarkson. Roosevelt had not anticipated the outburst brought on by the Vick appointment; in fact, his main purpose was to receive the support of Republican state organizations, not to aid or appoint Negroes. Senator Pritchard had a solid organization behind him that did not need rebuilding. Why rebuff the support of a well-knit group for a nonexistent entity? Roosevelt answered this problem by acceding to the North Carolina Senator's demands; hereafter, he turned a deaf ear to Clarkson's advice.

While T. R. followed Clarkson's policy, another uproar occurred in November of 1902. This time it took place in the ranks of Alabama Republicans. Roosevelt removed a Collector of Internal Revenue for anti-Negro activities. In place of this "lily white," he appointed a man who advocated the admittance of the Negro to the Republican Party. Postmaster Payne declared that the President will not tolerate "expulsion of any section of our people [Republicans] by reason of their race or color." At about this time, Roosevelt made an appointment that angered the South. He nominated a Negro doctor for a position in Charleston, South Carolina.

The Negro, Dr. William D. Crum, was selected to fill the Collectorship of the Port of Charleston. Many southerners considered it a disgrace for a Negro to serve in such a high official post in the "Cradle of the Confederacy." Dr. Crum had been appointed as Postmaster for the city by President Benjamin Harrison, but withdrew when protests became too great. Despite the sentiment against the Negro physician, the President continued to support his nomination. The Senate refused to confirm the appointment until January, 1905.

While the Crum appointment was in the public eye, another incident occurred that added fuel to the controversy over Negro rights. The town of Indianola, Mississippi, forced a Negro postmistress, Mrs. Minnie Cox, to resign her position. Mrs. Cox had been appointed by President Harrison. Roosevelt demanded that Mrs. Cox be returned to office; however, the town refused to accept the Negro lady. Raucous meetings were held in Indianola and threatening messages were issued. T. R. responded by closing the post office. Many southerners called Roosevelt's action autocratic and unconstitutional. The President answered with a statement on equal rights and the selection of public officials regardless of color.

The Indianola incident, and the others reported above, caused a verbal outbreak on the Negro question that had not occurred in years. One southerner charged the President with stirring "up a frenzy of race feeling such as the South had not exhibited since Reconstruction." Senator John L. McLaurin, a Mississippi Democrat, contended that Mrs. Cox was at best of "good Negro character." On the opposing side, the Negro Afro-American Council commended the President "to the affection and confidence of our people, regardless of party affiliation."

In Congress, Senator McLaurin stated that "the white people of Mississippi don't want negro postmasters appointed to give them out their mail." Senator John C. Spooner charged that a "brutal and lawless element" forced Mrs. Cox to resign. Congressman Edgar Crumpacker introduced a resolution to investigate the entire matter—it did not receive any consideration. John Bankhead, an Alabama Democrat, rebuked Spooner, Crumpacker, and Roosevelt. He declared that the President's attitude toward the Negro was disgusting and condemned T. R.'s anti-"lily white" actions. In Memphis, Tennessee a group of Confederate veterans refused to march in a parade honoring Roosevelt. Senator Arthur Pue Gorman, a Democrat, from Maryland, alleged that T. R. had pushed the race issue to the foreground; an issue that should remain undisturbed.

Condemnation not only came from the South, but from other areas of the nation. Northern moderates, such as *The New York Times,* criticized Roosevelt's actions. This northern newspaper rebuked the President for reviving the race issue and activating a matter that President McKinley had caused to be "dormant."

Roosevelt did not let these barbs go unanswered, nor did he lack support. He roared that the "square deal" covers all areas of American life: "I certainly cannot treat mere color as a bar to holding office, any more than I could so treat creed or birthplace." T. R. could not fathom the South's outbursts—"I confess I am wholly unable to understand" its protests. Negroes will be appointed so long as they are of "high character and good capacity," the President growled.

Leading Negroes came to Roosevelt's defense. Bishop W. B. Derrick declared that the President had opened the "door of hope" to the Negro. He urged the formation of a group to back T. R.—"Roosevelt Invincibles." The Bishop piled praise upon the President and his party, and denunciations were laid at the door of the Democrats. In addition, the Negro Republicans of Alabama applauded the administration's policy. The *Nation* praised the President and reprimanded his congressional critics.

But these actions were the last concrete steps Roosevelt took in behalf of the Negro. His deeds, thereafter, received the wrath rather than the support of most Negroes. These later actions were to be inconsistent with Roosevelt's earlier statements in behalf of equal rights for the Negro. But this discrepancy is more apparent than real. When T. R.'s private letters are examined much more light is shed upon his actions. A consistency emerges in his Negro policy that existed throughout his years in the White House. Political necessity appears to be the main motivation behind Roosevelt's policy.

The President, after some reflection, questioned the wisdom of the Washington Dinner, Crum's appointment, and similar pro-Negro actions. He did not understand why the South reacted so angrily to his policy: "Not a law has been passed or threatened affecting the negro or affecting the southern white in his relation to the negro during the three years that the South has been indulging in hysterics over me." He claimed that the number of Negro officeholders, "which was insignificant even under McKinley, has been still further reduced." He then stated his qualms about the Washington and Crum incidents:

> It may be that it would have been better for me not to have Booker Washington at dinner. It may be that it would have been better not to have originally

nominated Crum for the Charleston collectorship. Personally I think I was right in both instances. But even if I was wrong, to say that the South's attitude is explained by these two acts is to say that the South is in a condition of violent chronic hysteria.

He admitted to his novelist friend, Owen Wister, that these two incidents were not "politically expedient," though contending they were justified.

While Roosevelt may have been disturbed by the South's protests, he was incensed by the utterances of northern liberals. He charged that Oswald Garrison Villard, Rollo Ogden, and Charles Francis Adams were "irrational" on the Negro question; he doubted their "sincerity and common sense." The *"Evening Post* crowd" was rebuked for "hypocrisy and mendacity about the colored question."

Roosevelt did not stop at questioning his policy, he expressed doubts as to the Negro's equality with the white: "I entirely agree with you that as a race and in the mass they [Negroes] are altogether inferior to the whites." He regarded Booker T. Washington as one of the "occasionally good, well-educated, intelligent and honest colored men," who should be given the right to vote.

Roosevelt could not help thinking of the Negro as a group, "which are bad enough by nature." He caught himself upon the horns of a dilemma in the following statement:

> I would not be willing to die for what I regard as the untrue abstract statement that all men are in all respects equal, and are all alike entitled to the same power; but I would be quite willing to die . . . for the proposition that each man has certain rights which no other man should be allowed to take away from him.

How can one deny equality to strive for the same power, and yet cry for equal access to other rights? Roosevelt established a premise whereby all rights could be denied to certain persons. When power is given to mere humans to deny other humans "certain rights" that they themselves enjoy, the door to equal opportunity is shut. Roosevelt's statements constantly gave the impression of inconsistency, whereas, in reality, the issue to him was a problem in logistics not in conflicting philosophies. He did not regard race as irrelevant, as having no bearing on the equality or inequality of man; in fact, his praise of the "occasionally good" Negro like Booker T. Washington supports his position on the racial inequality of man. Thus, a constant belief in the innate difference of racial groups dominates Roosevelt's philosophy of man and society.

The actions that ran against Roosevelt's philosophy can be explained by political necessity; for example, his dealings with the "lily whites" were politically motivated. In Alabama, T. R. opposed the anti-Negro group that favored Hanna, whereas, in North Carolina, he gradually gave his support to the "lily whites." Roosevelt denied to Hanna that his Negro policy was conceived out of political considerations. What emerges is that the President was under the influence of Clarkson and Payne from late 1901 until mid-1903; these two men believed that Roosevelt should appeal to the Negroes of the North. An anti-"lily white" policy they believed would win the support of both Negroes and pro-Negro southern delegations. Work against the "lily white" state organizations and replace them with pro-Negro groups, concluded Clarkson. Roosevelt followed this advice in his Alabama appointments and in his early opposition to Pritchard in North Carolina; however, he came to the conclusion that he was injuring himself politically by these actions. For example, the "lily whites" in North Carolina were angered; they threatened to desert T. R.'s camp. Roosevelt—it appears—reassessed his position and discarded Clarkson and Payne's policy.

By mid-1903, Roosevelt had abandoned his "fight" against the "lily whites." The retreat had begun in December, 1902 and was completed by March, 1903. At no time after the latter date did Clarkson and Payne exercise any influence on the President pertaining to the Negro question. Roosevelt's concession to the "lily whites," and his final abandonment of the Clarkson-Payne position, can be seen in a letter to Booker T. Washington in 1904:

> The safety for the colored man in Louisiana is to have a white man's party which shall be responsible and honest, . . . in which he shall not be the dominant force.

Why did Roosevelt turn his ear from the words of Clarkson? First, and foremost, the Surveyor-General's advice did not work. His policy was receiving too much attention and was injuring Roosevelt's popularity throughout the South; in fact, some moderate northerners condemned T. R.'s actions. Roosevelt was faced with the detrimental political consequences of a policy that too many people condemned. Fear of losing the 1904 presidential nomination to Mark Hanna plagued T. R.'s mind. What Hanna lacked in popular appeal he possessed in political power. Roosevelt was the figure that captured the heart of the people, but Hanna was the one man who could prevent T. R. from winning the Republican nomination in 1904. Hanna's political power disturbed and harried Roosevelt. The Negro question was a problem that could determine the vote of southern Republican delegations. Hanna controlled both "lily white" and mixed delegations; therefore, Roosevelt concluded that he must follow a similar policy. If an anti-Negro policy could secure the vote of a delegation, he would use it; and, on the opposite side, if a pro-Negro program meant the control of a delegation, this was the policy to follow. Thus

Clarkson's proposals were to be scuttled and in their place a state by state policy was adopted.

Roosevelt's second term did not bring any change in his Negro policy; however, his public statements became more and more anti-Negro. At a Lincoln Day Dinner in 1905, Roosevelt delivered a speech that was applauded throughout the South. He continually invoked the word moderation; saying that he always had adhered to such a policy and that both the North and South should follow. "Clear sighted men" of the North, of which he was one, understood the South's problem. These men—and T. R.—will not press down upon the South any crown of thorns. The relations between the races must be adjusted so that the "backward race be trained . . . that it may enter into the possession of true freedom while the forward race is enabled to preserve unharmed" its high civilization. No doubt the process "must necessarily be slow," continued the President; "it is a problem demanding the best thought, the utmost patience." Then he echoed the words of Booker Washington—"the prime requisite of the Negro race is moral and industrial uplifting"; politics is secondary. The lazy and shiftless Negro is more of a danger to his race than the aggressive acts of white men, roared Roosevelt. At the end of his speech, T. R. gave a cry that many southerners had echoed in the marbled chambers of Congress: "Race purity must be maintained."

At first glance, this speech appears to be inconsistent with Roosevelt's earlier actions; however, if his private statements are understood this dichotomy disappears. The Lincoln Day Speech, at most, was a radical public departure, but it was consistent with Roosevelt's utterances contained in his private letters.

After his inauguration, Roosevelt took a trip southward and spread his spirit of moderation. He praised the grey as well as the blue. Did not the South know about his mother's southern birth? He informed every southern city of this fact; possibly hoping southerners would associate his beloved mother with their city. The presidency, continued the President, is only effective when its holder is half northern and half southern. By virtue of his maternal and paternal lines he fulfilled the geographic requirement. These statements were reiterated southward and southward. The South got the point—T. R. would not fight for Negro rights.

In the middle of his second term, Roosevelt committed an act which aroused the ire of the Negro community—he summarily dismissed a battalion of Negro soldiers accused of "shooting up" the town of Brownsville, Texas. Whether this action was anti-Negro or was unjust, is not within the scope of this paper. But if the discharge of these soldiers was anti-Negro, it did not mark an innovation in Roosevelt's policy. It was merely the extension of a policy devised far earlier.

Certain conclusions can be made from the material presented. Firstly, Theodore Roosevelt did not believe in the equality of man. He pictured certain races as "inferior," one of which was the Negro. The Negro to Roosevelt was "bad enough by nature." Secondly, he believed that certain Negroes were "occasionally good" and "well-educated," but the group did not or could not attain this position. A third point in Roosevelt's philosophy was that a majority of the Negroes should not be enfranchised; in fact, only one per cent should be permitted to vote. Finally, Roosevelt abandoned his fight for Negro rights —which was incidental to his political policy—by mid-1903 at the latest, not in 1905 or 1906 as some historians have contended.

Editorials from *Crisis*

The editor of *Crisis* between 1910 and 1934 was W. E. B. DuBois, the first Negro to receive a Ph.D. in history from Harvard University. Although he criticized many of Booker T. Washington's policies, DuBois believed in the possibility of accommodation with the white community during the long years of his association with the NAACP. At the end of his long career, however, he turned away from the problems of the American Negro to those of the emerging African nations. Embittered, DuBois died in Ghana in 1963 at the age of 95. The following editorials illustrate his accommodation phase.

THE PROPER WAY.

The editor of the Cleveland *Gazette* names three main points of attack for any national association which aims to help colored people:

1. Disfranchisement.
2. Interstate "Jim Crow" cars.
3. Lynchings.

This is perfectly true, and the National Association for the Advancement of Colored People recognizes this and is straining every nerve to attack these evils. As to disfranchisement we are making every effort to get the proper case before the Supreme Court. We have already helped by briefs and contributions the Oklahoma case, and when it comes before the court we have offered the services of two of the most eminent lawyers in the United States. We are represented on the counsel of the Mississippi "Jim Crow" case; the briefs are being examined by our lawyers, and we are making every effort to get the question before the court in the right way.

From "The Proper Way," *Crisis*, Vol. V (March 1913), pp. 238–239; "Emancipation," *Crisis*, Vol. V (January 1913), pp. 128–129; "Close Ranks," *Crisis* (July 1918), p. 111.

But the *Gazette* should know that cases before the Supreme Court are delicate matters. It does not do to rush into court with any haphazard case. If anyone has a case or knows of a case which will bring out the proper points we should be glad to have it. Theoretically, it would seem very easy to settle such matters. Practically, it is very hard, but we propose to keep at it.

As to lynching, there are four things to do: Publish the facts, appeal to the authorities, agitate publicity and employ detectives. Every one of these things we have done. THE CRISIS publishes the facts monthly over the protest of sensitive readers. We have sent telegrams and appeals to governors, sheriffs and the President; we have held mass meetings; we have sent distinguished writers and investigators; we have secured publicity in prominent magazines, and we spent thousands of dollars in putting Burns' detectives on the Coatesville matter. What else can we do? We want suggestions. Meantime we shall keep up our present agitation.

Some folk seem to imagine that the walls of caste and prejudice in America will fall at a blast of the trumpet, if the blast be loud enough. Consequently, when an association like the National Association for the Advancement of Colored People does something, they say querulously: "But nothing has happened." They ought to say: Nothing has yet happened, for that is true and that is expected. If in fifty or a hundred years THE CRISIS can point to a distinct lessening of disfranchisement, and an undoubted reduction of lynching, and more decent traveling accommodations, this will be a great, an enormous accomplishment. Would God all this could be done to-morrow, but this is not humanly possible.

What is possible to-day and to-morrow and every day is to keep up necessary agitation, make unfaltering protest, fill the courts and legislatures and executive chambers, and keep everlastingly at the work of protest in season and out of season. The weak and silly part of the program of those who deprecate complaint and agitation is that a moment's let up, a moment's acquiescence, means a chance for the wolves of prejudice to get at our necks. It is not that we have too many organizations; it is that we have too few effective workers in the great cause of Negro emancipation in America. Let us from this movement join in a frontal attack on disfranchisement, "Jim Crow" cars and lynching. We shall not win to-day or to-morrow, but some day we shall win if we faint not.

EMANCIPATION.

Fifty years ago, on the first day of January, 1863, the American people, by the hand of Abraham Lincoln, took the first formal and legal step to remove the unsightly shackles of slavery from the footstool of American liberty. They did not do this deed deliberately and with lofty purpose, but being forced into a war for the integrity of the Union, they found themselves compelled in self-defense to destroy the power of the South by depriving the South of slave labor and drafting slaves into Northern armies.

Once having realized that Liberty and Slavery were incompatible, the nation yielded, for a moment, leadership to its highest ideals: it gave black men not simply physical freedom, but it attempted to give them political freedom and economic freedom and social freedom. It knew then, as it knows now, that no people can be free unless they have the right to vote, the right to land and capital and the right to choose their friends. To call a man free who has not these rights is to mock him and bewilder him and debase him. This the nation knew, and for a time it tried to be true to its nobler self. But social reform costs money and time, and if it seeks to right in a generation three centuries of unspeakable oppression it faces a task of awful proportions. Facing this task and finding it hard, the nation faltered, quibbled and finally is trying an actual *volte-face*. It has allowed the right to vote to be taken from one and a half out of two million black voters. It has allowed growing land monopoly and a labor legislation that means peonage, child labor and the defilement of women. And above all it has insisted on such barriers to decent human intercourse and understanding between the races that to-day few white men dare call a Negro friend.

The result of this silly and suicidal policy has been crime, lynching, mob law, poverty, disease and social unrest. But in spite of this the Negro has refused to believe that the present hesitation and hypocrisy of America is final. Buoyed then by an unfaltering faith, he accumulates property, educates his children, and even enters the world of literature and art. Indeed, so firm has been his faith that large numbers of Negroes have even assented to waive all discussion of their rights, consent to present disfranchisement and do just as far as possible exactly what America wants them to do. But even here let there be no mistake; with Negro agitators and Negro submissionists there is the one goal: eventual full American citizenship with all rights and opportunities of citizens. Remove this hope and you weld ten million men into one unwavering mass who will speak with one voice.

Yet, after fifty years of attempted liberty, the reactionary South and the acquiescent North come forward with this program:

1. The absolute disfranchisement of all citizens of Negro descent forever.
2. The curtailment and regulation of property rights by segregation.

3. Strictly limited education of Negro children as servants and laborers.
4. The absolute subjection of Negro women by prohibition of legal marriage between races.
5. The eventual driving of the Negro out of the land by disease, starvation or mob violence.

Every single item in this program has powerful and active support in the halls of legislatures, in the courts of justice, in the editorial rooms of periodicals, and in the councils of Southern secret societies.

There are many organizations working against this program, but in most cases the opposition is not vigorous and direct, but apologetic and explanatory, and based on temporary philanthropic relief, rather than eternal justice. We have friends of the Negro who oppose disfranchisement by a program of partial and temporary and indefinite disfranchisement; who tell the Negro to buy property and ignore ghetto legislation; who believe in caste education and hotly accuse others who do not of being ashamed of work; who would preserve one foolish white woman if it costs the degradation of ten innocent colored girls, and who would greet the death of every black man in the world with a sigh of infinite relief.

The National Association for the Advancement of Colored People almost alone stands for a frank, open, front, forward attack on the reactionary Southern program. It demands a nation-wide fight for human rights, regardless of race and color; it calls for real democracy, social and economic justice, and a respect for women which is not confined to women of one privileged class.

In this fight we want your help. We need it desperately. The nation needs it. How in Heaven's name shall Liberty and Justice survive in this land if we do not oppose this program of slavery and injustice? Abraham Lincoln began the emancipation of the Negro-American. The National Association for the Advancement of Colored People proposes to complete it.

CLOSE RANKS.

This is the crisis of the world. For all the long years to come men will point to the year 1918 as the great Day of Decision, the day when the world decided whether it would submit to military despotism and an endless armed peace—if peace it could be called—or whether they would put down the menace of German militarism and inaugurate the United States of the World.

We of the colored race have no ordinary interest in the outcome. That which the German power represents today spells death to the aspirations of Negroes and all darker races for equality, freedom and democracy. Let us not hesitate. Let us, while this war lasts, forget our special grievances and close our ranks shoulder to shoulder with our own white fellow citizens and the allied nations that are fighting for democracy. We make no ordinary sacrifice, but we make it gladly and willingly with our eyes lifted to the hills.

Letters of Negro Migrants of 1916–1918

The years 1910–1920 were a period of intensive Negro migration to northern cities. Chicago became home to many southern blacks. In 1910, some 44,000 Negroes lived in the city; ten years later, the number increased to over 109,000. The prewar migrants had taken jobs as porters, janitors, and domestic servants. The war migrants became laborers at Swift, Armour, Pullman, and International Harvester. For many, the *Chicago Defender*, leading Chicago Negro newspaper, was a source of advice and comfort as these anonymous letters to the editor show.

Dallas, Tex., April 23, 1917.

Dear Sir: Having been informed through the Chicago Defender paper that I can secure information from you. I am a constant reader of the Defender and am contemplating on leaving here for some point north. Having your city in view I thought to inquire of you about conditions for work, housing, wages and everything necessary. I am now employed as a laborer in a structural shop, have worked for the firm five years.

I stored cars for Armour packing co. 3 years, I also claims to know something about candy making, am handy at most anything for an honest living. I am 31 yrs. old have a very industrious wife, no children. If chances are available for work of any kind let me know. Any information you can give me will be highly appreciated.

From "Letters of Negro Migrants of 1916–1918," *Journal of Negro History*, Vol. IV (1919), pp. 291–294, 297–298, 308, 333–334. Reprinted by permission of The Association for The Study of Negro Life and History, Inc.

SAVANNAH, GA., April 24, 1917.

Sir: I saw an advertisement in the Chicago Ledger where you would send tickets to any one desireing to come up there. I am a married man with a wife only, and I am 38 years of age, and both of us have so far splendid health, and would like very much to come out there provided we could get good employment regarding the advertisement.

WINSTON-SALEM, N. N., April 23, 1917.

Dear Sir: Colored people of this place who know you by note of your great paper the Age and otherwise desire to get information from you of jobs of better opportunities for them and better advantages.

You will do us a great favor to answer us in advance.

MOBILE, ALA., June 11, 1917.

Dear Sir: Will you please send me the name of the society in Chicago that cares for colored emigrants who come north seeking employment sometime ago I saw the name of this society in the defender but of late it does not appear in the paper so I kindly as you please try and get the name of this society and send the same to me at this city.

MOBILE, ALA., April 27, 1917.

Sir: Your advertisement appearing in the Chicago Defender have influenced me to write to you with no delay. For seven previous years I bore the reputation of a first class laundress in Selma. I have much experience with all of the machines in this laundry. This laundry is noted for its skillful work of neatness and ect. We do sample work for different laundries of neighboring cities, viz. Montgomery, Birmingham and Mobile once or twice a year. At preseant I do house work but would like to get in touch with the Chicago ———. I have an eager desire of a clear information how to get a good position. I have a written recommendation from the foreman of which I largely depend upon as a relief. You will do me a noble favor with an answer in the earliest possible moment with a description all about the work.

JACKSONVILLE, FLA., 4–25–17.

Dear Sir: in reading a copy of the Chicago defender note that if i get in touch with you you would assist me in getting imployment. i am now imployed in Florida East coast R R service road way department any thing in working line myself and friends would be very glad to get in touch with as labors. We would be more than glad to do so and would highly appreciate it the very best we can advise where we can get work to do, fairly good wages also is it possible that we could get transportation to the destination. We are working men with familys. Please answer at once. i am your of esteem. We are not particular about the electric lights and all i want is fairly good wages and steady work.

PENSACOLA, FLA., April 28, 1917.

Dear Sir: I seen in the Chicago Defender where men was wanted in small towns near Chicago at fair wages. As i want to lokate in the north i thought it very nessary to consult you in the direction of this work. hoping to receive from you full pertikulars i a wate a reply.

ATLANTA, GA., April 30, 1917.

Sir: I would thank you kindly to explain to me how you get work and what term I am comeing to Chicago this spring and would like to know jest what to do would thank and appreciate a letter from you soon telling me the thing that I wont to know.

VICKSBURG, MISS., May the 5th, 1917.

Sir: Just wants you to give me a few words of enfermation of labor situations in your city or south Dakota grain farms what is their offers and their adress. Will thank you for any enfermation given of same.

FULLERTON, LA., April 28, 1917.

Dear sir: I was reading about you was neading labor ninety miles of Chicago what is the name of the place and what R R extends ther i wants to come north and i wants a stedy employment ther what doe you pay per day i dont no anything about molding works but have been working around machinery for 10 years. Let me no what doe you pay for such work and can you give me a job of that kind or a job at common labor and let me no your prices and how many hours for a day.

MARCEL, MISS., 10/4/17.

Dear Sir: Although I am a stranger to you but I am a man of the so called colored race and can give you the very best or reference as to my character and ability by prominent citizens of my community by both white and colored people that knows me although am native of

Ohio whiles I am a northern desent were reared in this state of Mississippi. Now I am a reader of your paper the Chicago Defender. After reading your writing ever wek I am compell & persuade to say that I know you are a real man of my color you have I know heard of the south land & I need not tell you any thing about it. I am going to ask you a favor and at the same time beg you for your kind and best advice. I wants to come to Chicago to live. I am a man of a family wife and 1 child I can do just any kind of work in the line of common labor & I have for the present sufficient means to support us till I can obtain a position. Now should I come to your town, would you please to assist me in getting a position I am willing to pay whatever you charge I dont want you to loan me not 1 cent but *help* me to find an occupation there in your town now I has a present position that will keep me employed till the first of Dec. 1917. now please give me your best advice on this subject. I enclose stamp for reply.

BEAUMONT, TEX., May 14, 1917.

My dear Sir: Please write me particulars concerning emigration to the north. I am a skilled machinist and longshoreman.

ST. PETERSBURG, FLA., May 31, 1917.

Dear Sir: pleas inform me of the best place in the north for the colored people of the South, I am coming north and I want to know of a good town to stop in. I enclose stamp for reply.

SANFORD, FLA., April 27, 1917.

Dear Sir: I have seen through the Chicago Defender that you and the people of Chicago are helping newcomers. I am asking you for some information about conditions in some small town near Chicago.

There are some families here thinking of moving up, and are desirous of knowing what to expect before leaving. Please state about treatment, work, rent and schools. Please answer at some spare time.

NEW ORLEANS, LA., April 30, 1917.

Dear Sir: Seeing you ad in the defender I am writing you to please give me some information concerning positions—unskilled labor or hotel work, waiter, porter, bell boy, clothes cleaning and pressing. I am experienced in those things, especially in the hotel line. am 27 years of age, *good health*—have a wife—wish you could give me information as I am not ready to come up at present. would be thankful if you could arrange with some one who would forward transportation for me and wife. would be very glad to hear from you as soon as convenient. Thanking you in advance for interest shown me.

NEW ORLEANS, LA., April 23, 1917.

Dear Sir: Reading a article in the 21st issue of the Chicago Defender about the trouble you had to obtain men for work out of Chicago and also seeing a advertisement for men in Detroit saying to apply to you I beg to state to you that if your could secure me a position in or around Chicago or any northern section with fairly good wages & good living conditions for myself and family I will gladly take same and if ther could be any ways of sending me transportation I will gladly let you or the firm you get me position with deduct transportation fee out of my salary. as I said before I will gladly take position in northern city or county where a mans a man here are a few positions which I am capable of holding down. Laborer, expirance porter, butler or driver of Ford car. Thaking you in advance for your kindness, beg to remain.

CEDAR GROVE, LA., April 23, 1917.

Dear Sir: to day I was advise by the defendent offices in your city to communicate with you in regards to the labor for the colored of the south as I was lead to beleave that you was in position of firms of your city & your near by surrounding towns of Chicago. Please state me how is the times in & around Chicago place to locate having a family dependent on me for support. I am informed by the Chicago Defender a very valuable paper which has for its purpose the Uplifting of my race, and of which I am a constant reader and real lover, that you were in position to show some light to one in my condition.

Seeking a Northern Home. If this is true Kindly inform me by next mail the next best thing to do Being a poor man with a family to care for, I am not coming to live on flowry Beds of ease for I am a man who works and wish to make the best I can out of life I do not wish to come there hoodwinked not knowing where to go or what to do so I Solicite your help in this matter and thanking you in advance for what advice you may be pleased to Give I am yours for success.

P.S. I am presently imployed in the I C RR. Mail Department at Union Station this city.

PALESTINE, TEX., Mar. 11th, 1917.

Sirs: this is somewhat a letter of information I am a colored Boy aged 15 years old and I am talented for an artist and I am in search of some one will Cultivate my talent I have studied Cartooning therefore I am a Cartoonist and I intend to visit Chicago this summer and I want to keep in touch with your association and too from you knowledge can a Colored boy be an artist and make a white man's salary up there I will tell you more and also send a fiew samples of my work when I rec an answer from you.

TOPEKA, KANSAS, May 1st, 1917.
The Editor of The Chicago Defender.

My Dear Sir: Being a regular reader of your most valuable paper (The Defender) I am impressed with the seeming unlimited interest that paper is taking in the welfare of the army of emigrants comeing from the south.

This alone without the knowledge of its incomparable service as a link in the chain that should bind our people together more closely through out the country. should demand its presence in every negro home of this country. In keeping in touch with the doings of our people in the east and northern states through the Defender. To the Majority of the Middle western race people it seem quite improbable that oppertunities for good wage earning positions such as factory work and too a chance for advancement would be given to the workers of our race.

Such conditions in this part of the country to my knowledge is rare. Noteing in the issue of last weeks paper through the investigation into certain matter concerning our people some appearantly well organized league found openings for negro workmen in some parts of Wis. and Ill. that could not be filled.

As I for one that am not satisfied to content myself with little and to remain in the same old rut for the sake of lengthy assiation and fair treatment I am making My appeal to you in your wide aquaintence with conditions to help me to take advangage of an oppertunity that I might other wise miss.

I am mechanically inclined also with the advantage of a course with the International Correspondance School in Automobile work and with several years experience. I am not afraid of any kind of work that pays.

Will kindly ask you to help me all you can at my expense and I will be very grateful to you.

GONZALES, TEXAS, May 28, 1917.
NEW YORK AGE, New York, N.Y.

Gentlemen: I wish to know if a man from the south come north, such as common laborer, stationery engineer, gasoline engineer, fireman or janitor able to care for heating plants ets. and able to pay his own way there, is there a likelihood of finding lucrative employment?

I would be plased to have you advise me on the same as myself and several other men of good morals and sober habits and who are able to bear our own expenses would like to better our conditions by coming North.

If you can advise us or Know of any one or place that we can get the desired information please give us the benefit of the same.

Find stamp enclosed for answer.

HOUSTON, TEXAS, April 20, 1917.

Dear Sir: wanted to leave the South and Go and Place where a man will Be any thing Except A Ker I thought would write you for Advise As where would be a Good Place for a Composedly young man That want to Better his Standing who has a very Promising young Family.

I am 30 years old and have Good Experence in Freight Handler and Can fill Position from Truck to Agt.

would like Chicago or Philadelphia But I dont Care where so long as I Go where a man is a man

MEMPHIS, TENN., May 12 8 17.

Dear Sir: I am a constant reader of your paper which can be purchased here at the Panama Cafe news stand. Mr. ——— at present I am employed as agent for the Interstate Life and acc'd ins. Co. but on account of the race people leaving here so very fast my present job is no longer a profitable one. I have a number of young friends in your city who are advising me to come to Chicago and I have just about made up my mind to come. but before leaving here I wanted to ask Some advice from you along certain lines. I am buying property here and taking up notes each month on Same these notes now are aroun $14 per month. and with my present Salary and the unusual high price on everything I can't possibly protect myself very long against a foreclosure on above mentioned property on account of my Salary being less than $50.00 per month. Mr. ——— do you think I could come to your city with myself and wife rent this place out here and better my condition financially? I am strong and able to do anything kind of work so long as the Salary is O.K. I have a fair experience as a meat cutter and can furnish the best of reference from business houses one of them is Swift & Co of this city. I hope you can understand me clearly, it is my aim to make an honest living and would not dream of any other method. I am prepared to leave here at any time and must go Some place but Chicago is the place that impress me most. and having the confidence in you as a great race man I am writing you for your honest opinion concerning the facts in the matter. Many thanks for the information in today's paper under the Caption ("Know thyself") hoping this will meet with your hearty Cooperation.

P. S. What is about the average salaries paid there for unskilled laborers and what is board and room rent? if I come would it be advisable to come alone and Secure location and everything and then have my wife come later?

William Tuttle □ Views of a Negro During "the Red Summer" of 1919

The year 1919 was a period of considerable unrest for postwar America. A wave of strikes swept the nation; the government suppressed radicals in an extra-legal manner, and over twenty race riots erupted from one coast to another. In late July a racial incident involving the death of a Negro youth on a South Side Chicago beach ignited into a riot that lasted five days. Altogether, 16 Negroes and 15 whites died, and well over 500 Chicagoians sustained serious injury. It took six regiments of state militiamen and a cooling rain to subdue the violence. The following document is a letter from Stanley B. Norvell, a Chicago Negro war veteran, to the editor of the *Chicago Daily News*, Victor Lawson, concerning the causes of the riot.

My dear Mr. Lawson:

As the cause of the Negro in America is one that is nearer and dearer to my heart than any other, it has become an obsession with me, and for that reason I am taking the liberty of inflicting upon you this unsolicited treatise on the subject. It is my fond hope that these unlettered lines—which are intended to throw a little light upon the controversy from the dark side—may be of some little service to you and your worthy commission, as data. . . .

I take it that the object of this commission is to obtain by investigation and by conference the cause or causes of the friction between the

From "Views of a Negro During the Red Summer of 1919," ed. William Tuttle, *Journal of Negro History*, Vol. LI (July 1966). Reprinted by permission of The Association for The Study of Negro Life and History, Inc.

two races that started the molecules of race hatred into such violent motion as to cause the heterogenous mixture to boil over in the recent race riots.

Few white men know the cause, for the simple reason that few white men know the Negro as an entity. On the other hand, I daresay that almost any Negro that you might meet on the street could tell you the cause, if he would, for it is doubtful—aye, very doubtful—if he would tell you, because Negroes have become highly suspicious of white men, even such white men as they deem their friends ordinarily. The Negro has always been and is now largely a menial dependent upon the white man's generosity and charity for his livelihood, and for this reason he has become an expert cajoler of the white man and a veritable artist at appearing to be that which he is not. To resort to the vernacular, "conning" the white man has become his profession, his stock in trade. Take for example the Negro in Chicago—and Chicago is fairly representative—sixty per cent of the male Negro population is engaged in menial and servile occupations such as hotel waiters, dining car waiters, sleeping car porters, barbershop porters, billiard room attendants, etc., where "tips" form the greater part of their remuneration. Thirty per cent are laborers and artisans, skilled and unskilled, governmental and municipal employees; while the remaining ten per cent are business and professional men.

Unfortunately it is always by the larger class—the menial, servitor and flunkey class—that the race is judged. Even at that, we would not object to being judged by this class of our race, if those who did the judging had a thorough knowledge of the individuals who make up this class. Unfortunately they have not this knowledge nor can they get it except through the instrumentality of just such a commission as that to which you gentlemen have been assigned. The white man of America knows just about as much about the mental and moral calibre, the home life and social activities of this class of colored citizens as he does about the same things concerning the inhabitants of the thus far unexplored planet of Mars. If any white man were to be asked what he thought of George the porter on the Golden State Limited; or of James the waiter on the Twentieth Century diner; or of Shorty who gives him his billard cue at Mussey's; or of Snowball who polishes his boots at the Palmer House; or of that old gray-haired relic of by-gone days . . . who withholds his hat and menaces him with a long-handled whisk broom until he capitulates with a nickel; I say were you to ask any white man concerning these dusky servitors he would tell you that he was either honest or dishonest, that he was either industrious or lazy, that he was smart or stupid as the case might be. He will discuss him in a general superficial sort of way and if you press him further you will be surprised to know that in spite of his years of aquaintance with the subject he knows absolutely nothing about intellect, ability, ambitions[,] the home life and environment of one with whom he has come into daily contact for years. He is just a "nigger" and he takes him for granted, as a matter of course. . . .

In hotels, barber shops and billiard rooms where the patrons come in regularly, Sambo has a chance to get well acquainted with them. . . . He knows just what each one's business is and where it is located. He knows just where each one lives and in what circumstances. . . . He knows just how much each one is going to give him. There are some that never give him anything but still he likes them immensely because they treat him with kindness and consideration. There are some who tip him most liberally whom he despises because they are always making some aspersion about his race or because they always want him to clown and demean himself in order to get their money. . . . He knows that if he says, "Yas sah, Boss," and grins that you will vote him a "good nigger" and give him something; but were he to say, "Very good, sir," you would not only give him anything but would probably take a dislike to him and consider him supercillious. . . .

I can walk down the "Boul Mich" and be surveyed by the most critical of Sherlock Holmes's and I will wager that none of them can accurately deduce what I am or what I represent. They cannot tell whether I am well off or hard up; whether I am educated or illiterate; whether I am a northerner or a southerner; whether I am a native born Negro or a foreigner; whether I live among beautiful surroundings or in the squalor of the "black belt." I defy the shrewdest of your pseudo detectives to know whether I am a reputable citizen or whether I am a newly arrived crook. They cannot tell by looking at me what my income is. . . . The point is that I am only an ordinary, average Negro and that the white man is constantly making the mistake of discounting us and rating us too cheaply. He should wake up to the fact that brain is not peculiar to any race or nationality but is merely a matter of development.

This in a measure explains how the American white man knows less about the American Negro than the latter does about the former. . . .

The further causes of the apparent increased friction between the two races, in my opinion is due to the gradual, and inevitable evolution—metamorphosis, if you please—of the Negro. The Negro has also progressed in knowledge by his study of the white man, while the white man blinded by either his prejudice or by his indifference has failed to study the Negro judiciously, and as a consequence, he knows no more about him than he did fifty years ago and still continues to judge him and to formulate opinions about him by his erstwhile standards. Today we have with us a new Negro. A brand new Negro, if you please. What opportunities have you better class white people for getting into and observing the homes of the better class of colored people[?] Yet the duties of the colored man in his menial capacities gives him an insight of your home life. As a suggestion, if I may be permitted to make one, I suggest that the white members of this commission make it their business to try to obtain an opportunity through some of the colored members of the commission to visit the homes of some of our better class people. You will find that "Uncle Tom" that charming old figure of literature contemporary with the war of the rebellion is quite dead now and that his prototypes are almost as extinct as is the great auk, the dodo bird, old Dobbin and the chaise, and the man who refused to shave until William Jennings Bryan was elected. You will have committed an unpardonable faux pas if you should happen to call any eminently respectable old colored lady "mammy" or "auntie," and yet there still remain many misguided and well-intentioned folks of the white race who still persist in so doing. This was all brought about by education. . . . When a young colored boy of Chicago goes through the eight grades of grammar school and wins the cherished Victor F. Lawson diploma; then through a four year high school course and wins a university scholarship; and then goes to college and wins a degree . . . and is highly popular and well received among his fellow classmates, it is a very difficult thing for him to get it into his head that he is inferior to anybody that has no more knowledge, ability nor money than himself. Regardless of what the eminent sociologists may say, and the fiery and usually groundless claims of the southern negrophile [negrophobe] to the contrary notwithstanding, there is no amount of logic, nor philosophy, nor ethnology, nor anthropology, nor sociology that can convince him to his own satisfaction that he is not the possessor of all the lesser and major attributes that go to make up a good citizen by all of the standards which our republican conventions hold near and dear.

Take the late war for example, and consider the effect that it has had upon the Negro, by and large. I believe that the mental attitude of the Negro that went to war is comparable in a certain degree to the mental attitude of most of the Negroes throughout the country; so far as the awakenings are concerned. The Negro of this country has gone through the same evolution that the white man has, in his own way; and in a large percentage of the total, that way is not far removed from the way the white man's mind thought out the matter or is thinking it out, especially the soldier mind. The Negro of our country . . . the Negro of the mass I mean, is comparable in his awakening and in his manner of thought after that awakening, to these white boys who went to war. The white soldiers—being young—had but little thought of anything but their immediate concerns, and the Negro, until lately, had but little thought of anything but his immediate concerns—being segregated. How I loathe that word.

Since the war the Negro has been jolted into thinking by circumstances. . . . [Negroes] have learned that there were treaties and boundaries and Leagues of Nations and mandatories, and Balkan states, and a dismembered Poland, a ravished Belgium, a stricken France, a soviet Russia and a republic in Ireland and so on, and they have . . . for the first time in their lives taken a peep of their own volition and purely because they wanted to know, into the workings of governmental things of those other countries, and have tried to reason out the possible real cause of all of this bloodshed and woe and misery along such international, allied and foreign government and other vague lines.

Now then, this has logically—and we are nebulously logical, despite what the southern white says about us—brought us round to a sort of realization of how our government was made and is conducted. I venture to claim that any average Negro of some education, if closely questioned, and the questions were put to him in simple understandable form, will tell you that he finally has come to know that he counts as a part of his government, that he is a unit in it. It took a world war to get that idea into general Negro acceptance, but it is there now. Centuries of the dictum, which heretofore not many of us disputed, that, "This was a white man's country and that we were destined to always be hewers of wood and carriers of water," was set aside by circumstances and conditions and reactions and reflexes and direct contacts of this war. Negroes were pulled out of their ordinary pursuits all over the country and called upon to do things that they had to do because there was nobody at hand to do them, and those circumstances induced an awakening that must inevitably continue for all time.

The five hundred thousand Negroes who were sent overseas to serve their country were brought into contacts that widened both their perceptions and their perspectives, broadened them, gave them new angles on life, on government, and on what both mean. They are now new men and world men, if you please. . . .

What the Negro wants and what the Negro will not be satisfied with until he gets is that treatment and that recognition that accords him not one jot or tittle less than that which any other citizen of the United States is satisfied with. He has become tired of equal rights. He wants the same rights. He is tired of equal accommodations. He wants [the] same accommodations. He is tired of equal opportunity. He wants the same opportunity. He must and will have industrial, commercial, civil and political equality. America has already given him these inalienable rights, but she has not always seen to it that he has received them. America must see that the Negro is not deprived of any right that she has given him otherwise the gift is bare, and in view of her recent international exploits she will stand in grave danger of losing her national integrity in the eyes of Europe and she will be forced to admit to her European adversaries that her constitution is but a scrap of paper.

Social equality—that ancient skeleton in the closet of the southern negrophile [negrophobe], whose bones are always brought out and rattled ominously whenever the Negro question is discussed—is in no way a factor in the solution of the problem, but is a condition that will quite naturally exist when the problem is eventually solved—just a little prior to the millenium. Leastwise considering the unsettled condition of the world at large, the white man of this country has a great deal more to be sensibly alarmed about than the coming of social equality. Looking into the future I can see more ominous clouds on the horizon of this country's destiny than the coming of social equality.

When the Negro ponders the situation—and now he is beginning to seriously do that—it is with a feeling of poignant resentment that he sees his alleged inferiority constantly and blatantly advertised at every hand, by the press, the pulpit, the stage and by the glaring and hideous sign-boards of segregation. Try to imagine, if you can, the feelings of a Negro army officer, who clothed in the full panoply of his profession and wearing the decorations for valor of three governments, is forced to the indignity of a jim-crow car and who is refused a seat in a theatre and a bed in a hotel. Think of the feelings of a colored officer, who after having been graduated from West Point and having worked up step by step to the rank of colonel to be retired on account of blood pressure—and other pressure—in order that he might not automatically succeed to the rank of general officer. Try to imagine the smouldering hatred within the breast of an overseas veteran who is set upon and mercilessly beaten by a gang of young hoodlums simply because he is colored. Think of the feelings in the hearts of boys and girls of my race who are clean, intelligent and industrious who apply for positions only to meet with the polite reply that, "We don't hire niggers." Think how it must feel to pass at the top of the list and get notice of appointment to some nice civil service position that is paid for out of the taxes of the commonwealth, and upon reporting to assume the duties thereof, to be told that there has been a mistake made in the appointment.

When you think of these things, and consider them seriously it is easy to see the underlying, contributory causes of the friction that led up to the recent racial troubles. It is a well known fact that civilization is but a veneer which lightly covers the surface of mankind; that if slightly scratched, with the right kind of tool, a man will turn into a bloodthirsty savage in the twinkling of an eye. The overt act that is alleged to have started the recent conflagration, would not have in itself been sufficient to have ignited and exploded such vials of wrath had not the structure of society been long soaked in the inflammable gasolene of smouldering resentment.

As soon as the white man is willing to inform himself about the true status of the Negro as he finds him today, and is willing to take off the goggles of race prejudice and to study the Negro with the naked eye of fairness, and to treat him with justice and equity, he will come to the conclusion that the Negro has "arrived" and then voila, you have the solution to the problem.

We ask not charity but justice. We no longer want perquisites but wages, salary and commissions. Much has been said anent the white man's burden. We admit to having been a burden, just as an infant that cannot walk is at one time a burden. But in the natural order of things the infant soon ceases to be a burden and eventually grows up to be a crutch for the arm that once carried him. We feel that now we are able to take our first, feeble diffident steps, and we implore the white man to set his burden down and let us try to walk. Put us in your counting rooms, your factories and in your banks. The young people who went to school with us and who learned the three R's from the same black-board as ourselves will surely not object to working with us after we have graduated. If they do, it will only be because they are not yet accustomed to the new conditions. That is nothing. People soon become accustomed to new things and things that seem at first preposterous soon become commonplace. We have surely proven by years of unrequited toil and by constant and unfaltering loyalty and fealty that we are worthy of the justice that we ask. For God's sake give it to us!

Eugene K. Jones □ Cooperation and Opportunity

The riots of 1919 failed to diminish the flow of Negro migrants to the North. By 1923, Charles S. Johnson, editor of *Opportunity*, observed that "anxious eyes are casting southward again." Black labor was being imported into Pittsburgh, Wheeling, and Youngstown, and a "new migration indeed seems imminent." The following editorial—written by Eugene K. Jones, Executive Secretary of the Urban League—illustrates that race riots did not reduce a faith in accommodation.

The National Urban League for nearly twelve years has sought to merit a reputation as a doer of things worth while in the interest of the relations between the Negro and the white races in America. Its field work has in the main consisted of efforts to raise the standards of living among Negroes. Its slogan has been "Not Alms, but Opportunity." It has sought to make its contribution towards elevating the Negro in the social scale, the motive being to make it easier for theNegro to assimilate the cultural advantages of American civilization and to aid more Negroes of capacity and talent to emerge from the mass of their fellows of less promise.

The League has also attempted to make available to white people information on the Negro that would tend to clear up many of the mooted questions about the Negro.

The whites of America may be classified in several interesting groups according to their attitude toward the Negro: First—the indifferent group, or those who have given no thought to the Negro; those who have not come in contact with "the problem" and who therefore

From Eugene K. Jones, "Cooperation and Opportunity," *Opportunity*, Vol. I (January 1923), pp. 4–5. Reprinted with permission of the National Urban League, Inc., from *Opportunity: Journal of Negro Life*.

have not thought much about it. If pressed for an opinion members of this group would naturally be thrown into one of the other classes. Second, those who consciously detest and distrust all things Negroid either through a prejudice which has no foundation or as a result of unpleasant personal experiences with Negroes. Third, those who through a sense of justice cannot avoid the feeling that the Negro should be included in the unfortunate peoples to whom they extend their sympathy. They would like not to include the Negro but must in order to reconcile their attitudes to their theories of individual rights. So they believe, in the Negro with certain reservations. They believe in Negroes having their "man's chance" but segregated in the enjoyment of their rights in schools, pleasure parks or public recreational centers, in restaurants and in certain lines of employment. Fourth, those who believe in the application of the principle of justice and equality to all men, the Negro included. Except in the case of certain individuals with the spirit of martyrs these persons despite their beliefs are forced through convention and the social orders of the day to abide in practice largely by the requirements of a practical and tolerant society.

The League has sought to reach representatives of all of these groups in a spirit of co-operation.

Cooperation or good fellowship between the racial elements in America presupposes the existence of an inclination on the part of members of each race to meet the members of other races on a platform of good will. It assumes the existence of an intelligence and a standard of living common to both races, members of which observe in each other similar interests and ideals. The whites sooner or later, no matter what their present status or environment, are vouchsafed in time a chance to rise above their present level. Such is not the case with the Negro in anything like the same degree that it obtains for the whites. His case calls for drastic and special attention, not only to secure for him the operation of improvement programs, educational in character involving the whole race, but to promote the establishment of agencies dealing with fundamentals, agencies which more or less are common among the whites but among Negroes practically non-existent, such as day nurseries, settlement houses and health clinics.

The Urban League feels that the Negro, as a group, must be brought up to a higher social plane so that he can accept his rightful place in society as his opportunities come. His leaders must be trained and given a chance to gain wider experience with his fellows. The League furnishes a field of labor for these leaders. In many cases such potential leaders as executives of the League are men short of forty, and many just turning thirty. They see life from a new angle and are preparing new fields for their fellow-race members. They attempt programs which require great faith and energy. They have helped to revolutionize social work among Negroes, which has changed from the street-corner missionary type of work to the up-to-date scientific social service.

Many Negro churches have caught the vision and are building community churches and are adding social service features to their religious programs. In many cities representatives of or persons recommended by the League are appointed on Mayor's Emergency Relief or Unemployment Committees. Community movements of whatever character are not considered complete in most cities where the League works if recognition is not given to the needs of Negro citizens.

In the past this service has been promoted and publicity on achievements has been secured in a desultory, hit-or-miss fashion. Experiences have been exchanged between communities through correspondence and an occasional conference where representatives of various organizations have met to exchange ideas. The first method —that of correspondence—is a slow process. The second, that of occasional conferences—is inadequate because only a very few representatives from each organization get the direct benefit. The League feels that the very generous space which has been given to it by the newspapers and magazines has been of great help. But the League should not and could not command as much space to express its ideals as the importance of its mission justifies. The reports on its investigations and research work alone call for considerable space if only the practical parts of its findings are presented. The League therefore has launched on a new venture which should have the whole-hearted support and encouragement of all white and colored people who are interested in the scientific treatment of "the problem" and who wish to see more "cooperation" between the races.

"OPPORTUNITY" as a name has been adopted for our new magazine because it carries with it the idea presented by the League's motto "Not Alms, but Opportunity." "OPPORTUNITY'S" Editor is Charles S. Johnson, Director of the League's Department of Research and Investigations who was Associate Director of the Chicago Race Relations Commission which has recently published its report on the Causes of the Chicago Race Riots with recommendations for improvement in race relations. He is eminently qualified through both training and experience to edit a "journal of Negro Life" which will depict Negro life as it is with no exaggerations. We shall try to set down interestingly but without sugar-coating or generalization the findings of careful scientific surveys and the facts gathered from research, undertaken not to prove preconceived notions but to lay bare Negro life as it is.

Adam Clayton Powell, Sr. □ The Church In Social Work

Traditionally, the Negro minister has occupied an important role in the black community. He was often their intellectual as well as moral leader. Congregations placed great emphasis upon dynamic preaching, and a truly articulate pastor could become an influential force for social improvement. Such was the case of Adam Clayton Powell, Sr., father of the flamboyant Harlem Congressman. Born in 1865 in Franklin County, Virginia, the elder Powell was educated at Virginia Union University. From 1908–1937, he served as pastor of the Abyssinian Baptist Church of Harlem. Reverend Powell died in 1953.

The church must enlarge its religious activities if it is to retain the respect and support of intelligent men. Christianity is more than preaching, praying, singing and giving; it is all of these but a great deal more. The purpose of the Christianity of Jesus as revealed in the New Testament is to supply man's social as well as spiritual needs. The church is being called upon to give the world a Christianity of deeds as well as a Christianity of creeds. Very few people ask any more "What the church believes?" but "What the church is doing for the amelioration of the condition of mankind?" The majority of people care very little about church doctrines. They are looking for a translation of the spirit of Jesus Christ in the everyday life of his professed followers. The church will never draw and hold the masses by essays on faith, but by showing her faith by her works.

From Rev. Adam Clayton Powell, Sr., "The Church in Social Work," Vol. I (January 1923), p. 15. Reprinted with permission of the National Urban League, Inc., from *Opportunity: Journal of Negro Life*.

The church has not discharged its obligations when it has hired a man to stand up twice one day in seven, and piously ram the Bible down the throats of the people. It must go into the highways and hedges during the week caring for the sick, the wounded, the distressed and all that are needy, and then on Sunday they will hear us and believe us when we tell them of "Jesus, the Mighty to save."

The Abyssinian Baptist Church of New York City is planning to carry out this larger program of applied Christianity. A $300,000 Church and Community House is being erected in Harlem, the most densely populated Negro Center in the world. This Church will be a kind of an intellectual go-between for the public schools and the higher institutions of learning. Thousands of Negroes are coming to Northern cities each year who are too old to be reached by the public schools and too poorly informed to enter universities. This large group had in it tremendous undeveloped possibilities. Thru the classes in English, Reading Circles and Lecture Courses that will be provided, there will be not only a vision of the great world in which we live, but a means by which they may helpfully relate themselves to a movement for world betterment.

The Church should be the social center of the community in which it is located. Man seeks the fellowship of other human beings, as surely as water seeks its level. If he cannot find the fellowship he craves with good men he will find it with bad ones. The majority of people who go to disreputable places do not go because they desire to do wrong, but for fellowship. The Church should cease criticising and abusing people for spending their evenings in questionable places until it has given them a place to socialize in a wholesome environment. The Church which will grip and hold men in the future will be the Church that vitally relates itself to every problem of the masses. This does not mean that emphasis will be shifted from man's spiritual to his social needs. It is the paramount duty of the Church to Christianize the social order. The Church, therefore, which undertakes to carry out a large social program must be more spiritual than the one which deals simply in emotional religion. The world has gone wild like an uncaged beast of the jungle and there seems to be no power in science, politics, diplomacy, or economics to gird it. Only the social reign of God can bring order out of man's social confusion.

2

The Twenties and the New Negro

Richard Sherman □ The Harding Administration and the Negro: An Opportunity Lost

In 1920, many Negroes greeted the return of the Republican party to power with enthusiasm. Their confidence was understandable in the light of the discriminating practices of the Wilson administration —which had insisted upon segregating railroad workers—and which had done little to stop lynching. And after James Cox, the Democratic presidential candidate, accused the Republican nominee of being the tool of black radicals, there seemed little doubt that Warren Harding was preferable, especially after he had denounced lynching. In this essay, Professor Richard B. Sherman examines Harding's attitudes toward the Negro.

With the return of the Republicans to power in 1921 many Americans hoped that a new era in race relations would begin. Although disappointed by the record of the GOP since McKinley, Negroes were deeply embittered by the discriminatory practices of the Wilson administration. Thus most colored voters supported the Republicans in 1920. But in return they expected a reversal of at least the worst Democratic racial practices. And a few optimists, counting upon the influence of an enlarged and somewhat more independently inclined Negro electorate in the North, anticipated considerably more. They saw in the Republican revival an opportunity for the Party of Lincoln to recommit itself to the principles of equality and to rebuild its ancient alliance with the Negro.

From Richard Sherman, "The Harding Administration and the Negro: An Opportunity Lost," *Journal of Negro History* (July 1964). Reprinted by permission of The Association for The Study of Negro Life and History, Inc.

Despite such hopes the attitude of the GOP leaders in 1920 was not at first very encouraging. Harding's knowledge of racial problems was negligible. And like the other Republican presidential aspirants, he was reluctant to express precise opinions about matters of concern to American Negroes. For example, in February, 1920, the NAACP sent out a questionnaire to seventeen men mentioned as presidential possibilities asking for their opinion on a federal anti-lynching law, disfranchisement, Jim Crow cars in interstate travel, American intervention in Haiti, aid to education without color discrimination, service of Negroes in the armed forces, and segregation in the civil service. Only three men responded, and not one answered the questions asked. Senator Harding stated that he didn't believe in taking a stand on categorical questions, Senator Miles Poindexter affirmed his belief in "maintaining the legal rights and opportunities of all our citizens," and General Leonard Wood replied that his reported attitude toward colored officers was "enemy propaganda." Such responses were hardly reassuring.

Furthermore, the Republican National Convention paid very limited attention to Negro demands. The credentials committee, for example, decided in favor of lilywhites in several disputed delegation cases. Moreover, the convention passed a resolution that was designed to reduce the number of delegates from Southern states, and in so doing to weaken the black and tan parties and thus facilitate their reorganization by lilywhites. Five Negroes, including James Weldon Johnson of the NAACP, did sit on a platform advisory committee. But as Johnson later observed, that duty proved to be "quite an empty honor." The 1920 platform had only one plank of direct concern to Negroes, that on lynching. "We urge Congress," it said, "to consider the most effective means to end lynching in this country which continues to be a terrible blot on our American civilization." While this was vague, nevertheless it was the most specific recommendation of its sort to appear in a Republican platform in years.

During the campaign Republican leaders did make some effort to woo the colored voters. Thus they appointed Negro advisers for each section of the country, and in Ohio, the home state of both the Republican and Democratic presidential candidates, they conducted a drive to register Negro women. As a result the race issue became particularly important in that state. The Ohio Democrats attacked the Republicans for being too friendly to the Negro, and issued intimidating pamphlets, such as "A Timely Warning to the White Men and Women of Ohio," and "The Threat of Negro Domination." Democratic Vice-Presidential candidate Franklin D. Roosevelt angrily accused the Republicans of appealing to race hatreds and prejudices, while standard-bearer James M. Cox asserted that behind Harding was "the

Afro-American party, whose hyphenated activity has attempted to stir up troubles among the Negroes upon false claims that it can bring social equality."

While Cox was alienating colored voters by such remarks, Harding took the time to comment sympathetically on racial issues and to consult with Negro spokesmen at his home in Marion, Ohio. His acceptance speech, delivered on July 22, sounded a fairly positive note. "I believe the Federal government should stamp out lynching and remove that stain from the fair name of America." Moreover, continued Harding, "I believe the Negro citizens of America should be guaranteed the enjoyment of all their rights, that they have earned the full measure of citizenship bestowed, that their sacrifice in blood on the battlefields of the republic have entitled them to all of freedom and opportunity, all of sympathy and aid that the American spirit of fairness and justice demands." Actually, a careful reading of Harding's speech shows that the only specific recommendation it made concerning the Negro was that on lynching. Still the tone was vastly different from that used by Cox.

During the campaign Harding also criticized United States intervention in the Negro republic of Haiti. Prompted by charges of American atrocities, the board of directors of the NAACP voted in March, 1920, to send their field secretary, James Weldon Johnson, to Haiti to investigate. On return from a six weeks' visit Johnson wrote a damaging report of the occupation that appeared in the pages of *The Crisis, The Christian Herald,* and *The Nation.* On August 9, Johnson journeyed to Marion, Ohio, to discuss the matter with Harding, and a few weeks later the Republican candidate attacked the Wilson administration's Haitian policy. Secretary of the Navy Daniels countered by ordering a hearing by a naval board of inquiry, but the NAACP considered this investigation a mere whitewash and continued to press for American withdrawal. Thus the Haitian situation had embarrassed the Democrats, while Harding's public statements were relatively encouraging to concerned Negroes. What course a Republican administration would take, once it returned to power, remained to be seen.

Probably most Negro voters approached the Presidential election in fairly conventional terms and supported the Party of Lincoln. Nevertheless a growing number of Negro leaders preached the doctrine of political independence. The position taken by W. E. B. DuBois was suggestive of this spirit. Just before the Republican National Convention he published an article in *The Nation* instructing his readers that in a close election Negro votes in several Northern states would hold the balance of power. He also pointed out that Negroes had "longstanding grievances against the Republican Party, and it cannot therefore count on the absolute necessity of a black man voting Republican." If DuBois had hoped that his article might influence the Republicans at Chicago, the outcome of the convention proved him wrong. And the fiery editor returned such insolence in kind. "Neither candidate," he wrote in the August issue of *The Crisis,* "is a friend of the Negro nor of democracy. Neither convention was fair to us . . . We are, therefore, under no obligations. We are free of entangling alliances." The next month DuBois noted that while only the Farmer-Labor and Socialist parties took a decent stand on behalf of the Negro, neither could win. And as it might be a great danger to have a major party triumph without Negro aid, his advice was to vote for either party for President—he stated no preference—but to pay special attention to Congress, where one should "*vote for friends of our race and defeat our enemies.*"

Thus Negro enthusiasm for Harding was less than overwhelming. Yet if he had actually promised very little, at least Harding had been willing to listen in a friendly manner to Negro spokesmen. James Weldon Johnson, for example, noted that his "two interviews with Mr. Harding at Marion established a cordial relationship." And during the campaign Harding had been informed of a number of issues that the Negro community considered vital. Furthermore, the instruction process continued after the election. On January 15, 1921, Johnson met again with the President-elect at Marion and spoke about Negro disfranchisement, the Klan, lynching, Haiti, the appointment of an interracial commission, and pardon for the Houston rioters. Harding in turn invited him to come to Washington after the inauguration to discuss racial matters.

On two occasions before he took office Harding met with delegations of Negroes at St. Augustine, Florida, to discuss the race situation in the South. One interview, which had been arranged by James Weldon Johnson, took place on February 22, with a group headed by Captain James W. Floyd of Jacksonville. Another meeting was held at the instigation of Dr. Robert Moton, head of Tuskegee Institute, who hoped to establish contacts with the White House similar to those he had developed under Wilson. An appointment was finally secured for Dr. Moton, who was accompanied by Dr. Will Alexander of the Commission on Interracial Cooperation, John J. Eagan, president of the American Cast Iron Pipe Company and chairman of the C. I. C., the Reverend Ashby Jones, and Dr. Thomas J. Woofter from the staff of the C. I. C. After some confusion the group was ushered into Harding's suite in the Ponce de Leon Hotel. It was soon apparent that Harding's knowledge of the Southern racial situation was abysmal. Not only had he never heard of Dr. Moton, but he was ignorant even of Tuskegee Institute and Booker T. Washington. Harding, who apparently thought that the members of the delegation were job-seeking politicians, embarrassed the group by his discussion of politics and his cursing. Upon leaving, Dr. Moton commented to his associates: "I'm afraid we'll have to see the President-elect again sometime. We have completely failed." Dr. Woofter then added, "If you'd eliminate damn from that fellow's vocabulary he couldn't do anything but stutter."

James Weldon Johnson was more successful. Meeting with the new President on April 4, 1921, Johnson spoke "frankly of the great unrest among colored people and their dissatisfaction with conditions which allowed lynching, disfranchisement, peonage and other forms of racial injustice." At the same time Johnson gave Harding a memorandum prepared by the NAACP which asked that he recommend action to end lynching, that the Department of Justice investigate peonage, that the government investigate Negro disfranchisement in the South, that a national interracial commission be appointed to study race relations, that Congress investigate the American occupation of Haiti, that the administration appoint colored assistant secretaries in the Departments of Labor and Agriculture, and that the President abolish by executive order racial segregation in government departments in Washington and in the Civil Service. Harding's knowledge of the Negro was undoubtedly meager. But thanks especially to the efforts of James Weldon Johnson and the NAACP he possessed a list of actions desired by many colored Americans. Whether President Harding and the Republican administration would demonstrate a serious commitment to that program was another matter.

Harding's message to a special session of Congress on April 12 aroused hope in even some usually skeptical observers. In it he called upon Congress "to wipe the stain of barbaric lynching from the banners of a free and orderly representative democracy," and he cautiously noted, but did not explicitly recommend, the proposal for an interracial commission to study race relations. Actually a careful reading of the message reveals that Harding was very vague, that he failed to mention most of the issues brought up by James Weldon Johnson, and that even in regard to lynching he declined to recommend specifically the passage of the Dyer bill then before Congress. But the tone seemed warmly sympathetic, and even W. E. B. DuBois was elated. "This is the strongest pronouncement ever made by a President in a message to Congress," he wrote. "It offers hope that the eleven years of effort during which the NAACP has been stinging the conscience of America by bringing to light the conditions affecting the Negro, are about to bear fruit."

DuBois' unusual optimism was short-lived. And if his temperament was more volatile than most, his growing disappointment in the Harding administration was shared by many other Negroes. By the early summer of 1921 DuBois noted bitterly that nothing had been done about the interracial commission and that work on the antilynching bill was going on at a languid pace. Furthermore, he regarded Harding's consideration of Taft for the Supreme Court as "almost disastrous." After his message of April 12, 1921, Harding never again pressed Congress for legislation desired by Negroes. He was silent on the subject in both of his annual messages to Congress in December, 1921 and 1922. And Congress, which was firmly controlled by the Republicans, showed little concern for matters important to the Negro, with the exception of the antilynching bill. It was not that Harding was hostile. His public statements, while often pretty general, were usually friendly, and on the occasions when he met with Negro delegations his manner was warm and cordial. But his understanding of racial problems was superficial, and in dealing with them he lacked a sense of moral urgency or of strong political necessity. The result was that the two and a half years of Harding's abbreviated administration saw little progress in matters of concern to the Negro community.

Harding's most extensive public statement about the race problem in the United States was made on October 26, 1921, in a speech to several thousand Negroes and whites assembled at Woodrow Wilson Park in Birmingham, Alabama. In its wordy and repetitious style the address was vintage Harding. But he did make some positive statements that attracted considerable attention. As for the two races, he observed that:

> Politically and economically there need be no occasion for great and permanent differentiation, for limitations of the individual's opportunity, provided that on both sides there shall be recognition of the absolute divergence in things social and racial. When I suggest the possibility of economic equality between the races, I mean it precisely the same way and to the same extent that I would mean it if I spoke of equality of economic opportunity as between members of the same race. In each case I would mean equality proportional to the honest capacities and deserts of the individual.
>
> Men of both races may well stand uncompromisingly against every suggestion of social equality. Indeed, it would be helpful to have the word "equality" eliminated from this consideration; to have it accepted on both sides that this is not a question of social equality, but a question of recognizing a fundamental, eternal and inescapable difference. . . .
>
> Take the political aspect. I would say let the black man vote when he is fit to vote; prohibit the white man voting when he is unfit to vote. . . .
>
> On the other hand I would insist upon equal educational opportunity for both. . . . There must be such education among the colored people as will enable them to develop their own leaders, capable of understanding and sympathizing with such a differentiation between the races as I have suggested. . . . Racial amalgamation there cannot be. Partnership of the races in developing the highest aims of all humanity there must be if humanity, not only here but everywhere, is to achieve the ends which we have set for it.

Reaction to the speech was mixed. Some observers felt that Harding's comments about political and economic equality were bold, particularly as they were delivered in the deep-South city of Birmingham. A number of Southern newspapers commented favorably. But many Southern Congressmen denounced it vigorously. The comment of Senator Harrison of Mississippi, who assailed the encouragement to political equality as "a blow to the white civilization of this country that will take years to combat," was typical of such sentiment. Among Negroes one of the most favorable reactions was that of Dr. Robert R. Moton of Tuskegee who called the speech "the most important utterance on this question by a President since Lincoln," which contained a platform that can be supported by both whites and Negroes. And from quite different quarters came praise from Marcus Garvey. Many articulate Negroes, however, were far from pleased. W. E. B. DuBois tried hard to be fair. He commended the President for calling for political, educational, and economic equality, but he strongly regretted the comments about social equality which devaluated the effect of the message. Others were less reserved. "The President's speech supports the worst Negro-phobist element of the South," cried the *New York Crusade*. And Professor Kelly Miller, in an open letter to Harding, found his emphasis upon racial differences as "calculated in the long run to do the Negro as great harm as the Taney Dictum. . . ."

Certainly Harding's reference to "social equality" was unfortunate. He had said enough about political, educational and economic rights to arouse the ire of the Negrophobes to a degree that could not be assuaged by other remarks about eternal differences. Harding should have known, but apparently did not, that "social equality" was an extremely vague expression that was frequently raised as a great bugaboo by those who opposed virtually any amelioration of the Negro's condition. As James Weldon Johnson observed, "It is never defined; it is shifted to block any path that may be open; it is stretched over whole areas of contacts and activities; it is used to cover and justify every form of restriction, injustice, and brutality practiced against the Negro. The mere term makes cowards of white people and puts Negroes in a dilemma." Doubtless Harding felt it was politic to include comments about racial differences and to proscribe social equality in his Birmingham speech. It may have won him some applause. But whatever his intent this aspect was in fact evidence of his superficial understanding of the goals of American Negroes.

In the meantime Congress responded in a dilatory fashion to the programs desired by Negroes. Harding had referred to two items in his April 12 message, an interracial commission and action against lynching. A bill to create the first was introduced, but it died in committee, and Harding made no motion to create a commission by executive order. Action on a federal anti-lynching law, the number one item on the NAACP's agenda, was eventually carried further, although it too failed. Since 1918 bills had been introduced by Representative Leonidas Dyer of Missouri and others to no avail. But given the apparently sympathetic position of the Republican Party and Harding in 1920 and 1921, prospects for passage brightened. If Harding did not specifically endorse the Dyer bill in his April 12 message, his Attorney General, Harry M. Daugherty, wrote to the chairman of the House Judiciary Committee, on August 9, 1921, supporting it and giving his unofficial opinion in favor of its constitutionality. On October 20 the committee reported favorably, and after some sharp debate the bill passed the House on January 26, 1922, by a vote of 231 to 119.

The House action was acclaimed by Negroes, at times a little extravagantly. It was, said an NAACP statement, "one of the most significant steps ever taken in the history of America." But the real test lay ahead in the Senate. For several months the bill was bottled up in the Judiciary Committee, which finally reported favorably on June 30. Not until late in November did it get to the floor of the Senate where a resolute group of Southern Democrats filibustered until the Republican leaders surrendered early in December. This defeat was a bitter pill. Not only had most Republicans failed to put up a determined fight, but in the opinion of James Weldon Johnson, who had led the NAACP campaign for the bill, they seemed to feel that it was enough merely to be formally on record in favor of it, and let the Southerners take the blame if it failed. To such Republicans passage was almost a secondary matter. Moreover, Harding failed to exert pressure on behalf of the bill during any crucial period. On December 3, 1922, the day before the Senate abandoned the measure, Johnson wired Harding asking him to stand firm in opposing the filibuster. Harding's secretary, George B. Christian, answered on December 8, asserting that the President favored the Dyer bill and blaming the Democrats for its failure. This was little comfort. In a subsequent letter to Christian, Johnson described the "feeling of chagrin and resentment" held by Negroes. "This lukewarmness on the part of the Republicans is as much resented by the colored people as the aggressive tactics of the Southern Democrats." And Johnson concluded by specifically taking Harding to task for his failure to urge passage of the bill, or even to mention it favorably, at the time it was being considered by the Senate. On the same date Oswald Garrison Villard, who was a member of the NAACP's Board of Directors, wrote to the President about the great resentment among colored people, and warned him that they "have lost their faith in both the old parties, as well they may, and are turning in other directions." Villard recommended revival of the race commission idea, which he suggested might offset some of their sense of being betrayed as well as to serve a needed function of collecting data. But nothing came of this proposal. Thus both of Harding's initial two recommendations on the race issue came to naught.

While Harding had referred only to the interracial commission and antilynching measures in his April 12 message, favorable action on other matters would certainly have salvaged some of the reputation of his administration with Negroes. The second item on James Weldon Johnson's memorandum concerned peonage. On April 9, 1921, the Justice Department notified the NAACP that it was investigating peonage in all parts of the United States. It reported later that the crime was found "to exist to a shocking extent in Georgia, Alabama, and some parts of Texas," but that it had managed to prosecute successfully a number of cases. The Department continued to make investigations, although subsequent crises, such as the 1927 Mississippi flood, revealed the degree to which peonage still existed. But for the time being the government had directed some attention to the problem.

The attack upon Negro disfranchisement, however, got little support from either Harding or other Republican leaders, despite the President's comments on political equality in his Birmingham address. After the 1920 election the House Census Committee took up the charge of disfranchisement, during hearings on a bill for Congressional reapportionment, and heard the testimony of NAACP representatives. The only Congressman showing serious concern over the Negro's plight was George H. Tinkham of Massachusetts who proposed a Congressional investigation into disfranchisement and enforcement of the second section of the fourteenth amendment providing for reduction in representation of a state in which the right to vote was denied. On May 6, 1921, Tinkham introduced a resolution along these lines, which he claimed was constitutionally privileged and therefore entitled to immediate consideration. But the Speaker, Frederick H. Gillett, ruled unfavorably on this point of order, a ruling that the Republican-controlled House upheld by a 286 to 47 vote. Reintroduced as a regular resolution the proposal was lost in committee. In October, 1921, Tinkham also was unsuccessful in an effort to amend the reapportionment bill so as to reduce the representation of the disfranchising states. The Republican majority in Congress failed in 1921, and throughout the decade, to deal with the problem of Negro disfranchisement in the South. And there is no indication that Harding exerted any effort to rectify this injustice.

The fifth point in James Weldon Johnson's memorandum concerned American occupation of Haiti. After the election the lame duck Congress failed to respond to demands for an investigation. Finally, however, Medill McCormick of Illinois was appointed head of a Senate committee of inquiry which began hearings in August, 1921. Its final report issued on June 26, 1922, found little of a basic nature to condemn, although it did suggest some corrections designed to improve the efficiency of the American supervision. James Weldon Johnson considered the Senate action purely a whitewash. DuBois put it more strongly: *"If ever a Senator deserved defeat for betrayal of the Negro race, Medill McCormack is that man."* Whitewash or not, the investigation failed to achieve what the Negro critics desired —a condemnation of American intervention that would lead to eventual withdrawal. The handling of the Haitian issue by the Republicans was thus far from satisfactory to concerned Negroes. As the historian of Haitian-American relations has concluded, "President Harding had been shocked by Wilsonian interference in the domestic affairs of Haiti, but in 1922 his administration prepared to strengthen and expand the Wilsonian system of control."

Of more immediate interest to American Negroes was the question of federal government employment. Johnson's memorandum had asked Harding to appoint colored assistant secretaries of Labor and Agriculture, but the request got nowhere. As for Negro appointments generally, the results were also disappointing. Negroes naturally hoped that with the return of the Republicans to power the Wilson administration's practices of neglect and discrimination would be sharply reversed, and that Negroes would regain posts they had traditionally held. But it soon became obvious that there was to be no dramatic change. Harding was slow to appoint Negroes to office, particularly in the South. The first significant appointment was not made until June 28, 1921, when Harding nominated Henry Lincoln Johnson, a Negro National Committeeman from Georgia, to be Recorder of Deeds for the District of Columbia. By July, 1921, DuBois was complaining that with one exception Harding had made no Negro appointments of consequence. And DuBois was not the only person to become discouraged. For example, shortly before Harding's death a group of Negro Republicans from eighteen states led by Dr. George E. Cannon of Jersey City, New Jersey, met at Atlantic City in a mood strongly critical of the Republican administration. Some threatened a bolt from the GOP. "President Harding," charged Dr. Cannon, "has given less recognition to the colored race than previous Republican presidents." Clearly Harding had been very cautious in the matter of appointments, and if he finally restored some of the traditional posts, he failed to consider Negroes for positions of a higher grade or level of responsibility. By the 1920's Negro leaders rightly expected more from a Republican administration.

The last point of James Weldon Johnson's memorandum concerned the abolition of racial segregation in the federal government and civil service. Probably nothing had engendered as much bitterness against Wilson in American Negroes as did the segregationist policies introduced during his administration. Much could be corrected by executive order, and much was hoped for when the Republicans returned to power. But to the chagrin of the colored population in the two and a half years of Harding's presidency little seems to have been accomplished. While Harding received some protests, evidence of the continued practice of segregation in government departments was also shown by the numerous petitions against it directed to his successor, Calvin Coolidge. As late as June, 1926, the NAACP adopted a resolution at its annual conference that read: "We are astonished to note under President Coolidge and the Republican administration a continuation of that *segregation* of colored employees in the departments at Washington which was begun under President Wilson." In 1923 the District of Columbia branch of the NAACP investigated the problem, but its findings were limited by the reluctance on the part of colored clerks to make the facts known for fear of losing their jobs. The NAACP sent a white agent to check secretly in 1925, and it conducted another investigation in 1928. By that time it was able to report some improvement, despite the continued existence of much segregation. However, it was evident that rather than abolishing segregation the Republicans had maintained it or in some instances actually increased it.

By 1923 it was clear that with few exceptions little had been done to implement the program presented to Harding by James Weldon Johnson in April, 1921. Moreover, other matters could be noted, such as the hesitant response to the threat of the Ku Klux Klan, or the handling of the staffing of the new Negro veterans hospital at Tuskegee, a problem that clouded the final days of Harding's administration. But the conclusion is obvious. With the return of the GOP to power, Negroes learned that they could by no means count upon the Republican leaders to support their battle for fuller citizenship.

In his initial message Harding had shown some sympathy for the Negro's plight. From then on, however, Harding and the Republican-controlled Congress simply did not deliver. Original hopes gave way to disappointment and frustration. "May God write us down as asses," bemoaned W. E. B. DuBois in the spring of 1922, "if ever again we are found putting our trust in either the Republican or the Democratic Parties." Increasingly Negro leaders counseled political independence. In a "Message to Colored Americans," adopted on September 4, 1923, the NAACP recommended scrapping "allegiance to any party on historical grounds" and urged "a new political emancipation."

And at its annual conference in June, 1924, the NAACP passed a resolution urging Negroes to disregard party labels. It assailed the Republicans for their numerous failures and endorsed the third party idea. "Nothing," it concluded, "will more quickly bring the old parties to a clear realization of their obligations to us and the nation than a vigorous third party movement." In the next few weeks several other prominent Negroes bolted the GOP for Davis or LaFollette. While the rank and file of Negro voters remained true to their old party allegiance in 1924, the discontent expressed by so many leaders was ominous. It was evidence of the failures of the Harding administration to reconstruct firmly the Republican Party's ties to the Negro, and a forewarning of the massive defection that was to come.

Harding's failure may be explained partly in terms of his lack of awareness of the urgency behind the demands of an increasing number of Negro leaders. In 1921 the NAACP intended its program to be one for immediate action, not merely long-range planning. But the problem was not all due to ignorance. Like all Presidents, Harding was pressured by many, often irreconcilable elements. At the time there was much talk among Republican leaders of the opportunities for their party in the South. To encourage this new Republicanism meant rebuilding lilywhite state organizations at the expense of the traditional black and tan groups. And it also meant that national Republican leaders had to be cautious about responding too obviously to the demands of Negro groups like the NAACP. Such a Southern policy was a difficult and potentially dangerous gamble. It conflicted with the GOP's historic ideals in regard to the Negro, and it was hard to reconcile with the desire to capitalize on the political potential of the Negro population in Northern cities which, beginning with migrations during the World War, had been expanding at a prodigious rate. The result was a dilemma for which no satisfactory resolution was possible. Like Harding in his Birmingham speech, the party failed to make a firm commitment to either a Northern or a Southern policy, and so in the long run it failed in both quarters. The great new Southern Republicanism remained largely an illusion, while Negroes learned that the devotion of the Party of Lincoln its historic equalitarian principles was far from complete.

Long before Wilson, Negro leaders had been grumbling about the Republican Party's neglect, or virtual abandonment, of the Negro. But the bitterness engendered by Democratic policies encouraged them to look once more to the GOP. Continued failures by the Republicans could only stimulate the small but growing movement for political independence. Harding's opportunity was to convince the Party that its fortunes could best be promoted by striving to advance its historic ideals. It would have required a liberal party orientation that looked more to the urban masses than to the farm or Wall Street. The Negro, the historic ally of the GOP, and now an increasingly significant component of the urban population, was the bridge to this new orientation. But this would have required a deeper commitment to civil rights and a more prescient leadership than was offered by Harding and his Republican colleagues. Their failure added greatly to the Negro's disillusionment in the GOP, and made all the more likely his later desertion.

Alain Locke □ The New Negro

Art critic, author, and editor, Alain Locke was the first Negro American to be named a Rhodes Scholar. Born in 1886, he taught philosophy for many years at Howard University. Locke's works include *The Negro in America,* a biography of Frederick Douglass, and many articles. Locke died in 1954.

In the last decade something beyond the watch and guard of statistics has happened in the life of the American Negro and the three norns who have traditionally presided over the Negro problem have a changeling in their laps. The Sociologist, the Philanthropist, the Race-leader are not unaware of the New Negro, but they are at a loss to account for him. He simply cannot be swathed in their formulae. For the younger generation is vibrant with a new psychology; the new spirit is awake in the masses, and under the very eyes of the professional observers is transforming what has been a perennial problem into the progressive phases of contemporary Negro life.

Could such a metamorphosis have taken place as suddenly as it has appeared to? The answer is no; not because the New Negro is not here, but because the Old Negro had long become more of a myth than a man. The Old Negro, we must remember, was a creature of moral debate and historical controversy. His has been a stock figure perpetuated as an historical fiction partly in innocent sentimentalism, partly in deliberate reactionism. The Negro himself has contributed his share to this through a sort of protective social mimicry forced

From *The New Negro: An Interpretation,* ed., Alain Locke (New York: Albert and Charles Boni, 1925), pp. 3–16.

upon him by the adverse circumstances of dependence. So for generations in the mind of America, the Negro has been more of a formula than a human being—a something to be argued about, condemned or defended, to be "kept down," or "in his place," or "helped up," to be worried with or worried over, harassed or patronized, a social bogey or a social burden. The thinking Negro even has been induced to share this same general attitude, to focus his attention on controversial issues, to see himself in the distorted perspective of a social problem. His shadow, so to speak, has been more real to him than his personality. Through having had to appeal from the unjust stereotypes of his oppressors and traducers to those of his liberators, friends and benefactors he has had to subscribe to the traditional positions from which his case has been viewed. Little true social or self-understanding has or could come from such a situation.

But while the minds of most of us, black and white, have thus burrowed in the trenches of the Civil War and Reconstruction, the actual march of development has simply flanked these positions, necessitating a sudden reorientation of view. We have not been watching in the right direction; set North and South on a sectional axis, we have not noticed the East till the sun has us blinking.

Recall how suddenly the Negro spirituals revealed themselves; suppressed for generations under the stereotypes of Wesleyan hymn harmony, secretive, half-ashamed, until the courage of being natural brought them out—and behold, there was folk-music. Similarly the mind of the Negro seems suddenly to have slipped from under the tyranny of social intimidation and to be shaking off the psychology of imitation and implied inferiority. By shedding the old chrysalis of the Negro problem we are achieving something like a spiritual emancipation. Until recently, lacking self-understanding, we have been almost as much of a problem to ourselves as we still are to others. But the decade that found us with a problem has left us with only a task. The multitude perhaps feels as yet only a strange relief and a new vague urge, but the thinking few know that in the reaction the vital inner grip of prejudice has been broken.

With this renewed self-respect and self-dependence, the life of the Negro community is bound to enter a new dynamic phase, the buoyancy from within compensating for whatever pressure there may be of conditions from without. The migrant masses, shifting from countryside to city, hurdle several generations of experience at a leap, but more important, the same thing happens spiritually in the life-attitudes and self-expression of the Young Negro, in his poetry, his art, his education and his new outlook, with the additional advantage, of course, of the poise and greater certainly of knowing what it is all about. From this comes the promise and warrant of a new leadership. As one of them has discerningly put it:

> We have tomorrow
> Bright before us
> Like a flame.
>
> Yesterday, a night-gone thing
> A sun-down name.
>
> And dawn today
> Broad arch above the road we came.
> We march!

This is what, even more than any "most creditable record of fifty years of freedom," requires that the Negro of to-day be seen through other than the dusty spectacles of past controversy. The day of "aunties," "uncles" and "mammies" is equally gone. Uncle Tom and Sambo have passed on, and even the "Colonel" and "George" play barnstorm rôles from which they escape with relief when the public spotlight is off. The popular melodrama has about played itself out, and it is time to scrap the fictions, garret the bogeys and settle down to a realistic facing of facts.

First we must observe some of the changes which since the traditional lines of opinion were drawn have rendered these quite obsolete. A main change has been, of course, that shifting of the Negro population which has made the Negro problem no longer exclusively or even predominantly Southern. Why should our minds remain sectionalized, when the problem itself no longer is? Then the trend of migration has not only been toward the North and the Central Midwest, but city-ward and to the great centers of industry—the problems of adjustment are new, practical, local and not peculiarly racial. Rather they are an integral part of the large industrial and social problems of our present-day democracy. And finally, with the Negro rapidly in process of class differentiation, if it ever was warrantable to regard and treat the Negro *en masse* it is becoming with every day less possible, more unjust and more ridiculous.

In the very process of being transplanted, the Negro is becoming transformed.

The tide of Negro migration, northward and city-ward, is not to be fully explained as a blind flood started by the demands of war industry coupled with the shutting off of foreign migration, or by the pressure of poor crops coupled with increased social terrorism in certain sections of the South and Southwest. Neither labor demand, the boll-weevil nor the Ku Klux Klan is a basic factor, however contributory any or all of them may have been. The wash and rush of this human tide on the beach line of the northern city centers is to be explained primarily in terms of a new vision of opportunity, of social and economic freedom, of a spirit to seize, even in the face of an extortionate and heavy toll, a chance for the improvement of conditions. With each successive wave of it, the movement of the Negro becomes more and more a mass movement toward the larger and the more democratic chance—in the Negro's case a deliberate flight not only from countryside to city, but from medieval America to modern.

Take Harlem as an instance of this. Here in Manhattan is not merely the largest Negro community in the world, but the first concentration in history of so many diverse elements of Negro life. It has attracted the African, the West Indian, the Negro American; has brought together the Negro of the North and the Negro of the South; the man from the city and the man from the town and village; the peasant, the student, the business man, the professional man, artist, poet, musician, adventurer and worker, preacher and criminal, exploiter and social outcast. Each group has come with its own separate motives and for its own special ends, but their greatest experience has been the finding of one another. Proscription and prejudice have thrown these dissimilar elements into a common area of contact and interaction. Within this area, race sympathy and unity have determined a further fusing of sentiment and experience. So what began in terms of segregation becomes more and more, as its elements mix and react, the laboratory of a great race-welding. Hitherto, it must be admitted that American Negroes have been a race more in name than in fact, or to be exact, more in sentiment than in experience. The chief bond between them has been that of a common condition rather than a common consciousness; a problem in common rather than a life in common. In Harlem, Negro life is seizing upon its first chances for group expression and self-determination. It is—or promises at least to be—a race capital. That is why our comparison is taken with those nascent centers of folk-expression and self-determination which are playing a creative part in the world to-day. Without pretense to their political significance, Harlem has the same rôle to play for the New Negro as Dublin has had for the New Ireland or Prague for the New Czechoslovakia.

Harlem, I grant you, isn't typical—but it is significant, it is prophetic. No sane observer, however sympathetic to the new trend, would contend that the great masses are articulate as yet, but they stir, they move, they are more than physically restless. The challenge of the new intellectuals among them is clear enough—the "race radicals" and realists who have broken with the old epoch of philanthropic guidance, sentimental appeal and protest. But are we after all only reading into the stirrings of a sleeping giant the dreams of an agitator? The answer is in the migrating peasant. It is the "man farthest down" who is most active in getting up. One of the most characteristic symptoms of this is the professional man himself migrating to recapture his constituency after a vain effort to maintain in some Southern corner what for years back seemed an established living and clientele. The clergyman following his errant flock, the physician or lawyer trailing his clients, supply the true clues. In a real sense it is the rank and file who are leading, and the leaders who are following. A transformed and transforming psychology permeates the masses.

When the racial leaders of twenty years ago spoke of developing race-pride and stimulating race-consciousness, and of the desirability of race solidarity, they could not in any accurate degree have anticipated the abrupt feeling that has surged up and now pervades the awakened centers. Some of the recognized Negro leaders and a powerful section of white opinion identified with "race work" of the older order have indeed attempted to discount this feeling as a "passing phase," an attack of "race nerves" so to speak, an "aftermath of the war," and the like. It has not abated, however, if we are to gauge by the present tone and temper of the Negro press, or by the shift in popular support from the officially recognized and orthodox spokesmen to those of the independent, popular, and often radical type who are unmistakable symptoms of a new order. It is a social disservice to blunt the fact that the Negro of the Northern centers has reached a stage where tutelage, even of the most interested and well-intentioned sort, must give place to new relationships, where positive self-direction must be reckoned with in ever increasing measure. The American mind must reckon with a fundamentally changed Negro.

The Negro too, for his part, has idols of the tribe to smash. If on the one hand the white man has erred in making the Negro appear to be that which would excuse or extenuate his treatment of him, the Negro, in turn, has too often unnecessarily excused himself because of the way he has been treated. The intelligent Negro of to-day is resolved not to make discrimination an extenuation for his shortcomings in performance, individual or collective; he is trying to hold himself at par, neither inflated by sentimental allowances nor depreciated by current social discounts. For this he must know himself and be known for precisely what he is, and for that reason he welcomes the new scientific rather than the old sentimental interest. Sentimental interest in the Negro has ebbed. We used to lament this as the falling off of our friends; now we rejoice and pray to be delivered both from self-pity and condescension. The mind of each racial group has had a bitter weaning, apathy or hatred on one side matching disillusionment or resentment on the other; but they face each other to-day with the possibility at least of entirely new mutual attitudes.

It does not follow that if the Negro were better known, he would be better liked or better treated. But mutual understanding is basic for any subsequent coöperation and adjustment. The effort toward this will at least have the effect of remedying in large part what has been the most unsatisfactory feature of our present stage of race relationships in America, namely the fact that the more intelligent and representative elements of the two race groups have at so many points got quite out of vital touch with one another.

The fiction is that the life of the races is separate, and increasingly so. The fact is that they have touched too closely at the unfavorable and too lightly at the favorable levels.

While inter-racial councils have sprung up in the South, drawing on forward elements of both races, in the Northern cities manual laborers may brush elbows in their everyday work, but the community and business leaders have experienced no such interplay or far too little of it. These segments must achieve contact or the race situation in America becomes desperate. Fortunately this is happening. There is a growing realization that in social effort the co-operative basis must supplant long-distance philanthropy, and that the only safeguard for mass relations in the future must be provided in the carefully maintained contacts of the enlightened minorities of both race groups. In the intellectual realm a renewed and keen curiosity is replacing the recent apathy; the Negro is being carefully studied, not just talked about and discussed. In art and letters, instead of being wholly caricatured, he is being seriously portrayed and painted.

To all of this the New Negro is keenly responsive as an augury of a new democracy in American culture. He is contributing his share to the new social understanding. But the desire to be understood would never in itself have been sufficient to have opened so completely the protectively closed portals of the thinking Negro's mind. There is still too much possibility of being snubbed or patronized for that. It was rather the necessity for fuller, truer self-expression, the realization of the unwisdom of allowing social discrimination to segregate him mentally, and a counter-attitude to cramp and fetter his own living—and so the "spite-wall" that the intellectuals built over the "color-line" has happily been taken down. Much of this reopening of intellectual contacts has centered in New York and has been richly fruitful not merely in the enlarging of personal experience, but in the definite enrichment of American art and letters and in the clarifying of our common vision of the social tasks ahead.

The particular significance in the re-establishment of contact between the more advanced and representative classes is that it promises to offset some of the unfavorable reactions of the past, or at least to re-surface race contacts somewhat for the future. Subtly the conditions that are molding a New Negro are molding a new American attitude.

However, this new phase of things is delicate; it will call for less charity but more justice; less help, but infinitely closer understanding. This is indeed a critical stage of race relationships because of the likelihood, if the new temper is not understood, of engendering sharp group antagonism and a second crop of more calculated prejudice. In some quarters, it has already done so. Having weaned the Negro, public opinion cannot continue to paternalize. The Negro to-day is inevitably moving forward under the control largely of his own objectives. What are these objectives? Those of his outer life are happily already well and finally formulated, for they are none other than the ideals of American institutions and democracy. Those of his inner life are yet in process of formation, for the new psychology at present is more of a consensus of feeling than of opinion, of attitude rather than of program. Still some points seem to have crystallized.

Up to the present one may adequately describe the Negro's "inner objectives" as an attempt to repair a damaged group psychology and reshape a warped social perspective. Their realization has required a new mentality for the American Negro. And as it matures we being to see its effects; at first, negative, iconoclastic, and then positive and constructive. In this new group psychology we note the lapse of sentimental appeal, then the development of a more positive self-respect and self-reliance; the repudiation of social dependence, and then the gradual recovery from hyper-sensitiveness and "touchy" nerves, the repudiation of the double standard of judgment with its special philanthropic allowances and then the sturdier desire for objective and scientific appraisal; and finally the rise from social disillusionment to race pride, from the sense of social debt to the responsibilities of social contribution, and offsetting the necessary working and commonsense acceptance of restricted conditions, the belief in ultimate esteem and recognition. Therefore the Negro to-day wishes to be known for what he is, even in his faults and shortcomings, and scorns a craven and precarious survival at the price of seeming to be what he is not. He resents being spoken of as a social ward or minor, even by his own, and to being regarded a chronic patient for the sociological clinic, the sick man of American Democracy. For the same reasons, he himself is through with those social nostrums and panaceas, the so-called "solutions" of his "problem," with which he and the country have been so liberally dosed in the past. Religion, freedom, education, money—in turn, he has ardently hoped for and peculiarly trusted these things; he still believes in them, but not in blind trust that they alone will solve his life-problem.

Each generation, however, will have its creed, and that of the present is the belief in the efficacy of collective effort, in race co-operation. This deep feeling of race is at present the mainspring of Negro life. It seems to be the outcome of the reaction to proscription and prejudice; an attempt, fairly successful on the whole, to convert a defensive into an offensive position, a handicap into an incentive. It is radical in tone, but not in purpose and only the most stupid forms of opposition, misunderstanding or persecution could make it otherwise. Of course, the thinking Negro has shifted a little toward the left with the world-trend, and there is an increasing group who affiliate with radical and liberal movements. But fundamentally for the present the Negro is radical on race matters, conservative on others, in other words, a "forced radical," a social protestant rather than a genuine radical. Yet under further pressure and injustice iconoclastic thought and motives will inevitably increase. Harlem's quixotic radicalisms call for their ounce of democracy to-day lest to-morrow they be beyond cure.

The Negro mind reaches out as yet to nothing but American wants, American ideas. But this forced attempt to build his Americanism on race values is a unique social experiment, and its ultimate success is impossible except through the fullest sharing of American culture and institutions. There should be no delusion about this. American nerves in sections unstrung with race hysteria are often fed the opiate that the trend of Negro advance is wholly separatist, and that the effect of its operation will be to encyst the Negro as a benign foreign body in the body politic. This cannot be—even if it were desirable. The racialism of the Negro is no limitation or reservation with re-respect to American life; it is only a constructive effort to build the obstructions in the stream of his progress into an efficient dam of social energy and power. Democracy itself is obstructed and stagnated to the extent that any of its channels are closed. Indeed they cannot be selectively closed. So the choice is not between one way for the Negro and another way for the rest, but between American institutions frustrated on the one hand and American ideals progressively fulfilled and realized on the other.

There is, of course, a warrantably confortable feeling in being on the right side of the country's professed ideals. We realize that we cannot be undone without America's undoing. It is within the gamut of this attitude that the thinking Negro faces America, but with variations of mood that are if anything more significant than the attitude itself. Sometimes we have it taken with the defiant ironic challenge of McKay:

> Mine is the future grinding down to-day
> Like a great landslip moving to the sea,
> Bearing its freight of debris far away

Where the green hungry waters restlessly
Heave mammoth pyramids, and break and roar
Their eerie challenge to the crumbling shore.

Sometimes, perhaps more frequently as yet, it is taken in the fervent and almost filial appeal and counsel of Weldon Johnson's:

O Southland, dear Southland!
Then why do you still cling
To an idle age and a musty page,
To a dead and useless thing?

But between defiance and appeal, midway almost between cynicism and hope, the prevailing mind stands in the mood of the same author's *To America*, an attitude of sober query and stoical challenge:

How would you have us, as we are?
  Or sinking 'neath the load we bear,
Our eyes fixed forward on a star,
  Or gazing empty at despair?

Rising or falling? Men or things?
  With dragging pace or footsteps fleet?
Strong, willing sinews in your wings,
  Or tightening chains about your feet?

More and more, however, an intelligent realization of the great discrepancy between the American social creed and the American social practice forces upon the Negro the taking of the moral advantage that is his. Only the steadying and sobering effect of a truly characteristic gentleness of spirit prevents the rapid rise of a definite cynicism and counter-hate and a defiant superiority feeling. Human as this reaction would be, the majority still deprecate its advent, and would gladly see it forestalled by the speedy amelioration of its causes. We wish our race pride to be a healthier, more positive achievement than a feeling based upon a realization of the shortcomings of others. But all paths toward the attainment of a sound social attitude have been difficult; only a relatively few enlightened minds have been able as the phrase puts it "to rise above" prejudice. The ordinary man has had until recently only a hard choice between the alternatives of supine and humiliating submission and stimulating but hurtful counter-prejudice. Fortunately from some inner, desperate resourcefulness has recently sprung up the simple expedient of fighting prejudice by mental passive resistance, in other words by trying to ignore it. For the few, this manna may perhaps be effective, but the masses cannot thrive upon it.

Fortunately there are constructive channels opening out into which the balked social feelings of the American Negro can flow freely.

Without them there would be much more pressure and danger than there is. These compensating interests are racial but in a new and enlarged way. One is the consciousness of acting as the advance-guard of the African peoples in their contact with Twentieth Century civilization; the other, the sense of a mission of rehabilitating the race in world esteem from that loss of prestige for which the fate and conditions of slavery have so largely been responsible. Harlem, as we shall see, is the center of both these movements; she is the home of the Negro's "Zionism." The pulse of the Negro world has begun to beat in Harlem. A Negro newspaper carrying news material in English, French and Spanish, gathered from all quarters of America, the West Indies and Africa has maintained itself in Harlem for over five years. Two important magazines, both edited from New York, maintain their news and circulation consistently on a cosmopolitan scale. Under American auspices and backing, three pan-African congresses have been held abroad for the discussion of common interests, colonial questions and the future co-operative development of Africa. In terms of the race question as a world problem, the Negro mind has leapt, so to speak, upon the parapets of prejudice and extended its cramped horizons. In so doing it has linked up with the growing group consciousness of the dark-peoples and is gradually learning their common interests. As one of our writers has recently put it: "It is imperative that we understand the white world in its relations to the non-white world." As with the Jew, persecution is making the Negro international.

As a world phenomenon this wider race consciousness is a different thing from the much asserted rising tide of color. Its inevitable causes are not of our making. The consequences are not necessarily damaging to the best interests of civilization. Whether it actually brings into being new Armadas of conflict or argosies of cultural exchange and enlightenment can only be decided by the attitude of the dominant races in an era of critical change. With the American Negro, his new internationalism is primarily an effort to recapture contact with the scattered peoples of African derivation. Garveyism may be a transient, if spectacular, phenomenon, but the possible rôle of the American Negro in the future development of Africa is one of the most constructive and universally helpful missions that any modern people can lay claim to.

Constructive participation in such causes cannot help giving the Negro valuable group incentives, as well as increased prestigé at home and abroad. Our greatest rehabilitation may possibly come through such channels, but for the present, more immediate hope rests in the revaluation by white and black alike of the Negro in terms of his artistic endowments and cultural contributions, past and prospective. It must be increasingly recognized that the Negro has already made very substantial contributions, not only in his folk-art, music especially, which has always found appreciation, but in larger, though humbler and less acknowledged ways. For generations the Negro has been the peasant matrix of that section of America which has most undervalued him, and here he has contributed not only materially in labor and in social patience, but spiritually as well. The South has unconsciously absorbed the gift of his folk-temperament. In less than half a generation it will be easier to recognize this, but the fact remains that a leaven of humor, sentiment, imagination and tropic nonchalance has gone into the making of the South from a humble, unacknowledged source. A second crop of the Negro's gifts promises still more largely. He now becomes a conscious contributor and lays aside the status of a beneficiary and ward for that of a collaborator and participant in American civilization. The great social gain in this is the releasing of our talented group from the arid fields of controversy and debate to the productive fields of creative expression. The especially cultural recognition they win should in turn prove the key to that revaluation of the Negro which must precede or accompany any considerable further betterment of race relationships. But whatever the general effect, the present generation will have added the motives of self-expression and spiritual development to the old and still unfinished task of making material headway and progress. No one who understandingly faces the situation with its substantial accomplishment or views the new scene with its still more abundant promise can be entirely without hope. And certainly, if in our lifetime the Negro should not be able to celebrate his full initiation into American democracy, he can at least, on the warrant of these things, celebrate the attainment of a significant and satisfying new phase of group development, and with it a spiritual Coming of Age.

Claude McKay □ If We Must Die

Born in Jamaica in 1890, Claude McKay studied at Tuskegee and at Kansas State University. In 1917, he published "Harlem Dancer" in *Seven Arts* and was later an associate editor of *Liberator*. *Harlem Shadows* was his first major American publication. McKay died in 1948.

If we must die, let it not be like hogs
Hunted and penned in an inglorious spot,
While round us bark the mad and hungry dogs,
Making their mock at our accursèd lot.
If we must die, O let us nobly die,
So that our precious blood may not be shed
In vain; then even the monsters we defy
Shall be constrained to honor us though dead!
O kinsmen! we must meet the common foe!
Though far outnumbered let us show us brave,
And for their thousand blows deal one deathblow!
What though before us lies the open grave?
Like men we'll face the murderous, cowardly pack,
Pressed to the wall, dying, but fighting back!

George S. Schuyler □ The Negro-Art Hokum

Born in 1895, George S. Schuyler has been a persistent voice of criticism within the black community. His long career as a journalist —which began in the 1920's with his association with the radical *Messenger*—continues today in his columns for the *Pittsburgh Courier,* where he continues to write acerbically about the white and black community. In this essay, Schuyler denies that Negro artists should explore themes solely within the confines of the black community.

Negro art "made in America" is as non-existent as the widely advertised profundity of Cal Coolidge, the "seven years of progress" of Mayor Hylan, or the reported sophistication of New Yorkers. Negro art there has been, is, and will be among the numerous black nations of Africa; but to suggest the possibility of any such development among the ten million colored people in this republic is self-evident foolishness. Eager apostles from Greenwich Village, Harlem, and environs proclaimed a great renaissance of Negro art just around the corner waiting to be ushered on the scene by those whose hobby is taking races, nations, peoples, and movements under their wing. New art forms expressing the "peculiar" psychology of the Negro were about to flood the market. In short, the art of Homo Africanus was about to electrify the waiting world. Skeptics patiently waited. They still wait.

From George S. Schuyler, "The Negro-Art Hokum," *The Nation,* (June 1926), pp. 262–263.

True, from dark-skinned sources have come those slave songs based on Protestant hymns and Biblical texts known as the spirituals, work songs and secular songs of sorrow and tough luck known as the blues, that outgrowth of ragtime known as jazz (in the development of which whites have assisted), and the Charleston, an eccentric dance invented by the gamins around the public market-place in Charleston, S. C. No one can or does deny this. But these are contributions of a caste in a certain section of the country. They are foreign to Northern Negroes, West Indian Negroes, and African Negroes. They are no more expressive or characteristic of the Negro race than the music and dancing of the Appalachian highlanders or the Dalmatian peasantry are expressive or characteristic of the Caucasian race. If one wishes to speak of the musical contributions of the peasantry of the South, very well. Any group under similar circumstances would have produced something similar. It is merely a coincidence that this peasant class happens to be of a darker hue than the other inhabitants of the land. One recalls the remarkable likeness of the minor strains of the Russian mujiks to those of the Southern Negro.

As for the literature, painting, and sculpture of Aframericans—such as there is—it is identical in kind with the literature, painting, and sculpture of white Americans: that is, it shows more or less evidence of European influence. In the field of drama little of any merit has been written by and about Negroes that could not have been written by whites. The dean of the Aframerican literati is W. E. B. Du Bois, a product of Harvard and German universities; the foremost Aframerican sculptor is Meta Warwick Fuller, a graduate of leading American art schools and former student of Rodin; while the most noted Aframerican painter, Henry Ossawa Tanner, is dean of American painters in Paris and has been decorated by the French Government. Now the work of these artists is no more "expressive of the Negro soul"—as the gushers put it—than are the scribblings of Octavus Cohen or Hugh Wiley.

This, of course, is easily understood if one stops to realize that the Aframerican is merely a lampblacked Anglo-Saxon. If the European immigrant after two or three generations of exposure to our schools, politics, advertising, moral crusades, and restaurants becomes indistinguishable from the mass of Americans of the older stock (despite the influence of the foreign-language press), how much truer must it be of the sons of Ham who have been subjected to what the uplifters call Americanism for the last three hundred years. Aside from his color, which ranges from very dark brown to pink, your American Negro is just plain American. Negroes and whites from the same localities in this country talk, think, and act about the same. Because a few writers with a paucity of themes have seized upon imbecilities of the Negro rustics and clowns and palmed them off as authentic and characteristic Aframerican behavior, the common notion that the black American is so "different" from his white neighbor has gained wide currency. The mere mention of the word "Negro" conjures up in the average white American's mind a composite stereotype of Bert Williams, Aunt Jemima, Uncle Tom, Jack Johnson, Florian Slappey, and the various monstrosities scrawled by the cartoonists. Your average Aframerican no more resembles this stereotype than the average American resembles a composite of Andy Gump, Jim Jeffries, and a cartoon by Rube Goldberg.

Again, the Aframerican is subject to the same economic and social forces that mold the actions and thoughts of the white Americans. He is not living in a different world as some whites and a few Negroes would have us believe. When the jangling of his Connecticut alarm clock gets him out of his Grand Rapids bed to a breakfast similar to that eaten by his white brother across the street; when he toils at the same or similar work in mills, mines, factories, and commerce alongside the descendants of Spartacus, Robin Hood, and Erik the Red; when he wears similar clothing and speaks the same language with the same degree of perfection; when he reads the same Bible and belongs to the Baptist, Methodist, Episcopal, or Catholic church; when his fraternal affiliations also include the Elks, Masons, and Knights of Pythias; when he gets the same or similar schooling, lives in the same kind of houses, owns the same makes of cars (or rides in them), and nightly sees the same Hollywood version of life on the screen; when he smokes the same brands of tobacco and avidly peruses the same puerile periodicals; in short, when he responds to the same political, social, moral, and economic stimuli in precisely the same manner as his white neighbor, it is sheer nonsense to talk about "racial differences" as between the American black man and the American white man. Glance over a Negro newspaper (it is printed in good Americanese) and you will find the usual quota of crime news, scandal, personals, and uplift to be found in the average white newspaper—which, by the way, is more widely read by the Negroes than is the Negro press. In order to satisfy the cravings of an inferiority complex engendered by the colorphobia of the mob, the readers of the Negro newspapers are given a slight dash of racialistic seasoning. In the homes of the black and white Americans of the same cultural and economic level one finds similar furniture, literature, and conversation. How, then, can the black American be expected to produce art and literature dissimilar to that of the white American?

Consider Coleridge-Taylor, Edward Wilmot Blyden, and Claude McKay, the Englishmen; Pushkin, the Russian; Bridgewater, the Pole; Antar, the Arabian; Latino, the Spaniard; Dumas, *père* and *fils*, the

Frenchmen; and Paul Laurence Dunbar, Charles W. Chestnut, and James Weldon Johnson, the Americans. All Negroes; yet their work shows the impress of nationality rather than race. They all reveal the psychology and culture of their environment—their color is incidental. Why should Negro artists of America vary from the national artistic norm when Negro artists in other countries have not done so? If we can foresee what kind of white citizens will inhabit this neck of the woods in the next generation by studying the sort of education and environment the children are exposed to now, it should not be difficult to reason that the adults of today are what they are because of the education and environment they were exposed to a generation ago. And that education and environment were about the same for blacks and whites. One contemplates the popularity of the Negro-art hokum and murmurs, "How come?"

This nonsense is probably the last stand of the old myth palmed off by Negrophobists for all these many years, and recently rehashed by the sainted Harding, that there are "fundamental, eternal, and inescapable differences" between white and black Americans. That there are Negroes who will lend this myth a helping hand need occasion no surprise. It has been broadcast all over the world by the vociferous scions of slaveholders, "scientists" like Madison Grant and Lothrop Stoddard, and the patriots who flood the treasury of the Ku Klux Klan; and is believed, even today, by the majority of free, white citizens. On this baseless premise, so flattering to the white mob, that the blackamoor is inferior and fundamentally different, is erected the postulate that he must needs be peculiar; and when he attempts to portray life through the medium of art, it must of necessity be a peculiar art. While such reasoning may seem conclusive to the majority of Americans, it must be rejected with a loud guffaw by intelligent people.

Langston Hughes □ The Negro Artist and the Racial Mountain

Langston Huges was born in Joplin, Missouri in 1902 and graduated from Lincoln University in Pennsylvania. His first poem appeared in *Crisis* in 1921. A prolific writer of poems and short stories, Hughes served as a merchant seaman and later wrote a column for the *Chicago Defender*. He died in 1967.

One of the most promising of the young Negro poets said to me once, "I want to be a poet—not a Negro poet," meaning, I believe, "I want to write like a white poet"; meaning subconsciously, "I would like to be a white poet"; meaning behind that, "I would like to be white." And I was sorry that young man said that, for no great poet has ever been afraid of being himself. And I doubted then that, with his desire to run away spiritually from his race, this boy would ever be a great poet. But this is the mountain standing in the way of any true Negro art in America—this urge within the race toward whiteness, the desire to pour racial individuality into the mold of American standardization, and to be as little Negro and as much American as possible.

But let us look at the immediate background of this young poet. His family is of what I suppose one would call the Negro middle class: people who are by no means rich yet never uncomfortable nor hungry —smug, contented, respectable folk, members of the Baptist church. The father goes to work every morning. He is a chief steward at a

From Langston Hughes, "The Negro Artist and the Racial Mountain," *The Nation,* (June 1926), pp. 692–694.

large white club. The mother sometimes does fancy sewing or supervises parties for the rich families of the town. The children go to a mixed school. In the home they read white papers and magazines. And the mother often says "Don't be like niggers" when the children are bad. A frequent phrase from the father is, "Look how well a white man does things." And so the word white comes to be unconsciously a symbol of all the virtues. It holds for the children beauty, morality, and money. The whisper of "I want to be white" runs silently through their minds. This young poet's home is, I believe, a fairly typical home of the colored middle class. One sees immediately how difficult it would be for an artist born in such a home to interest himself in interpreting the beauty of his own people. He is never taught to see that beauty. He is taught rather not to see it, or if he does, to be ashamed of it when it is not according to Caucasian patterns.

For racial culture the home of a self-styled "high-class" Negro has nothing better to offer. Instead there will perhaps be more aping of things white than in a less cultured or less wealthy home. The father is perhaps a doctor, lawyer, landowner, or politician. The mother may be a social worker, or a teacher, or she may do nothing and have a maid. Father is often dark but he has usually married the lightest woman he could find. The family attend a fashionable church where few really colored faces are to be found. And they themselves draw a color line. In the North they go to white theaters and white movies. And in the South they have at least two cars and a house "like white folks." Nordic manners, Nordic faces, Nordic hair, Nordic art (if any), and an Episcopal heaven. A very high mountain indeed for the would-be racial artist to climb in order to discover himself and his people.

But then there are the low-down folks, the so-called common element, and they are the majority—may the Lord be praised! The people who have their nip of gin on Saturday nights and are not too important to themselves or the community, or too well fed, or too learned to watch the lazy world go round. They live on Seventh Street in Washington or State Street in Chicago and they do not particularly care whether they are like white folks or anybody else. Their joy runs, bang! into ecstasy. Their religion soars to a shout. Work maybe a little today, rest a little tomorrow. Play awhile. Sing awhile. O, let's dance! These common people are not afraid of spirituals, as for a long time their more intellectual brethren were, and jazz is their child. They furnish a wealth of colorful, distinctive material for any artist because they still hold their own individuality in the face of American standardizations. And perhaps these common people will give to the world its truly great Negro artist, the one who is not afraid to be himself. Whereas the better-class Negro would tell the artist what to do, the people at least let him alone when he does appear. And they are not ashamed of him—if they know he exists at all. And they accept what beauty is their own without question.

Certainly there is, for the American Negro artist who can escape the restrictions the more advanced among his own group would put upon him, a great field of unused material ready for his art. Without going outside his race, and even among the better classes with their "white" culture and conscious American manners, but still Negro enough to be different, there is sufficient matter to furnish a black artist with a lifetime of creative work. And when he chooses to touch on the relations between Negroes and whites in this country with their innumerable overtones and undertones, surely, and especially for literature and the drama, there is an inexaustible supply of themes at hand. To these the Negro artist can give his racial individuality, his heritage of rhythm and warmth, and his incongruous humor that so often, as in the Blues, becomes ironic laughter mixed with tears. But let us look again at the mountain.

A prominent Negro clubwoman in Philadelphia paid eleven dollars to hear Raquel Meller sing Andalusian popular songs. But she told me a few weeks before she would not think of going to hear "that woman," Clara Smith, a great black artist, sing Negro folksongs. And many an upper-class Negro church, even now, would not dream of employing a spiritual in its services. The drab melodies in white folks' hymnbooks are much to be preferred. "We want to worship the Lord correctly and quietly. We don't believe in 'shouting.' Let's be dull like the Nordics," they say, in effect.

The road for the serious black artist, then, who would produce a racial art is most certainly rocky and the mountain is high. Until recently he received almost no encouragement for his work from either white or colored people. The fine novels of Chestnutt go out of print with neither race noticing their passing. The quaint charm and humor of Dunbar's dialect verse brought to him, in his day, largely the same kind of encouragement one would give a sideshow freak (A colored man writing poetry! How odd!) or a clown (How amusing!).

The present vogue in things Negro, although it may do as much harm as good for the budding colored artist, has at least done this: it has brought him forcibly to the attention of his own people among whom for so long, unless the other race had noticed him beforehand, he was a prophet with little honor. I understand that Charles Gilpin acted for years in Negro theaters without any special acclaim from his own, but when Broadway gave him eight curtain calls, Negroes, too, began to beat a tin pan in his honor. I know a young colored writer, a manual worker by day, who had been writing well for the colored magazines for some years, but it was not until he recently broke into the white publications and his first book was accepted by a prominent New York publisher that the "best" Negroes in his city took the trouble to discover that he lived there. Then almost immediately they decided to give a grand dinner for him. But the society ladies were careful to whisper to his mother that perhaps she'd better not come. They were not sure she would have an evening gown.

The Negro artist works against an undertow of sharp criticism and misunderstanding from his own group and unintentional bribes from the whites. "O, be respectable, write about nice people, show how good we are," say the Negroes. "Be stereotyped, don't go too far, don't shatter our illusions about you, don't amuse us too seriously. We will pay you," say the whites. Both would have told Jean Toomer not to write "Cane." The colored people did not praise it. The white people did not buy it. Most of the colored people who did read "Cane" hate it. They are afraid of it. Although the critics gave it good reviews the public remained indifferent. Yet (excepting the work of DuBois) "Cane" contains the finest prose written by a Negro in America. And like the singing of Robeson, it is truly racial.

But in spite of the Nordicized Negro intelligentsia and the desires of some white editors we have an honest American Negro literature already with us. Now I await the rise of the Negro theater. Our folk music, having achieved world-wide fame, offers itself to the genius of the great individual American Negro composer who is to come. And within the next decade I expect to see the work of a growing school of colored artists who paint and model the beauty of dark faces and create with new tecnhique the expressions of their own soul-world. And the Negro dancers who will dance like flame and the singers who will continue to carry our songs to all who listen—they will be with us in even greater numbers tomorrow.

Most of my own poems are racial in theme and treatment, derived from the life I know. In many of them I try to grasp and hold some of the meanings and rhythms of jazz. I am sincere as I know how to be in these peoms and yet after every reading I answer questions like these from my own people: Do you think Negroes should always write about Negroes? I wish you wouldn't read some of your poems to white folks. How do you find anything interesting in a place like a cabaret? Why do you write about black people? You aren't black. What makes you do so many jazz poems?

But jazz to me is one of the inherent expressions of Negro life in America: the eternal tom-tom beating in the Negro soul—the tom-tom of revolt against weariness in a white world, a world of subway trains, and work, work, work; the tom-tom of joy and laughter, and pain swallowed in a smile. Yet the Philadelphia clubwoman is ashamed to say that her race created it and she does not like me to write about it.

The old subconscious "white is best" runs through her mind. Years of study under white teachers, a lifetime of white books, pictures, and papers, and white manners, morals, and Puritan standards made her dislike the spirituals. And now she turns up her nose at jazz and all its manifestations—likewise almost everything else distinctly racial. She doesn't care for the Winold Reiss portraits of Negroes because they are "too Negro." She does not want a true picture of herself from anybody. She wants the artist to flatter her, to make the white world believe that all Negroes are as smug and as near white in soul as she wants to be. But, to my mind, it is the duty of the younger Negro artist, if he accepts any duties at all from outsiders, to change through the force of his art that old whispering "I want to be white," hidden in the aspirations of his people to "Why should I want to be white? I am a Negro—and beautiful!"

So I am ashamed for the black poet who says, "I want to be a poet, not a Negro poet," as though his own racial world were not as interesting as any other world. I am ashamed, too, for the colored artist who runs from the painting of Negro faces to the painting of sunsets after the manner of the academicians because he fears the strange unwhiteness of his own features. An artist must be free to choose what he does, certainly, but he must also never be afraid to do what he might choose.

Let the blare of Negro jazz bands and the bellowing voice of Bessie Smith singing Blues penetrate the closed ears of the colored near-intellectuals until they listen and perhpas understand. Let Paul Robeson singing Water Boy, and Rudolph Fisher writing about the streets of Harlem, and Jean Toomer holding the heart of Georgia in his hands, and Aaron Douglas drawing strange black fantasies cause the smug Negro middle class to turn from their white, respectable, ordinary books and papers to catch a glimmer of their own beauty. We younger Negro artists who create now intend to express our individual dark-skinned selves without fear or shame. If white people are pleased we are glad. If they are not, it doesn't matter. We know we are beautiful. And ugly too. The tom-tom cries and the tom-tom laughs. If colored people are pleased we are glad. If they are not, their displeasure doesn't matter either. We build our temples for tomorrow, strong as we know how, and we stand on top of the mountain, free within ourselves.

3

Depression, New Deal, and World War II

Leslie H. Fishel, Jr. □ The Negro and the New Deal

By 1932, many Negroes declared that their political debt to the Republican party had been paid, and voted for Franklin D. Roosevelt. The new President, through the efforts of Harold Ickes and Mrs. Roosevelt, established close ties with various Negro leaders. In this essay, Leslie H. Fishel, Jr., Director of the State Historical Society of Wisconsin, explores the depth of that relationship.

The rhythm and the tone of the New Deal was set by the man in the White House, since Franklin D. Roosevelt was the spokesman and the master of his administration. His first public statement, the inaugural address of March 4, 1933, pierced the depression-fostered gloom and stabbed deftly and surely at the nation's physical and psychological ills. In stark contrast to his predecessor, Roosevelt recognized the prevailing despair, "the dark realities of the moment," and committed himself and his administration to a brighter future. He lashed out in Biblical terms against the profiteers and the selfish among the monied classes and laid down an emphasis which would characterize his administration more than he then realized: "The measure of the restoration lies in the extent to which we apply social values more noble than mere monetary profit." Identifying himself with the unemployed and underprivileged—"our greatest primary task is to put people to work"—he compared the depression to a war emergency and he warned that he was prepared to mobilize the resources of the federal government to fight it.

From *The Negro American: A Documentary History* by Leslie H. Fishel, Jr., and Benjamin Quarles. This article first appeared as "The Negro and the New Deal Era" in the *Wisconsin Magazine of History* (Winter 1964–5).

Like so many of FDR's speeches, including his informal radio fireside chats, the written version of this one paled on paper. His voice exuded warmth and a personal inflection which brought him close to his listeners. His own physical affliction and the way he bore it earned him deserved admiration and gave encouragement to those who had afflictions of their own, even a darker skin. John Gunther testified to Roosevelt's attraction for people as "concrete and intimate. . . . He set up goals in human terms that the average man could grasp for." The general public responded to his magnetism; one of his secretaries selected a list of salutations which were used on letters addressed to him, and they ran the gamut from "Dear humanitarian friend of the people" to "My Pal!" and "Dear Buddy." Almost all of his callers remarked on his personal charm and persuasiveness.

These characteristics of FDR the man, taken with his consummate ability to personalize his understanding of human exploitation and underprivilege, made him the most attractive President, for Negro citizens, since the Civil War. Robert Vann, publisher of the Negro weekly Pittsburgh *Courier,* who was brought into the 1932 campaign by some of Roosevelt's lieutenants, advised his race to "go home and turn Lincoln's picture to the wall. The debt has been paid in full." Yet, like Lincoln, Roosevelt's actual commitments to the American Negro were slim. He was more a symbol than an activist in his own right. His compassion, though real, was tempered by his own background, by the enormity of the decisions which came up to him, and by political considerations. An enthusiastic politician, he used political weights and measures on a political scale to judge the evidence, and the Negro was often found wanting. When Walter White, the executive secretary of the NAACP, obtained an audience through the good graces of Mrs. Eleanor Roosevelt to plead for the President's public support of the antilynching bill, FDR demurred because he needed Southern votes in Congress on other matters.

Nevertheless, the FDR image eventually became a favorable one; his picture hung in living rooms and infant sons carried his name. At first, though, Negroes waited to be shown. Their publications granted him the benefit of doubt when he spoke about justice and equality, in the hope that he was talking, too, to Negroes. He called lynching murder, remarked W. E. B. DuBois, and "these things give us hope." His acknowledgment, through his Secretary of Labor, of the National Urban League's survey of economic conditions among Negroes was, in the words of an *Opportunity* editorial, "an evidence of his deep interest in the Negroes' welfare." By midway through his first term, FDR had captured the admiration and affection of the Negro people and, with that, their votes. During the campaign of 1936, Negroes were outspoken in their support of the Democratic national ticket. Sixteen thousand Harlem residents traveled to Madison Square Garden in September of that year to attend a political rally, and sixty other cities held similar and simultaneous rallies. The New Yorkers mixed a rich fare of music and entertainment with leading New Dealers talking politics, but it was an African Methodist Episcopal Bishop, the Reverend C. Ransome, who symbolized the affair and its meaning by reading a "New Emancipation Proclamation." The vote in November was anticlimactic; the second Roosevelt had weaned the Negro away from the Republican party.

Roosevelt did not publicly associate himself with Negro projects or Negro leaders before 1935, but his programs and some of his associates were more aggressive. Early in 1933, he approved of a suggestion that someone in his administration assume the responsibility for fair treatment of the Negroes, and he asked Harold Ickes to make the appointment. A young white Georgian, Clark Foreman, came to Washington at Ickes' request to handle the task, and brought in as his assistant an even younger Negro of great promise, Robert C. Weaver. Foreman successfully made his way through the burgeoning maze of new agencies which were springing up and did a respectable job of calling to the attention of agency heads and their assistants an awareness of the special problems of Negroes. Along with Ickes, Daniel Roper, the Secretary of Commerce; Harry Hopkins, FDR's relief administrator; and Aubrey Williams, a Hopkins deputy, were sympathetic to committing the New Deal to work more generously with and for Negroes.

From the first, the various New Deal agencies carried the major burden of this emphasis, since they translated words into bread and butter, shelter and schooling. For the Negro, the most significant were the Federal Employment Relief Administration (FERA), the National Recovery Administration (NRA), the Works Progress Administration, later called the Work Projects Administration (WPA), the Agricultural Adjustment Administration (AAA), the Tennessee Valley Authority (TVA), the National Youth Administration (NYA), the Civilian Conservation Corps (CCC), and the public housing efforts of several agencies. There were others in the alphabetical jungle which assisted Negroes, as whites, in more specialized ways, such as the Federal Writers' Project and the Office of Education studies. The very number of agencies added credence to the emergent fact that, for the first time, the federal government had engaged and was grappling with some of the fundamental barriers to race progress.

It was one thing to engage and grapple with a problem at the federal level, and another thing to implement it at lower levels. Most of the New Deal agency programs ran afoul of local laws and customs and most of them capitulated on very practical grounds. As a consequence, Negroes vigorously attacked the inequities, even while they appreciated the limited benefits. FERA, the first New Deal agency to work directly to alleviate the plight of the destitute, tried by locally administered dole and work-projects to pump more money into circulation. Until the end of 1935, when it was abolished, it administered most of the direct relief and work relief programs which the New Dealers initiated, distributing about four billion dollars. Its progress was dogged by racial discrimination, since the design of projects and allocation of funds remained in local hands. Jacksonville, Florida, Negro families on relief outnumbered white families three to one, but the money was divided according to proportions of the total city population. Thus 15,000 Negro families received 45 per cent of the funds and 5,000 white families got 55 per cent. Along the Mississippi River, from Natchez to New Orleans, Negroes were passed over for skilled jobs and frequently received less than the stipulated minimum wage. When the state of Georgia squeezed out of the FERA administrator the right to fix hourly wages for Negroes below thirty cents an hour, *Opportunity* mounfully questioned, "Does this presage the end of that heralded concern for the Forgotten Man?"

If the relief program raised questions of discrimination, the NRA brought howls of indignation. In the words of a Negro labor specialist, the NRA administrator, General Hugh A. Johnson, was "a complete failure" for not properly recognizing the Negro. The industrial codes established under NRA deferred to geographic wage and employment consideration so that the Negro worker generally earned less money for equal time and was frozen out of skilled jobs. A young Negro lawyer, John P. Davis, organized the Joint Committee on National Recovery in the fall of 1933 to persuade federal authorities to rectify these policies. "It has filed briefs, made appearances at public hearings," he wrote, and "buttonholed administrative officers relative to the elimination of unfair clauses in the codes," but to little avail. In self-defense, NRA officials explained the difficulty in bucking local customs, pointing out also that the NRA was responsible only for industrial workers. Agricultural laborers, domestic servants, and the service trades were not included, and most of the unskilled workers were exempted by statute from wage and hour minimums. "It is not fair," wrote an NRA administrator in a Negro journal, "to blame the NRA for not curing all these ills, if such they be, within a year." Until the Supreme Court decreed its demise in the spring of 1935, the NRA was a favored whipping boy for Negroes, as well as for others. "The Blue Eagle," a Virginia newspaper observed, "may be [for Negroes] a predatory bird instead of a feathered messenger of happiness."

The TVA and the AAA came under fire in the early years of the New Deal for similar reasons. Negro critics raged at the all-white model towns, such as Norris, Tennessee, which were established in conjunction with TVA. Homes for white workers on the project were substantial, while Negro workers lived in substandard temporary barracks. Skilled jobs went first to whites and most labor crews were segregated. TVA, it appeared to two observers in 1934, "aims to maintain the *status quo*." A year later, the situation seemed little better. In one sample two-week period, Negroes were 11 per cent of the working force, receiving only 9.5 per cent of the payroll. Under AAA, Negro tenant farmers and sharecroppers, as the most dispensable laborers, suffered first from the crop-reduction policy and found themselves without employment. Concerned about the evolving discriminatory pattern, the NAACP in 1934 devoted a major share of its energy to trying to prevent white landlords from illegally depriving their Negro tenants of crop-reduction bonuses.

Two New Deal programs for young people operated with a minimum of discrimination: the CCC and the NYA. The CCC established segregated camps in the South and in some parts of the North; the great bulk of the integrated camps were in New England. By 1935, its peak year, CCC had over a half million boys in camp. In general, Negroes stayed in CCC camps longer than whites, were not moved up to administrative posts in camps as readily as whites, and were restricted to less than 10 per cent of the total enrollment. Since the proportion of young Negro men in need was substantively higher than this, the quota system was actually inequitable. The NYA, which Mary McLeod Bethune served as administrator of Negro affairs, was shaped to help young men and women in school and with schooling. It grew out of the university and college student relief program established under FERA, and by the end of its first six months, in late 1935, had distributed more than forty million dollars. Conforming to existing state and regional patterns, the NYA still managed to help a critical age group among Negroes.

The debit side of the New Deal's efforts to assist Negroes fell far short of its material and psychological credits. Never before had Negro leaders participated in government affairs as freely and as frequently. The Department of Commerce had E. K. Jones, on leave from the National Urban League; the NYA had Mrs. Bethune; Interior had William H. Hastie and Weaver; the Social Security Board had Ira DeA. Reid; Labor had Lawrence W. Oxley; the Office of Education had Ambrose Caliver, to mention a few. Never before had there been so great a stress on improving the education of Negroes. Many relief programs included elementary education and training classes as part of the regimen. Negro colleges and universities received funds for buildings. The Office of Education, along with other agencies, began an important study of the status of Negro education.

Professional opportunities opened up in government, although not at the rate at which Negroes were graduating from college. For the first time, Negroes were employed as architects, lawyers, engineers, economists, statisticians, interviewers, office managers, case aids, and librarians. Nonprofessional white-collar jobs, which had rarely been within reach of the race, now became available to trained stenographers, clerks, and secretaries. While many of these jobs centered around programs for Negroes within the government, such as Negro slum clearance projects, Negro NYA offices, and the like, they broke the dam which had hitherto kept Negroes out of these kinds of positions.

Harold Ickes, a former president of the Chicago chapter of the NAACP, was the first New Dealer to be recognized as a tried friend. He quickly ended discrimination in his department and set the example by placing professionally-trained Negroes in responsible positions. He first drew FDR's attention to Hastie as a candidate for the federal judge vacancy in the Virgin Islands, and Roosevelt made the appointment in 1937. Ickes appeared at predominantly Negro functions and in 1936, on the occasion of an address as Howard University, even went so far as to wear a University of Alabama hood with his cap and gown because "it seemed to have the best color effect. . . ." While Ickes could not breach established segregation patterns in housing, one-eighth of the federal housing projects planned before the end of 1935 were in mixed neighborhoods. Approximately one-half of them were in Negro slum areas and, thanks to the negotiating skill of Ickes' assistant, Robert C. Weaver, the contracts for a substantial portion of these called for the employment of both skilled and unskilled Negro workers.

Eleanor Roosevelt, the New Deal's conscience, made it her business to reaffirm by word and deed her faith in the equality of opportunity for all. She included Negro and mixed organizations on her itineraries, welcomed mixed groups of adults and children to the White House, and spoke up for the race at critical times. In 1936, as part of a long memo on political strategy in the presidential campaign, she urged party leaders to ask respected Negroes like Mrs. Bethune to participate among Negro groups. The penalty for her unflagging advocacy of the Negro's cause was abuse or occasionally embarrassing questions. As the European war spread after 1939, she confronted questions about the Negro's loyalty. "Rarely," she told a group of New Jersey college women in 1940, "do you come across a case where a Negro has failed to measure up to the standard of loyalty and devotion to his country."

Eleanor Roosevelt was more than a symbol of the New Deal's conscience; she was a vehicle for approaching and influencing the

President. She performed this service for Walter White when the antilynching bill was before Congress. When the DAR refused to allow Marian Anderson to sing in Constitution Hall, Mrs. Roosevelt was the intermediary who secured permission to use the Lincoln Memorial for the concert. It was useful for the President to have his wife serve in these varying capacities, absorbing some of the criticism, supplying him with information he could get from no other source, and sparking his conscience, when that was needed. This relieved the President from having to punctuate his speeches and press conferences with references to the Negro. Before 1935, these were almost nonexistent; after 1935, they increased in frequence and directness, but Roosevelt did not directly commit himself, as his wife did, until his famous Executive Order 8802 of June, 1941, established a Fair Employment Practice Committee to supervise all defense-contract industries.

In many ways, 1935 seemed to be a pivotal year for the President's public statements to and about the Negro. His annual message to Congress in January asserted that "in spite of our efforts and in spite of our talk, we have not weeded out the overprivileged and we have not effectively lifted up the underprivileged." Uplift and underprivilege were two words which Negroes understood, two words which footnoted their history; yet Roosevelt did not mention the Negro specifically. Shortly after that, he told WPA state administrators that "we cannot discriminate in any of the work we are conducting either because of race or religion or politics," and although he went on to speak of political pressures, the word "race" was there for Negroes to see. In two other public statements later in the year, FDR paid lip service to the accomplishments of the race and by 1936, an election year, he proclaimed his policy that "among American citizens there should be no forgotten men and no forgotten races." The transformation was more one of degree than of conviction; Roosevelt was beginning to speak to the Negro, however rarely, rather than to lump him without identification into massive generalizations. But his eye was ever on the balance of political forces and he never voluntarily came out foursquare for the Negro.

In perspective, Roosevelt's circumspection on some domestic issues was less significant than his New Deal legislative program. Labor unions received substantial encouragement from Section 7a of NRA and from the Wagner Act, although the White House maintained an equivocal position toward both labor and management. The jump in union memberships and the rise of the Committee on Industrial Organization, first within the AF of L and later as the independent Congress of Industrial Organizations (CIO), gained impetus from the newly established right to strike and the newly created federal board to mediate labor disputes. A strengthened labor movement confronted, as one of its problems, the question of Negro members. Older unions such as the United Mine Workers and the International Ladies Garment Workers Union welcomed Negroes without distinction. When the CIO broke from the AF of L, its nucleus of unions including the new and somewhat fragile organizations in the automobile, rubber, and steel industries accepted Negroes on an equal basis, except in those localities where race friction was high. The United Textile Workers attempted to do the same, but the existence of textile plants in southern states made this task more onerous. It was not enough for a union to resolve, as the CIO did, to accept members without regard to race, creed, or color, or even, as the UAW and the organizing committees of the steelworkers did, to offer Negro workers a chance to join up. Negroes still hung back, alternately tempted and frightened by management's offers and threats. The wave of the future was with the industrial unions, and *Opportunity's* declaration to Negro steelworkers that it would be "the apotheosis of stupidity" for them to stay out of the union battling for recognizance in 1937, was prophetic. The success of the Brotherhood of Sleeping Car Porters, under the leadership of A. Philip Randolph, in gaining recognition as the bargaining agent with the Pullman Company after a twelve-year struggle, marked the beginning of the race's influence in national labor circles and on national labor policy. After his union was recognized, Randolph prodded the AF of L to grant it an international charter, making it an equal with other member unions, and he never eased up his fight to liberalize the AF of L's racial policies. Even though he was not persuasive enough to break down these craft and railway-union prejudices, Randolph emerged before World War II as a dominant voice in Negro circles and a power to be reckoned with in American unionism.

Of the many voices which spoke out for and against the race, none was more deceptive than that of the Communists. Before 1935, their ideology committed their followers to support a separate state for Negroes, the so-called Black Republic, and insisted that they work independent of all other groups toward this end. When the NAACP unsuccessfully defended the Scottsboro boys—nine young Negroes accused of rape on an Alabama freight train in 1931—the Communists abusively blamed the NAACP for the failure. With shrill bravado, they muscled the NAACP out of the picture and took over the defense. They were unsuccessful in court, but they publicized the case all over the world as an example of capitalistic exploitation and milked the American public for uncounted (and unaccountable) thousands of dollars. In 1935, the Communist ideology swung over to a united-front tactic, and they abandoned their attacks on existing non-Communist organizations and held out the carrot of co-operation. Their purpose was to mix with these organizations and either subvert them directly or gain control behind the scenes. The National Urban League and the NAACP quickly recognized the move for what it was and co-operated at a chilly distance. The League had to dissolve some of its worker's Councils, established in northern cities, because the Communists took them over. The NAACP agreed to work with Communist support on the Scottsboro case, but continued to warn against close co-operation.

Failing to engage the two dominant Negro organizations, the Communists jumped at the chance to work with these and other Negro groups through the newly formed National Negro Congress. The brainchild of New Deal critic John P. Davis, it was organized under the co-sponsorship of almost forty Negro organizations and met in Chicago in 1936 with close to 900 delegates. The Communists stayed in the background—Davis was sympathetic—and the resolutions were non-Stalinist, but Davis was elected executive secretary and maintained close touch with Communist leaders. The 1937 Congress met in Philadelphia with even larger crowds. But soon after that the more conservative organizations and individuals withdrew their sponsorship and the Congress, handicapped by lack of funds, began to crumble. Some local councils established by the Congress were active in Western cities, but after 1937 the Congress as a national group dwindled into impotence and in 1940 became an openly controlled Communist organization. This take-over followed the Stalin-Hitler pact and signalized the 180-degree pivot which American Communists were forced to execute, exploding the united front movement. Organizations like the NAACP which had worked with Communists at a distance suddenly found themselves subject to vituperative and irrational attack, but the vast majority of Negroes merely continued to ignore Communism as a method of achieving their goals.

With the exception of the church, the major Negro organizations felt the sting of mass apathy. "We recognize our lack of skill at mass appeal," NAACP's Roy Wilkins admitted in 1941. The national office of NAACP attracted men and women of an intellectual bent whose convictions on race matters had not changed with the seasons, since the organization was still dedicated to the abolition of segregation and discirimination. But the spark which had sent John Shillady, Walter White, and James Weldon Johnson into race-hatred areas, North and South, burned low. On the national level, the NAACP fought its battles in court, in Congress, and in the press, but not in communities where racism flourished. At local levels, it depended upon its branches, many of which were woefully weak in finances and leadership, to seek out and rectify racial problems of every description. Its base was too narrow for its superstructure, and its bones creaked from inaction at the community level; yet it thrived because it learned to speak the language of influence in political circles and because it chose wisely the cases of discrimination and segregation which it pursued through the courts. Indeed, the road to the 1954 desegregation decisions was charted, bulldozed, paved, and landscaped by the NAACP.

The National Urban League was tested during the depression and not found wanting. Its leadership was similar to that of the NAACP, except that to the extent that its goals were more specific, framed in terms of employment, family welfare, health, and education, it was accused of being more timid, dominated by white liberals, and hostile to trade unionism. Its chief executive, E. K. Jones, replied to these criticisms in a private memo in 1941. The League, he said, was not a Negro but "truly an interracial movement. . . . Any movement of this character which advocates understanding through conference and discussion must necessarily refrain from advocating mass action of one race calculated to force the other group to make concessions." Gunnar Myrdal, the Swedish sociologist whose monumental study of the Negro in America was published during World War II, found that the League worked actively with unions and held "the lead as a pro-union force among the Negro people." Urban League branches were beginning to receive local support from Community Funds, which gave them greater strength and a source for independent leadership. Taken together, these two Negro organizations, in spite of their lack of popular support, moved together in harmony along parallel paths to the great good of the race.

The Negro's church maintained its grip on the masses during these years as it had for centuries, but its hold was loosening. Strong in numbers and appeal, the church had inherent weaknesses which gradually reduced its potency in modern America. It was not one church but many, from the strong African Methodist Episcopal (AME) and African Methodist Episcopal Zion (AMEZ) to the independent colored branches of the Baptist denomination. To these were added smaller denominations and sects and store-front evangelical churches which dissipated the religious energies of the race. The differences were more personal than ideological; in fact, except for the split between the liberal and the fundamentalist churches—a split matched in white denominations—there was no basic theological difference. The churches' hierarchies stood in the way of closer cooperation. The Negro church was all-Negro and proudly so, a self-perpetuating, segregated institution which made no effort to reach across race barriers, individually or institutionally. In the North, this would have been troublesome for white churches, whose precepts were in advance of practice. Negro preachers generally stayed in Negro pulpits. In the South this would have been almost impossible. The Northern Negro church bred isolation; the Southern Negro church fostered accommodation. Fettered by a strain of fundamentalism and emotionalism, and weakened by the diffusion of denominations, the Negro church had little appeal for the younger generation. In the 1930's and 1940's it struggled without success to find a vehicle for its latent power, but its leadership had lost touch with the material and moral issues of the day. It failed to see its obligation as a participant in the fight for equal rights. "We are the policemen of the Negroes," a Southern colored preacher observed in 1941. "If we did not keep down their ambitions and divert them into religion there would be upheaval in the South." For the second third of the twentieth century, this message was anachronistic.

It would be simplistic to suggest as have some recent novelists, such as James Baldwin in *Go Tell It on the Mountain,* that the church's withdrawal for fear of upheaval led directly to upheaval, but there is a trace of truth in it. When Harlem rioted in 1935, *The Crisis* explained that only the patience of the Negro had delayed it that long. Patience was not enough to counter the "sneers, impertinence, and personal opinions of smart-aleck investigators, supervisors and personnel directors." Unemployment, rent gouging, and the belief that Harlem had not received its share of relief money snapped the uneasy calm; the riot erupted with a frenzied attack on whites and the purposeful looting of food and clothing stores. The prompt on-the-scene appearance of New York City's popular mayor, Fiorello H. La Guardia, helped restore rationality. When the United States entered World War II, Harlem still seethed from overcrowding, white insolence, and price gouging, and again rioting broke out, followed by riots in other cities, most notably Detroit. The hands of the clock had swung half circle and the Negro had learned from the white how to use violence and lawlessness when order and the law were not sufficient.

Toward the end of the 1930's the federal government turned more and more of its attention to the European conflict, the economy flourished as the industrial bastion of the embattled Allies, and the Negro had committed himself to the New Deal and to President Roosevelt. Polls in 1940 showed that Negro voters overwhelmingly supported Roosevelt for a third term, and the polls were right. The reason for this support was not difficult to surmise. Outside of what the Democratic Administration had tried to do directly and indirectly, the decade itself was marked with identifiable milestones of progress. In athletics, Jesse Owen was an Olympic champion, and Negro football players starred on many of the major college teams. Professional baseball still resisted, but its time was not far off. In interracial activities, conferences on a variety of subjects began to meet with overbearing regularity and, though self-consciously interracial, the pattern developed almost irrevocably. College students and adults met to talk about education, religion, economic matters, and of course, civil rights. Even in the South, the indomitable Mrs. Bethune organized an interracial conference at the college she founded, and the white University of Florida tentatively sent delegates. In the deep South, interracial conferences were held on a segregated basis; Eleanor Roosevelt told of attending one in Birmingham and inadvertently sitting in the colored section. "At once the police appeared to remind us of the rules and regulations on segregation. . . . Rather than give in I asked that chairs be placed for us with the speakers facing the whole group." White Southerners began to speak up for the Negro. They were still a small minority, but the mere fact that a white supervisor of schools in Georgia would admit to the inequalities of segregated schools, or a white North Carolina legislator would question a decreased appropriation for a Negro college, was a sign of change. The rise of Huey Long in Louisiana brought a different attitude, one of ignoring race differences without changing race relationships. The all-white Mississippi Education Association established a committee in 1938 to recommend ways in which students might study Negro life, and several Northern newspapers in 1940 editorially acknowledged the importance of Negro History Week. The tide had turned, and Negroes credited the turning to the New Deal.

The sudden shock of the surprise attack which drew the United States into World War II served more to expose sore spots than to blanket them in loyalty. In the First World War, the protests against unequal treatment were slow to develop and not widely heard, but the Second World War was different. Even before Pearl Harbor, clamors arose from the South warning that the Negro was not going to "come out of this war on top of the heap as he did in the last one." However distorted the comparison, the attitude was clear, and it influenced the government's decision to extend pre-Pearl Harbor patterns into the war period.

The Negro soldier remained separate in the armed services, and not always welcome. Judge William L. Hastie resigned as civilian aide to the Secretary of War in protest against the dissembling tactics of the Army Air Corps to keep the Negro on the ground. *The Crisis*, returning to a World War I cry, criticized the appointment of Southern white officers for Negro troops and the explanation that they could handle them better. When FDR queried Walter White about the carelessness of the Negro press and the consistency of its attack on the war effort, White replied that better treatment for Negroes in the armed services and the invitation of Negro editors to presidential press conferences and top briefings would clear up the problem.

White became an important man in the war effort and was finally sent overseas as a war correspondent in early 1944. He toured every major front in Europe and the Pacific and his reports did not make soothing reading. Wherever he went, he later wrote, "there was a minority of bigots who were more determined to force their bigotry on others than they were to win the war." This was particularly true of officers, both Northern and Southern. Separation, he found, bred this spirit, especially when key officers were "prejudiced or weak, or both." When Negroes and whites actually fought together, as they did during the Battle of the Bulge in December of 1944, attitudes changed, according to polls among white officers and men. "After the first day," a white South Carolinian admitted, "when we saw how they fought, I changed my mind." The top combat brass, such as General Dwight Eisenhower and Admiral Chester Nimitz, were willing to co-operate, but they were hemmed in by Washington orders and junior officer reluctance.

At home, the intense feelings bared by war boiled up with wearying constancy. In the spring of 1941, A. Philip Randolph organized the March on Washington movement which threatened to march if the White House did not declare for fair employment practices in defense industries. President Roosevelt issued his famous Executive Order 8802 in June, establishing the FEPC and the principle of government concern with employment discrimination. Randolph continued the movement during the war, but it lapsed as the older organizations themselves became more militant.

The prosperity of war industry and the proscriptive Southern mores once again attracted thousands of Negroes to Northern cities. The consequent overcrowding and war tension heated racism to the boiling point, as the riots in New York, Detroit, and Los Angeles demonstrated. For the Negro, racism was the same wherever it appeared. In Roy Wilkins' words, "it sounds pretty foolish to be *against* park benches marked 'Jude' in Berlin, but to be *for* park benches marked 'Colored' in Tallahassee, Florida." Negroes could not understand why whites drew distinctions between the Nazi ideology of Aryan supremacy and the American ideology of white supremacy. Even back in 1933, the *Crisis* expressed its "unholy glee" at Hitler's attack on the Jews: "Now that the damned include the owner of the [New York] *Times,* moral indignation is perking up." The paradox which Wilkins illustrated could only be resolved by a change of face on the part of white America.

The war itself, by drawing thousands of men and women into a collaborative effort with whites, made such a change possible. Negroes served in the armed services in all ratings and at all ranks, though segregated. War industries hired skilled Negro men and women at supervisory and managerial levels. Government used colored workers in great numbers and in more sensitive positions than ever before.

The Negro's political power was organized in an unprecedented manner during the wartime presidential election. The younger generation of Negro men and women who had grown up in prosperity and matured in depression were awakened to the infinite possibilities of an assimilated society, and from them came the trained leadership to plan the campaign.

The death of Roosevelt and the end of the war in 1945 terminated an era. The office of the Presidency now symbolized a concern for justice and equality for all Americans, including Negroes. The White House had taken a stand in favor of the principle of equal rights, although the practice had lagged. The new President, Harry S. Truman, a man of lesser parts, was to take the next practical step and declare in specifics his belief in the equality of men of whatever race under the law. Where Roosevelt concealed the particular in the general principle, Truman spoke out without check. Where Roosevelt used the excuse of war to delay integration, Truman used the excuse of peace to accelerate it. Where Roosevelt used the federal government to increase economic opportunities for all, Truman used the federal government to increase economic opportunities for Negroes. While the Truman Fair Deal never approximated the energy and the excitement of the Roosevelt New Deal, it was the former which capitalized on the Negro's readiness to take an equal place in American democracy.

Three major strands marked the period between the end of the war and the Supreme Court's 1954 desegregation decision. One related to the improving economic condition of the Negro, a second to the reports of three Presidential committees, and the third to the increasingly significant role of the United States Supreme Court in racial matters. The Negro's improving economic condition stemmed from a variety of causes. In microcosm, the successful introduction of Jackie Robinson into baseball's National League in 1947 is exemplary, since his breakthrough eventually opened the gates in almost every professional sport. In like manner, the appointment of Ira DeA.Reid to the faculty of New York University was a breakthrough in higher education of lesser quantity but equal quality. Other major universities and colleges eventually followed suit. The forceful policy of the CIO, led by the United Auto Workers, brought the AF of L into line. The Negro, Walter Reuther warned in late 1945, "should not allow his painful experiences with many of the old craft unions of the American Federation of Labor to embitter him against all labor unions." Both the Negro and the AF of L took the hint. Some craft unions still held out, generally by subterfuge, but the weight of the major unions and their two national federations swung unequivocally to the side of equal opportunity without regard to race.

Dark spots in the improving picture still plagued the nation. Housing was a special need and a particular irritant, since the restrictive convenant, even after the Supreme Court ruled in 1948 that it had no legal standing, was sufficient to block integrated neighborhoods, North and South. The Negro young people were restive under segregated conditions and their still limited economic opportunities. When Thurgood Marshall warned them in 1946 against a widespread disobedience movement on the grounds that it "would result in wholesale slaughter with no good achieved" and alienate public sympathy of "the cautious and the timid," his counsel only helped to delay student nonviolent protests for a decade. In those federal programs where local agencies exercised jurisdiction, the Negro was frequently abused, and President Harry S. Truman, early in 1947, asked his Civil Rights Committee to add this to its already full agenda.

In establishing the President's Committee on Civil Rights in December, 1946, Truman had already spoken in general terms about the preservation of civil liberties. It was, he stated, "a duty of every Government—state, Federal and local." But he pointed out that when state or local governments failed in their responsibilities, the obligation fell back on to the federal establishment. The committee was instructed to review what Truman called "these weak and inadequate statutes" and recommend new legislative or other methods to protect the civil rights of American citizens. The committee, a group of representative men and women under the chairmanship of industrialist Charles E. Wilson, published its *Report* the following year, the first intensive study of its kind by a government-appointed committee. It was a sweeping endorsement of federal activity in the civil rights area and a severe indictment of the many discriminatory practices found in state and local governments.

The *Report* had immediate and far-reaching repercussions. The President's Executive Order 9980 established a fair employment procedure within the government structure. Executive Order 9981 was even more significant since it, in effect, abolished discrimination in the armed services. The committee established by this order to study the situation and make recommendations published its report, *Freedom to Serve,* in 1950, by which time all three of the service branches had abolished the quota system of enlistment and segregation in any form, including separate units and limited opportunities. The Navy was first in its implementation, having started even before the President's order, and although the Army dragged its feet, the committee was satisfied that the order and its execution were effective. A year later, a third Executive Order, 10308, established a President's Committee to insure compliance by government contractors with contractual regulations prohibiting discrimination because of race, creed, color, or national origin. The committee's report was filed early in 1953.

The political reverberations to these dramatic steps by President Truman echoed in the halls of Congress and almost split the Democratic party asunder. In 1948, the Dixiecrats walked out of the Democratic convention in protest to the strong civil rights plank which the young junior Senator from Minnesota, Hubert Humphrey, had pushed through. Truman's election victory that year, in the face of the walkout and the left-wing Progressive Party, was convincing evidence that civil rights had attracted voter support. In Congress, this message from the electorate went unheeded; Southern Democrats and conservative Republicans, whose constituencies sent different messages to them, blocked all efforts to write civil rights into statute.

Outside of politics, the nation moved slowly but certainly away from segregated positions. Professional associations in southern states began, somewhat tentatively, to invite Negroes to membership—lawyers, social workers, nurses, and librarians. The state medical association in Florida stood alone in admitting colored doctors, while other dentists and teachers in the South remained aloof. The American Friends Service Committee began a four-year program in 1951 to eliminate segregation in Washington, D.C., and in Dallas, Texas, a year earlier, the theological seminary of Southern Methodist University opened its doors to Negro students. In the North, several states adopted open-occupancy laws for public housing, and in key cities like New York, Philadelphia, Detroit, and Washington, Negroes moved into upper- and middle-class neighborhoods without difficulty.

These were straws in the wind rather than set patterns. A full quota of segregation in education and housing, employment, and places of public accommodation still existed. But as the walls began to develop cracks, the role of the Supreme Court emerged as the most significant factor in the equation. Before the milestone decision of 1954, the Supreme Court had charted a course which led, almost inevitably, to that end.

Before World War II, the Supreme Court rendered decisions in three areas involving Negro rights. One was an outgrowth of a group effort by Negroes in Washington, D.C., to persuade a store which catered to Negroes to hire them. The Court determined that this was a labor dispute within the meaning of the Norris-La Guardia Act and that the New Negro Alliance was entitled to picket and pass out literature to accomplish its aim (New Negro Alliance *v.* Grocery Co., 1938). Southern efforts to exclude Negroes from jury service were undermined by the Court's decision in Smith *v.* Texas (1940) which, in the words of Justice Hugo Black, himself a Southerner, asserted that "for racial discrimination to result in the exclusion from jury service of otherwise qualified groups . . . violates our Constitution and the laws enacted under it. . . ." And in the field of education, where the NAACP had begun to place its major legal redress emphasis, the Court found for the petitioner, Lloyd Gaines, in Missouri *ex rel.* Gaines *v.* Canada (1938). Gaines had been refused admission to the University of Missouri Law School because he was a Negro. "The basic consideration," the Court said, "is not as to what sort of opportunities other States provide, or whether they are as good as those in Missouri, but as to what opportunities Missouri itself furnishes to white students and denies to negroes solely upon the ground of color."

The Court did not go beyond the limits of "separate but equal" facilities, but insisted, at the least, that equal facilities exist. Missouri hastened to appropriate a half million dollars for a Negro law school and invited Lloyd Gaines to use a two-room basement establishment in the interim. Before the NAACP could contest this dubious implementation by the state of Missouri, Gaines disappeared and the case was abandoned.

During and after the war, the Court continued to chip away at the encrustations of law which prevented Negroes from full participation as citizens. Its decisions in a series of cases involving the railroad brotherhoods, jury selection, the white primary, and the restrictive covenant generally favored the Negro. In 1948 and again in 1953, the Court made it patently clear that restrictive covenants were not enforceable, in any way, in any court of the land, federal or state. The states of Texas, Mississippi, and Georgia were instructed by the Court in separate decisions between 1947 and 1954 that "the Constitution requires only a fair jury selected without regard to race," and that the various devices used by these states and some of their local subdivisions denied minority groups the equal protection of the laws. In 1944, the Court overruled a 1935 decision and insisted that primaries were sufficiently related to official state actions, even if they were declared to be private, to be regulated by the Fifteenth Amendment. Nine years later, the Court asserted that a private county association of long standing which served as a pre-primary selector of nominees was subject to the same constitutional provision.

Negroes in general and the NAACP in particular could take some satisfaction in knowing that the Court was slowly opening basic rights, but in the area of education the progress was even more marked. The NAACP invested heavily of its time and funds in widening educational opportunities by court action. The University of Maryland in 1935 had capitulated at the graduate-school level with out taking the case to the Supreme Court. Three years later Missouri was instructed to educate a Negro law student, but its subterfuge worked so well that it tried it again in 1942 by establishing a two-room graduate school in journalism for one qualified Negro graduate student. The University of Oklahoma followed suit when the Supreme Court allowed Missouri's effort to stand, but the end was in sight. In

1950 Texas was told by the Court that its Negro law school had to be equal to that of the white University of Texas Law School, and the doors of the latter were duly opened to Negroes. In a parallel case, Oklahoma was rebuked for permitting a Negro student to be segregated within its state university, and the practice ceased. With a Supreme Court which read the Constitution as a document protecting the rights of all citizens and with the opening of universities at the graduate level, the time was ripe for an all-inclusive appeal for educational opportunities.

The twenty years between the inauguration of Franklin D. Roosevelt and the eve of the Supreme Court desegregation decision were the most revolutionary two decades in the history of the American Negro up to that time. In part, the elemental movements had little to do with race matters; depression, war, prosperity—these were not issues of black and white. Yet they determined a basic posture change: that whites and Negroes would work closely together on matters of national and international importance which had nothing to do with race. Perhaps the most startling development to emerge from these decades was that prominent Negroes began to assume responsibilities in government, business, labor, athletics, education, and the social services which had no connection with race. Negroes, finally, were working in critical jobs because they were needed, and not simply because they were Negroes. Ralph Bunche of the United Nations, Jackie Robinson of the Brooklyn Dodgers, Ira De A. Reid of Haverford College, to name just a sampling, were men who were doing their jobs—and who happened to be Negroes.

While this was the wedge, slowly to be driven into the grain of American society, pressures which mounted throughout these two decades supplied the hammer to drive it home. Some of these pressures were cumulative, like the development of substantial numbers of highly skilled and highly educated Negroes, and the steady flow of Negroes from farm to city, from South to North. Other pressures were selective, like the magnetism of FDR and the dogged determination of Harry S. Truman. There were economic forces, like the dawning awareness by retailers of the Negro market and the sudden realization by most unions that integration meant greater strength. Then, too, there were such forces as the quiet efforts of Southern liberals to make integration in higher education successful.

The Negro himself was a pressure on the wedge. Still smarting as a second-class citizen, more ready than ever to step up to equal citizenship, he used every resource available. Some were peaceful and passive, like the continuing desire for education and the calculated use of votes. Some were peaceful and active, like the push to break down labor union and employment barriers and the play to get more national publicity. Some were outside the law and violent. These efforts were not concerted and not always effective, but the total impact was pervasive. American society could no longer sit back, consoled by the thought that the Negro was not yet prepared. By the end of these two decades, he was ready, and in the decade to come, the young men and women of his race would make this clear.

Newell D. Eason □ Attitudes of Negro Families on Relief

The American Negro community never was nor is in complete agreement regarding solutions to racial problems. During the New Deal period, there were those who argued that relief programs failed to provide an adequate answer to the problems of the unemployed. Such a view is represented in the following article by Newell D. Eason, a professor of sociology and economics at Shaw University, Raleigh, North Carolina.

Throughout the country as a whole Negroes are on relief in almost twice as great a proportion to their number in the population as are whites. The percentage of the urban Negro receiving relief is three times that of the urban white population. Obviously, then, there are being created some very serious problems for social work in many parts of the country. The least obvious, and perhaps most serious, consequence of relief on Negro families relates to the changing attitudes of the members toward each other, toward work, toward the home and toward life.

The Negro family has only recently made the transition from the rural areas of the South to the city. With his loose familial and social organization, he has migrated en masse to the city and there has been literally dumped on relief. He has been thrown on the relief rolls just

From Newell D. Eason, "Attitudes of Negro Families on Relief," *Opportunity,* XIII (December 1935), pp. 367–369, 379. Reprinted with permission of the National Urban League, Inc., from *Opportunity: Journal of Negro Life.*

at the time that the Negro family was securing a degree of stability. Under the stimulus of relief new values are rising over the Negro families' horizon. As a result even his most fixed attitudes are changing. Modifications of these attitudes are in many cases imperceptible. They are none the less real.

In this study of the attitudes of Negro families on relief the questions may arise: are these attitudes representative? Do they represent a cross-section of Negro life? Do these attitudes hold true for more than the sixty-five cases studied? It is not held that these facts relating to the attitudes of Negro families on relief are characteristic of all Negro families on relief. These assertions are valid for the Negro population on relief in Watts, California; a population that is only recently removed from the farm life of the South. Differences or similarities in attitudes of other groups have not been noted. This, however, does not detract from the essential value of the selected facts.

When first applying for relief, Negroes make an energetic bid for a job. They vehemently declare it is work that they want, not relief. After they are placed on relief for awhile this attitude becomes less active. It soon dwindles to a refusal to work. They begin to cling to the minimum existence which seems to be guaranteed by the relief agency. They seem to discover that they have always worked too hard for such a small income so that the idea of receiving an equal sum with no labor attached has a catastrophic effect.

In many instances they refuse work under the most ridiculous pretext as in the following case of Mr. A:

"Mr. A had been on relief for six weeks. He had, before being placed on relief, asked energetically for a work assignment as a carpenter. He took the assignment fretfully. Three days later he turned in his assignment saying that the job wasn't 'constructive enough'."

Others refuse work on the grounds that "the job is too far," "I am not feeling well," "I haven't car fare."

Employers in case after case have undermined the Negroes' ambition as a worker by replacing them in their jobs with white workers. Employers have taken the attitude that "no Negro has a right to a job as long as there is a white man unemployed." This attitude finds support in the employers public at large. The Negro is then literally forced on relief. He accepts the relief as due recompense for lost opportunity. Because he falls in such large numbers on the relief rolls the general public views him as a chronic dependent. There are few attitudes that have done more to disorganize the Negroes' personality and family life than this attitude. His attitudes are conditioned by the reflection of himself as a chronic dependent that he thinks he sees in the white public. He turns whole heartedly to the relief agency. He finds this the easiest way to eke out an existence.

The general attitude of the families studied was so much an attitude of disgust for work until it leads to the belief that the Negro on relief is becoming pauperized faster than we ordinarily think. At any rate, normal attitudes toward work are not being preserved. If once the Negro looked upon work as a "necessary evil" he now looks upon it as an "unnecessary evil." He does not long to be occupied, he longs for more gifts. In only a few cases were there found Negroes trying to help themselves by gardening, taking in washing, etc. In no instance were any found occupying their time by making any little novelties to sell or trying to learn a new trade to follow on their own account. They were on the whole averse to any suggestion of self-help.

While once the Negro was fostering objectives which enlisted the support of the different members of the family, today under relief he is shifting the responsibilities of the home to the social agency. The members of the family no longer look to the father for the necessities of life. They seek out the social worker. If shoes, dresses, bed clothing, etc., are needed the members of the family do not turn to the father but to the visitor. If the wife feels that she needs a stove she does not cooperate with her husband to secure one, she asks her visitor to supply it. A good deal of emotional dependence can be seen in their attitudes. They look to the social worker for comfort, guidance and protection. The emotional reaction of members of families can be seen in the following case:

"The L's are a family of eight. Since coming to Los Angeles fifteen years ago. Mr. L. had been stable and reliable in providing for his family. He was assisted by William, aged nineteen, and Leon, aged eighteen. Mr. L owned two rickety Ford trucks; he and the boys were in the transfer business. The L's began receiving relief in June, 1934 to the amount of $12.00 per week. In November the project closed and the family became extremely dependent. The father decided that he wanted to move his family to a larger house and to a better neighborhood. This was accomplished. The family now paid $15.00 instead of $5.00. In January Mr. L began begging for clothing. The visitor secured clothing for the entire family from members of a social club who wished to do something for the deserving poor. Two weeks later Mr. L called in the district office loudly inquiring if he were to be turned into a Communist! He explained that his family needed furniture, shoes, and new clothing instead of secondhand ones. He spent his days hanging around the social agency begging for these things. Visitor called in his home two days later. No one answered the door bell. Visitor walked around to the rear. No one answered the knock. In and out of the building soiled clothing was rotting on the floor. Neighbor next door complained that the woman never washed the soiled clothing but left them out to be washed at a laundry."

After receiving relief for a while many members of the families seem unable to meet any situation. They become exceedingly dependent.

It was observed that women who have been on relief for any period of time lose interest in caring for the house. Whether or not the living conditions are purposefully left in a disgraceful manner in order to secure more sympathy from the social worker is difficult to discover. It seems more likely that with such unsanitary conditions and so much general decay prevalent that the cause must lay in an apathetic attitude.

Whenever these women were asked why they did not keep their houses cleaner they would reply, "I have no broom," "I have no soap," or "I am not well enough to do this house work." In some instances the mother placed the burden of cleaning the house entirely on the children.

There has developed a new cultural attitude that it is actually desirable for boys and girls to leave the parental home and establish independent residence as early as possible. It is desirable because it is much easier for both parent and the child to secure separate relief when living apart. Where once these young people found it advantageous living with their parents, or, at any rate, found it impossible to get away from them, they are, under our relief system, finding it not only possible but advantageous to leave their parental home. This may turn out to be a constructive attitude as it eliminates the difficulties and inevitable conflicts of the large household. It is, however, disturbing to see boys and girls leave home to live elsewhere in the belief that their families will not suffer, since in any case they receive only the minimum budget, and in order that they might receive separate aid. Undoubtedly the most serious handicap the Negro is suffering under relief is the growth of attitudes that are disorganizing the family life.

There seems to be a weakening of the tie between children and parents due to the fact that the children seek the things they want from the social worker rather than the parents. "In such a way is the child cheated out of normal family functioning and forced to look away from the family and even away from his own satisfying creative effort to the community to supply his wants." Children now proudly boast "that's my visitor," where once they boasted "that's my daddy." Parental authority as a result appears to be on the wane. The following case illustrates the loss of prestige by the father:

"The S's were a father-ruled family. All purchases for the home were made by Mr. S. His wife was not entrusted with a penny. Mr. S's slightest command was law to the three children aged fifteen, nine, and seven. They delighted in the father's prowess. Mr. S had been a blacksmith. He possessed a powerful physique. John was examined by the school doctor and was found under-weight, also with a tubercular tendency. Billy was under-weight. A quart of milk daily for each was recommended by the nurse. In order that the milk be purchased, $6.00 was added to the monthly check. Mr. S refused to cooperate. Family quarrels followed. Mrs. S would explain in the presence of the children that "the visitor has allowed the money but your father refuses to buy the milk." Mrs. S at last began besieging the office about the weekly check, stating that Mr. S refused to furnish necessary milk and vegetables. After several weeks of seeking cooperation unsuccessfully from Mr. S the payee on the check was changed to Mrs. S. The S's almost separated. Mr. S insisted that he was head of the house. He could manage his own affairs and that no woman could manage his money. All quarrels were carried on in the presence of the children. Anne Lou, aged fifteen, has refused for three weeks to speak to her father. John and Billy have informed their mother that they are not going to let their father beat them again but will go 'tell the office.'" The loss of prestige by the father often leads to the breakdown of family discipline.

The personalities of the parents and their interaction with the children certainly are not healthy under relief. With the parents begging in front of the children for gifts and in some instances inducing the children to beg the social worker for things they want certainly does not leave the child the better.

The Negro child, like other youth, slavishly imitate their parents in their general social attitudes because their parents help to set their social values. They are in reality but miniature copies of the attitudes and social values of their parents. What, then, is happening to the personalities of Negro children when they hear their parents presenting false claims and lying in order to get gifts and more gifts? It becomes impossible for them to develop those elemental social values of honesty, truth-telling and fair play so essential to the development of a healthy personality.

Negro families on relief have taken an attitude of resignation toward life. They have no plans. They are fatalistic toward the future. Either they have no hopes at all or hopes that are lightly taken. They are well characterized by a feeling of hopelessness, but not fear. They have no fear of the future because they feel that "somehow God will provide."

Those that have been on the relief rolls for some time have lost self confidence, self respect and the spirit of independence. It is alarming that so many of them have lost their sense of human dignity and yet do not suffer consciously as a result. At first members of the family felt humiliated because of the lowering of their status resulting from being recipients of relief, but it no longer distresses them. They ask, they beg, they say, "buy me," "get me," "give me," but they do not feel ashamed. When families accept relief with parasitic response, then the relief is doing more towards disorganizing the family life than poverty. Something of the attitude toward life is shown in the following case:

"Mr. and Mrs. F and their four children were on direct relief. They both felt that things would never be better. There was 'no use wearing out his shoes looking for a job.' The Negro has never had anything and never will. Mr. F says there is money enough for those who need it, but those who don't need it are doling it out and stealing half of that."

Members of these families have, further, developed an attitude which can be expressed approximately as: get as much given to you as you can. They don't think it harmful to try to get as much from the agency as possible. Their income while on relief has been decreased but there has been corresponding contraction in the psychological sphere of their wants. The result is that in many cases there has been a moral collapse resulting in prostitution, theft and utter disregard for the truth. They lie, using all manners of false pretenses, to get more relief. It is obvious that in seeking to qualify for the help they require that a conflict arises between their own conception of need and a necessarily arbitrary standard of eligibility.

Many of the members of these families feel that the government has appropriated a large sum of money for the poor folks so why should they not have it. One father said in the presence of his family, "the big folks are whacking it all off (the relief funds) and we poor folks have to get all the little that's left that we can." Others feel that the only reason they don't get more is that the social worker steals some of the checks.

The social cost of direct relief as indicated by these changing attitudes in Negro families is placing a tremendous task at the door of modern social work. Social workers dealing with these families are seldom qualified with the skill, insight and rare human understanding that is necessary to help these maimed Negro families struggle back to self respect and belief in themselves.

Relief alone is pauperizing Negro families, and is therefore doing more harm than good. It is turning approximately one-fifth of the Negro population into willing professional recipients of charity. Employment is itself a human need apart from the relation to subsistence. Wise social work will offer the unemployed person a chance to earn relief.

The reaction of children reflecting parental attitudes is one of the most disastrous results of relief on the Negro family. Society must later face the seared personality of children who have not had the elemental and essential social values of truth-telling, honesty, and fair play passed on to them. Society will for years to come face the embittered and crushed spirits of these children.

There is need for an effective social work among Negroes that will prevent the development of the attitudes that are emerging. There is need for a social work that will give "them a stronger economic foundation and a better appreciation of social values." There is need for a social work that will help Negro families struggle back to self respect for "without self respect it is almost impossible for persons to maintain the respect of other persons, for by suggestion his attitudes toward himself influence the attitudes of others toward him." Harmonious race relations therefore demand that we build rather than destroy the self-respect of all groups in order that there may be a decent way of life for all people.

Thyra J. Edwards □ Attitudes of Negro Families on Relief—Another View

Other observers disagreed with Professor Eason. In this selection, Thyra J. Edwards, a Chicago social worker, argues that relief plays a justifiably large role in the battle against poverty.

Several years ago a distinguished agriculturist from Tuskegee Institute was presented to the secretary of the Negro Branch Y.M.C.A. at Gary, Indiana. The secretary, recently migrated from Texas, looked up at his tall, broad shouldered visitor, acknowledged the introduction, and added facetiously, "Alabama, eh, where there are the meanest white folks in the world."

"The meanest white folks and the meanest Negroes," was the agriculturist's unperturbed rejoinder. "Throughout the States I have found that the Negro community is in every instance a parallel reflection of the local white community. The variation is in degree only. The essential social pattern is the same."

Briefly this simple incident points the untenability of the thesis posed rather generally by Negro students and students of the Negro in treating the Negro as an isolated phenomenon rather than an integral unit of the community and national life. Any premise that sets apart certain attitudes, reactions and behavior patterns as particularly and peculiar to any one racial or cultural group, be it Negro, Aryan or Jewish, is sociologically and anthropologically unsound. There are no

From Thyra J. Edwards, "Attitudes of Negro Families on Relief—Another View," *Opportunity*, XIV (July 1936), pp. 213–215. Reprinted with permission of the National Urban League, Inc., from *Opportunity: Journal of Negro Life*.

particular Negro emotions, reactions, or rhythms patterned by race exclusively. Unemployed Negroes and their families do not suffer a particularized hunger and exposure, nor do they react to it in a particular Negro fashion.

Unemployment has become, except for the Soviet Union, universal in extent. For the past seven years a very considerable segment of the American population has been sustained by public funds administered as Direct Relief, or as Work Relief Projects. In December 1935 there were, according to the conservative estimates of the American Federation of Labor, 11,401,000 employable persons in the United States separated from gainful employment. Mass unemployment of Negroes became acute by 1927 and by 1929 there were 300,000 employable Negroes separated from employment. A number which has continued to rise. The percentage of Negroes in this category usually exceeds the whites by from 30 per cent to 60 per cent. There is a similar disproportion in the relief population. Negroes constitute 9.4 per cent of the population while comprising 18.4 per cent of all relief cases, 17.8 per cent of all the Negroes in America being maintained by Public Relief funds. At present the Negro Relief population is 3, 864,000.

And what is the source of this desperate disproportion between the Negro population and the Negro Relief population in relation to the total American population and the total American Relief population? It is generally recognized that the Negro, as a marginal and a minority group, suffers intenser employment hazards through discrimination in wages, in work allotment and in the disbursement of Relief. There is a prevailing sentiment that Negroes should not be hired as long as there are white men without jobs. There are in addition other basic factors: the introduction of machinery into unskilled functions formerly predominantly performed by Negroes has displaced a mass of Negro workers; the reduction of production in the automotive and steel industries in which large numbers of Negroes were employed, has displaced other thousands; cessation of activity in building construction which previously absorbed a great bloc of Negro skilled and unskilled labor; the reduction of incomes of families employing numbers of servants and the widespread use of electrical household machinery has thrown domestic servants on the labor market. The disappearance of small business into which category all Negro business fell, has not only created unemployment but destroyed and blasted the hope of a separate "Negro economy." The destitution of the southern farm population affects some 2,000,000 Negro farmers, largely share croppers and tenant farmers. And the government's removal of acreage from cotton cultivation has increased the destitution and intensified the insecurity of this group.

Even in the more liberal urban centers there is discrimination and segregation in the assignment of Negroes to certain work projects and to camps. Chicago uses the Batavia Camp, exclusively for white men. There are exclusive "white" projects.

Now after seven years, Unemployment and Unemployment Relief can no longer be classified as emergencies. Yet Federal and local governments continue establishing temporary procedures, made work, and work programs of a few months' life span only. Such procedure is mere wishful thinking. For as distasteful as are unemployment and relief to the American temperament and to the American philosophy of individual thrift and industry and individual success the permanency of unemployment and the problem of caring for the unemployed population are now recognized and accepted by the American public.

If indeed then, the Negro, in the face of these preponderous odds, has recognized the potential permanence of sustained unemployment and has adjusted his attitudes to the enigma of want and suffering in the midst of an abundance ruthlessly destroyed under government authority, then he has displayed an astuteness that exceeds and anticipates that of the finance capitalists and the political administrators who continue tampering and pottering with half measures. For there is doubtful virtue in the gesture of pacing the sidewalks in a futile search for jobs that do not exist.

Despite this it is notable that men and women on relief beg for and accept jobs, project and work relief assignments—even when the wage offered is the mere equivalent of their relief budgets. It restores some of their self respect to handle cash and to purchase direct and be able to shop about without the stigma and discrimination attendant upon buying on disbursing orders.

With the establishment of the Works Progress Administration this job-eager attitude repeated itself. A few men have refused jobs under slight pretexts. But the great number have anxiously accepted jobs, any kind of jobs, most of them at the ridiculous wage of $55.00 a month for full time. In large families this amount was cruelly below even the relief budget and families suffered the delays attendant upon cases being reopened for supplementation. Men went to these jobs often so poorly clad that "unsocially minded" foremen sent them home off the outdoor jobs. Waiting rooms in some relief stations displayed a gruesome exhibit of crisping, cracked, frozen ears, bleeding hands and swollen, frost bitten feet.

These men, eagerly accepting any kind of work under any kind of circumstances, represent a trend, not a phenomenon. At the American Association of Social Workers' Delegate Conference in Washington, February 14th, Mrs. Roslyn Serota, Junior supervisor of the County

Relief Board of Philadelphia, Pa., reported that an impartial study of four urban centers disclosed that a very small proportion of job refusal (by the unemployed) is without justification. Physical disability, inability to perform the job offered, current employment, substandard wages are revealed as the common reasons for job refusals. Philadelphia has used a Job Refusal committee to define a bona-fide work offer and a "justifiable" refusal, and to hear complaints. Before presuming to indict the unemployed such boards of impartial hearing should be set up in every community dispensing to large units of the unemployed.

"They were on the whole," complains Mr. Newell Eason, referring to Negro families on Relief, "averse to any suggestion of self help."

Well, Watts, California, is remote from the experience and knowledge of the bulk of the American population. But in Chicago—the second city in the world for Negro population—the self-help efforts among Negroes are bravely defiant.

Last year a congested strip of Chicago's Black Belt comprising approximately nine city blocks and containing 1,349 households, a total of 4,422 individual souls was intensively studied and analyzed. There was the accustomed run of ice cream and watermelon venders and window washers and news hawkers. And in addition, up and down the walks were fish vendors, carrying long strings of perch hanging from their backs or pushing their "catch" in rude carts converted from discarded baby carriages. The "junk men" had the middle of the street. These latter have hitched themselves to carts which they have built out of wheels, usually found on dump heaps, and irregular scraps of board gotten from some building in the process of demolition.

A conversation with the fish vendor disclosed this: "Three pounds for two bits, Miss. But sometimes I walk all day to sell three pounds. They's so many o' us on the street, we jus' 'cuttin' each other's tho'ts. I works wid a partner. A white fellow from the West Side. He stays out to de Lake and sets the nets and catch 'em, an' I walk up an' down an' sells 'em. I gets a quarter outta ev'y dollar I sells. But fish don' bite ev'y day, Miss. 'Pends on how de wind blowin. Ef it ain't blowin' yo' way it jus' sweep de fish out toward de middle o' de Lake an dey don' bite. Fish don' bite ev'y day."

Behind the stone facade of the building down the street a colony of unemployed men and women have drifted in and settled. The building appears gruesomely debauched. Outside doors have disappeared so that it stands open always. Window apertures are stuffed with rags, old clothes, cardboard, wire netting, wooden doors, anything at hand. A side entrance formerly protected by a door is now barricaded by rusted bed springs, stoves and scraps of iron. Throughout the floors are rotted and in places broken out. On the stairways windows have become only great gaps where the cold packs in. All electric wiring has been torn out, all gas piping stripped. Various styles and sizes of coal stoves are used in the different individual "quarters." In the absence of flues these are piped through holes cut through to the outer walls of the building. Passing on the outside when several "quarters" have fires the adjoining vacant lot is a series of smoke puffs at various heights and levels.

Mr. Eason bemoans the wane of parental authority and the loss of prestige by the father. He cites the miserable example of Mr. S. clinging to the last vestige of medieval male dominance by arbitrarily denying the necessary milk to undernourished Billie even when the money had been especially provided for this. His sole explanation, "the visitor has allowed the money but your father refuses to buy the milk!" That is the strongest indictment of the contemporary family pattern. Parental rule by blind, unreasoning might of authority bulwarked by school, pulpit, press and by the mores, and ultimately conquered by Relief!

For in the past the complete economic dependence of women upon their husbands, children upon their parents, and in turn in sickness and old age, parents upon their children has tended to warp every fine, free impulse in familial relationships. It has created the nagging wife wheedling an underpaid husband for the little luxuries of life which his inadequate wage cannot provide. It has created the demand upon older sisters and brothers to sacrifice their own education to help support younger sisters and brothers.

And so instead of decrying this overthrow of the tyrant-parent the sociologist should rather hasten the day when in addition sickness and invalidity insurance, a comprehensive unemployment insurance act and adequate assistance for the aged will relieve the burden of poor relations on other poor relations.

The fact is that professional social workers have been in intimate daily contact with large segments of the unemployed population for more than five years now. They have had continual access to the case records of thousands of these families. They are thus in possession of facts to expose and explode these hair trigger conclusions branding the unemployed as malingerers, chiselers and indolent and hopeless parasites. Instead of the too ready indictment of the unemployed condemnation should, it would seem, be directed against the political economy that creates these conditions of mass unemployment and its attendant malnutrition, disease, overcrowding, immorality, delinquency and family disintegration.

Bonita Golda Harrison □ Social Security: What Does It Mean for the Negro?

Certain New Deal programs were not as effective for the Negro as they were for the white. In this document, Bonita G. Harrison, a graduate student at Atlanta University, discusses the inadequacies of the Social Security Act.

The Social Security Act is a very long and involved document and one which few citizens, including this writer, have either attempted or been able to understand in full. A perusal of the many digests which are available indicates that the law embodies old age pensions, unemployment insurance, and child dependency. The omission of health insurance from this bill, which was intended to care for citizens who through no fault of their own cannot take care of themselves, is an outstanding tribute to the lobbying power of the organized medical profession.

The most popular part of the Social Security Act is the old age pension phase. Benefits begin in 1942 and the federal regulations regarding state participation are very liberal—too liberal. The benefits provided by the federal old age annuities plan and the relatively small expenditures of the United States Public Health Service are the only benefits which may be secured without action by the state. Every

From Bonita Golda Harrison, "Social Security: What Does It Mean for the Negro?" *Opportunity,* XIV (June 1936), pp. 171–173. Reprinted with permission of the National Urban League, Inc., from *Opportunity: Journal of Negro Life.*

other benefit made possible by the Act can be realized only if the states pass the necessary laws designated by the Act. Tax payers of all states will contribute to the federal government to finance grants, but only states which pass laws designed to permit them to participate in the Act will receive benefits.

Unemployment insurance, another phase of the Act, may be secured only through state participation. To those unemployed today, the Act offers nothing. It does not cover workers in establishments of less than eight employees, agricultural workers, casual workers, seamen, persons in domestic service, public service employees, and employees of institutions operated for religious, charitable, scientific, literary, or educational purposes.

The third phase of the Act is designed to provide for dependent children who are not in institutions. This is to be provided through a subsidy to those states whose Mothers' Aid Legislation conforms with the Security Act. As of November 1, 1935, there were only twelve states eligible for this type of aid. Very little has been said about this phase of the Act because there is very little to it and very little that it can do in its present form. States must match the federal government dollar for dollar, and on the 1,000,000 dependent children potentially eligible under the Act, the states spent only $37,000,000.00 in 1934. This is an average of $37 per year per dependent child.

Let us examine the status of the Negro in relation to the needs which the Social Security Act will attempt to meet. In 1930 the proportion of Negro elders to Negro youth showed only a slight increase—but an increase nevertheless. Social scientists on President Hoover's Research Committee on Social Trends estimate that between 1930 and 1950 the proportion of Negroes under 20 is likely to decline over one-sixth, with increases of one-fourth at the ages of 45–65, and over three-fourths at older ages. Keeping in mind that old age benefits do not begin until 1942, this estimated increase in the proportion of Negro elders is important.

Passing to unemployment among Negroes we arrive at a subject where the least said the better. When we exclude agriculture where unemployment is practically negligible, we find that ten out of every one hundred workers are Negroes. In 1930, however, in the non-agricultural occupations, sixteen out of every one hundred workers unemployed were Negroes.

The providing of aid for dependent children is evidence of a recognition of the right of a child to the care of a home and a mother, or an approximate equivalent of such. Since women in industry and child labor are outgrowths of the inability of the husband and father, where there is such, to provide an adequate income, this is particularly important to the Negro group.

Verily, the Negro has the need, but no one believes that he will secure his full share of the benefits of the Act. In the first place, in 1930, 78 per cent of the Negroes lived in the states which will be ages passing laws which will enable their citizenry to share in the benefits to the Act. Secondly, politicians in Southern States will never pass these laws unless they are certain that they have devised means to foil Negro participation. In the third place, the Act, by leaving the administration of its various phases to the local communities, makes it easy for the southern whites to prevent Negroes from receiving benefits. For example: Alabama, the first state to receive federal approval for its child dependency set-up, has vested administration in the Board of Education. It is difficult to visualize Negroes getting their just desserts from a body which gives Negro children 8 per cent of the total amount expended for education when Negro children constitute 39 per cent of the total population six to thirteen years of age.

The Act made it even easier for southern politicians in its unemployment feature by not including in its benefits agriculture and domestic service, where 65 per cent of the gainfully employed Negroes were to be found in 1930. Of course, there are certain provisions to see that "sluggards" are not given benefits, and if not watched, many industrious Negroes will find themselves classified as "sluggards."

In its old age pension phase, the Act has the Negro beaten from the start by reason of the need for establishing proof of age. The lack of accurate birth registrations in Southern States is well known and for the Negro population there are hardly any registrations. The mid-wife problem further complicates the issue in the South. As of June 31, 1931, only seventeen states had passed old age pension laws and among these, the border state of West Virginia was the nearest approach to a Southern State. The slight chance of the Negro to participate in the child dependency feature has already been indicated in the state of Alabama. It seems the height of optimism to expect a group to change its lifelong policies simply because a law of a different name is passed. Dependent children, and especially Negro dependent children, had better not wait for Alabama and its sister states to aid them.

Announcements are coming from Washington concerning Civil Service examinations for jobs with the Social Security Board, and all indications point to the selection of a well-trained and impartial national personnel. But the struggle over administration is not in Washington, but in the local communities. It is there that the Act is to be interpreted and administered, and it is there that the local politicians will fasten their tentacles. The disfranchised Negro can hardly hope for social security without political security.

Old age pensions and the unemployment insurance are designed to take care of persons "who have been wage earners." It is an established fact that millions of people will never be reabsorbed by private industry, and a proportion out of proportion to their per cent of the total population will be Negroes. Many other Negroes who are reabsorbed will never share the benefits because of the marginal nature of their work as well as the exclusion of their jobs from the benefits of the Act. Social security under the Act is, therefore, impossible without economic security which the Negro does not possess.

In a section of the country where every Negro is a potential lynch law victim, and where there has been a continuous sabotaging of any efforts of the federal government to require compensation of the lynch victims' dependents, there is not likely to be much concern over the welfare of Negro children. Personal security, which does not exist for the Negro in the South, must precede social security.

Thus, Negroes cannot expect much in the way of social security when the majority of the Negro population does not have political economic or personal security. In the Negro's present position, social security can mean only the security of a monopoly on the bread and soup line, security of being exploited by employers when employed, security of being unemployed when there is no possibility of being exploited, and finally, the security of paying taxes and having them administered in such a manner that the payees received no parts of the benefits. Social security can mean that to the Negro. This brings to mind the following story which appeared in the columns of a newspaper writer on the staff of a metropolitan newspaper:

> . . . a party of wanderers came upon a deserted mound and a tomb on a hillside. The inscription on the tomb was still legible:
>
> ERECTED TO THE MEMORY OF
> DAVE
> A FAITHFUL WORKER
>
> It appears that one of the members of the party was a bit of a poet. . . . He suggested whimsically that the grave on the hill be consecrated as "The Tomb of The Unknown Worker" just as there was a tomb in memory of the Unknown Soldier.
>
> The Press exploited the idea. The population seized upon the point. In a year the little mound on the hillside had become a shrine, in ten years a mecca. Labor delegates toiled up the hills to lay wreaths on the mound, for the bones of the unknown worker were not regarded as the bones of one man. They came to be symbolic, embracing the laborers of the world.
>
> Each year on Labor Day . . . labor leaders gave solemn orations . . . bands played . . . women wept . . . wreaths were piled high. . . .
>
> And then, something curious happened. One Spring, just as a group of pilgrims had reached the tomb of the Unknown Worker, a mountain freshet came roaring down the slope, washed away the foundation of the shaft and tore away the mound. When the storm passed, the pilgrims gathered again at the tomb. The grave had been washed up, the sacred bones were exposed. The pil-

grims shrank away in horror. . . . They were the bones of an animal! The grinning skull was unmistakable . . . the bones of an ass!

A rumult of ironical laughter shook the world. For years the slaving millions had worshipped an ass.

Let us fervently hope, then, that in the face of our gross lack of political security, economic security, and personal security we shall not worship the bones of the ass of social security. LET US HOPE . . .

Roy Wilkins □ Through the 1937 Flood Area

The New Deal period was a time in which new leadership emerged in the black community. Roy Wilkins was among the younger leaders. Born in St. Louis in 1901, Wilkins received his BA at the University of Minnesota and was managing editor of the Kansas City *Call* from 1922–1931. In 1934, he became editor of *Crisis,* a position he occupied until 1949. Since 1955, Mr. Wilkins has been Executive Director of the NAACP. In this article, he discusses the flooding of the Mississippi in 1937 and how discrimination continued to work against the Negro even in times of disaster.

The small sedan nosed its way across the bridge to West Memphis, Ark. It was late dusk but there was still a dull gleam on the muddy water, a faint gray-brown reflection of the last rays of the sun.

"There she is," my host said, mixing his genders, "Old Man River, himself."

Yes, there she was. There he was. Old Man River, now, at Memphis, but up above through the valley, it had been the raging, grinding, implacable Ohio. Out there below me the strong current was still discernible. Deep, powerful movement was visible. But not the mad dash of the flood stage. Not the tearing torrent of two weeks ago.

Here it was getting on down to the gulf. The gauge, high up on the bluff read: 39¼F, meaning thirty-nine and a quarter feet and falling. Here it was only a brooding giant, flexing its muscles, sulking still, and threatening a little.

But back up the valley it had been different. My taxi driver in Cincinnati had shown me where the boats had landed people here and

From Roy Wilkins, "Through the 1937 Flood Area," *Crisis,* Vol. 44 (1937), pp. 104–106. 124–126. Reprinted with the permission of The Crisis Publishing Company.

there. Now there were trains, but then there had been none. The Union terminal plaza a lake. Yonder a water line on that house. Down that street, dry now and full of business, four feet of water.

And proud Louisville! High and low, black and white, mansion and shack—all had been helpless before the angry waters—those same waters mingled now under the bridge beneath my automobile, surging and sullen, but held in check and sent on their way by the great levee system.

"Yes," I replied to my host, bringing my mind back from the valley cities, " 'Old Man River.' We don't know, up in New York, what that song really means: "River Stay 'Way From My Door." Pretty significant to the people around here, I guess."

He said nothing. He did not have to. At the high stage the water had been within two feet of the roadway of the low part of the bridge. There was a barn crushed against the stone pillar of the Frisco railroad bridge. Far away across the backwater, which still lay in front of the big St. Francis levee, stretched the sandbagged tracks of the Rock Island line. Looming ahead of us on the concrete was a sign: Road closed by flood water. An old story to Memphis residents, but new to me.

As we turned about and ran back to Memphis, along Riverside drive where tomorrow I was to see by daylight the high water marks on the sodded banks in the park along Front street, I contrasted this Memphis with the Louisville I had left the day before. (Later both Louisville and Memphis were to seem like Paradise compared to Paducah.)

I had heard that race prejudice had taken a vacation in Louisville during the flood disaster, but such tales are hard to believe. The white natives are seldom to be trusted in their estimates of such matters; and the Negro residents are so conditioned to ill-treatment that their judgment is not always accurate.

But I found, to my amazement, that except for some few minor incidents likely to occur in any community, the city had waved aside any double standard of rescue and relief based on color. Negroes and whites were rescued, housed, clothed, fed, given medical attention, and transferred to other communities without discrimination. The Urban League was one of the telephone stations of the army units, being in direct communication with military headquarters. It organized a corps of workers to register refugees and issue food cards; and colored workers, including school teachers and students from the Louisville Municipal College for Negroes, attended to the needs of white and colored refugees alike.

It seems a little thing (and it is little, except in the Dixie white mind) this business of intelligent, competent courteous Negroes rendering skilled and semi-skilled "white collar" service to disaster-stricken whites as well as Negroes. The average person who has had everything swept away and who stands before a desk with nothing except the clothes on his back, is not very particular about the color of the man or woman who sits there ready and able to minister to his needs. The inexorable Ohio river taught Luoisville that humanity is humanity and that what counts is the stuff inside, not the label on the outside.

Doctors and nurses, black and white worked day and night. Long lines of white and colored people, mixed up together, shuffled in and out of clothing bedding and food stations. They got what they needed out of the huge stores available. There was no pile of good new clothing and bedding for white and old clothes and bedding for Negroes—like there was in Memphis.

At the height of the flood there was a hitch in the housing of Negro refugees in Louisville, but after an appeal by Mayor Miller (which sounded bad over the radio, but which was sincere and well-meant) the difficulty was soon straightened out. White residents in the exclusive, aristocratic sections of the city opened their homes to colored people. They fed them and housed them until the Red Cross could provide for them or until the refugees could return to their homes.

I rode down Louisville's Broadway which, a few weeks before, had looked like a Venetian canal. Up and down the streets, in Negro and white residential areas, the scars of the water were everywhere to be seen. Black oily water lines halfway up on some houses, up under the eaves of cottages. Dozens of pianos out on the lawns falling apart. Stacks of hardwood flooring. Piles of what had been over-stuffed furniture. Gas ranges. Bedsteads. Mute evidence of the awful ravages of the river.

And yet, the city was bounding back to normal with the amazing speed which seems a part of America. The downtown district was humming with activity. The people were cheerful, with the Negroes, as usual, the most cheerful of all. There was a sort of quiet philosophy about. They were all ready to start over and determined to do better. People staying with friends and relatives talked easily and naturally of when they would be back in their own homes. Skilled artisans and small contractors and even ordinary laborers were scurrying about from one rehabilitation job to another. I met one colored carpenter who had just put in a bid to repair a white church. Louisville was beating back—fast.

The American Red Cross had the job of rehabilitation well under way. Trained social workers were being brought in to supplement local workers. A few local colored workers were being employed, but none imported. Miss Helen Colwell, case superivsor for the Red Cross, said she could easily use ten trained Negro case workers, but they were not available and it was against the policy of the Red Cross to import them.

Of all the things I found on this trip, the employment policy of the Red Cross was the most irritating. In the administration of relief the Red Cross did everything within its power to see that there was no discrimination. In this it was successful, except in petty cases with minor prejudiced officials, but in a great disaster every little detail cannot be watched every moment, so the Red Cross deserves credit for a minimum of color line friction.

But when the critical period of readjustment and rehabilitation came, the Red Cross fell back on an almost lily white policy. It is in this period that families have to be interviewed, histories established, understanding built up, and needs met adequately. In this phase, trained Negro case workers could do a magnificent job. This does not say that all white.case workers are prejudiced or incapable of understanding Negroes, or that any Negro case worker is better than a white one in the same circumstances. But it is reasonable to believe that the needs of more Negro families would be better interpreted by colored case workers than would be well handled by whites.

The Red Cross is afraid of the white South, but it need not be *so* afraid. There are plenty of sensible, fair white people in the South and the Red Cross ought to listen to a few of them and take a gamble now and then. In Mississippi, no, but in Louisville, yes.

The Red Cross officials with whom I talked, including regional directors, medical directors and others, insisted that the Red Cross was a relief organization and its function was not to change prejudices or make over community customs and traditions. It is not organized to solve the race problem. They are correct, but it does seem that the Red Cross ought always to be seeking ways to improve the administration of relief and rehabilitation. One improvement would be the infiltration of trained Negro workers wherever possible into the Red Cross personnel and reserve.

The South is still pretty bad on the Negro question, but the day is long past when it can be said sweepingly that "the South" will not stand for this or that. Dixie is not as bad as it used to be and there are minorities here and there willing and even eager to do as well by the dark brother as does Boston, Mass.

It was in Memphis, on the matter of employment and differentials in pay that I had the most refreshing experience of my trip. For I met there a naïve and wholly unreconstructed southern woman, an assistant to the chief of Red Cross nurses. She did not ask me to sit down, nor did she ask me my name and the nature of my business. She talked always as she would to a client, or a child patient under her care. I was some colored man who thought I had a question to ask (but didn't, really) who thought I had a point to make, and with whom she must be patient, coolly polite, a little indulgent (they are like children, you know) and as brief as possible. I asked if it was true that white registered nurses were paid more than Negro registered nurses.

"Why, of course," she said instantly, in a broad southern drawl. "They can live cheaper than white nurses!"

There seemed nothing wrong with that argument to her. She meant it and believed it. She went on to explain that there had been a mix-up in Nashville—a "mistake"—whereby someone had started paying Negro nurses the same scale. I said we had had conplaints from Memphis about the lower scale.

"But," she said, amazed, "they are satisfied here. *We* haven't had any complaints. The complaints must have come from Nashville. Are you sure you have come to the right town?"

(Why don't you colored people get things straight? Don't you know the difference between Nashville and Memphis?)

I explained gently that I would not have come all the way from New York to Memphis if we had received complaints from Nashville.

She looked up, then, with just a flicker of a new estimation in her eye, and said:

"Well, I don't suppose you would, but we all make mistakes."

There was some talk that white and colored doctors did not receive the same pay for work done in the Memphis refugee stations and hospitals, but Dr. M. S. Lombard, genial, suave chief of doctors, would not be pinned down. He offered cigarettes, waved his hand at charts, drew out daily reports showing the number of cases treated and where and by whom. He called in a secretary and dictated a statement for the newspapers "correcting any impression that any more than a very few doctors had been paid."

But I am confident there was a wide difference in the pay of those white and colored doctors who were paid.

It was Memphis (Memphis just has to be near the bottom in practically everything affecting the two races) that forced Negroes to work on reinforcing the levees near the town when there were reports that the swollen waters might break them. I do not mean the convict labor used by Shelby county authorities. I mean that Memphis city officials and the Memphis police dragged Negro men off of Beale avenue (they should have let the name remain Beale *street*) with threats and intimidation and made them work day and night in the mud and rain carrying sandbags to save the threatened industrial plants in South Memphis.

The WPA paid the men 27 cents an hour, taking away some of the sting, but not all. Squad cars of police followed by trucks came down

Beale avenue, snatching men right and left, accepting no excuses. Any black man who happened to be walking along the street was taken. Police stood at the doors of moving picture theatres and as fast as men came out they were seized separated from their wives and girl friends, thrown into trucks and hustled to the levee behind a motorcycle escort. A well-known Beale avenue lunch counter, the "One Minute Lunch" was literally cleaned out by the police.

Some couples, hearing of the shanghaiing, refused to leave movie theatres and stayed in them all night. Men were forced to work in their good clothes, ruining suits, shoes, shirts and overcoats. Many had no work gloves. All took chances on death from pneumonia.

One cynical colored man admitted that whites worked on the levee also, but, said he: "They had all the soft jobs. All the white folks I saw were foremen and those who weren't regular foremen made little signs saying 'foreman' and pinned them on their coats."

Police Commissioner Clifford Davis granted me an interview, said he did not approve of what was done on Beale avenue and that as soon as he found out about it, he stopped it. (He stopped it as soon as the flood danger was past.)

The commissioner seemingly could not for the life of him explain how it was that uniformed Memphis police under his command could have shanghaied free citizens into forced labor without orders from someone higher up. He suggested rather lamely and hurriedly that "some deputy sheriff from out in the country got excited, came into town and got some policemen to help him round up men." I asked him if deputy sheriffs outside of Memphis had the authority to issue orders to his police force, but he was lighting a fresh cigar, at the time and didn't answer. It takes a lot of concentration to light a cigar.

Anyway, as I left, he sang me the old song: "The relations between the races are good in Memphis. I have a lot of friends among the colored people. We have good schools for them. They are fine citizens. I spoke at one of their churches just a short time ago, etc, etc."

(The school situation is nothing to brag about. I saw one ancient building crammed down in a warehouse, tenement-shack district, with no play space, with one trunk line railroad running in front of the school and another running almost in its back door. Not far away was a white school set on a terrace, with lawn and playground in abundance.)

The WPA administrator, S. T. Pease, is a nice old gentleman who seemed to be disturbed by the thought that there was anything irregular in recruiting the levee labor paid by his office. He said they had sent a request to him for 2,000 men and he had only 200 available. They agreed to get the men if he would pay them. He paid them and asked no questions about how they got on the payroll. He smokes a hefty pipe, does Mr. Pease, and good tobacco, and he was much more polite than most Memphis white folk.

The Army engineers had nothing to do with the forced labor. They did not look after the city levees. What labor they did use on river levees near Memphis was secured in the regular way through the WPA.

As for the actual administration of relief by the Red Cross in Memphis, it seemed to be as free of discrimination as one could expect. The higher officials tried hard to maintain equality. Good solid food was served in abundance. There was some discrimination in handing out clothing. Whites got good stuff and Negroes got what the white people thought was good enough for Negroes. There was a story going around that one town in Mississippi had 800 Negro refugees and several truckloads of good colthing were sent. When it arrived and the officials saw the quality, they sent it all back, saying their Negroes did not need anything.

The Memphis Red Cross did employ temporarily about a dozen colored people, some of them Le Moyne college students, as interviewers, clerks and junior social workers.

It was a cold, gray, wet Sunday when I came to Paducah, the city of 35,000 population which had been entirely inundated. Almost every resident, including the 7,000 colored citizens, had been evacuated to nearby and distant points.

It was a gray tale of woe I heard also, that Sunday. The only way out of the town was to Mayfield, Ky., about fifteen miles away. Here the people were sent in droves, and from there to other places.

Two colored doctors, G. A. Davis and P. M. Fernandez, driven from their homes by the water, went to Mayfield and offered to aid the Red Cross. They were accepted and worked day and night. But the Red Cross made no provision for their lodging and food. Finally they were given refugee food tickets and after working hours with the sick, had to stand in line to get tickets and then stand in line again to get food.

Meanwhile white doctors doing the same work had excellent, comfortable lodgings provided for them at Red Cross expense and good meals in regular restaurants or private boarding houses. To add insult to injury, Drs. Fernandez and Davis later were put on the Red Cross payroll—*at $65 a month.*

As Dr. Davis told me this tale in a quiet, but bitter tone, my mind went back to the Red Cross medical offices on the 25th floor of the Sterick building in Memphis. I thought of the rumor that white doctors in Memphis, comfortable and dry, working in established base hospitals, were being paid $350 a month. I recalled the rumor that colored doctors in Memphis had been offered $200 a month.

I looked again at the little man in front of me, the gray at his temples showing as he gazed across the campus of the West Kentucky Industrial college. He had on boots and there was mud caked around the bottom of his overcoat. He was talking calmly of the water that had covered the first floor of his house, ruining his office equipment and his instruments. He did not know exactly how much damage had been done his own home, for he had just come over from the firing line in Mayfield.

Sixty-five dollars a month. Already he had received a check for $32.50. And yet he did not know how it was with his own fortunes. What a picnic the doctors in Memphis were having! No telephone service here. Few cars. Few lights. Mud everywhere. Tents. Yet adults and babies were sick and had to have care. The Red Cross collected 20 millions of dollars for flood relief and Davis and Fernandez (and others for all I know) battled disease and misery and death, with no thought of themselves, for *sixty-five dollars a month.*

"Aid will be administered without discrimination," Admiral Cary T. Grayson, head of the Red Cross, had wired the N.A.A.C.P. This declaration had been echoed by every official with whom I had talked, but what about Paducah?

West Kentucky Industrial College, presided over by the veteran educator D. H. Anderson, and Dean T. R. Dailey, proved a God-send to the refugees. There were still 863 persons housed when I passed through. Medical attention had been skimpy and it was a miracle that no epidemic had broken out. The food was substantial. People slept on cots placed in every available space. The auditorium was a huge, one-room dormitory.

Red Cross work was just getting under way. Some of the people, whose homes could not be re-occupied, were to be housed in a tent colony just off the campus until some plans could be made for them. Louisville followed this same plan for those whose homes were destroyed.

David G. Linden, in charge of Red Cross work among Paducah's colored people, came to the job from Washington. Numerous whites, with and without Red Cross experience, were hired and imported by the Red Cross, but few, if any, trained Negro workers were employed. In fact, the Red Cross refused to employ trained Negro case workers in New York and send them into the South.

As an example of the efficiency of the white "case workers" on duty in Paducah, some of them rushed up to colored refugees who were just climbing out of trucks on the college campus. Bear in mind that the refugees had just been brought back to the city and had not as yet even seen their homes. Said the social workers:

"What is your name? Where do you live? How high did the water get in your house? How much damage do you think it did? How much furniture did you lose?"

All these questions to bewildered people whose last glimpse of their homes had been water rising in their front yards. How did they know what damage had been done?

And so I left Paducah, fighting bravely to get back to normal, and came up the river to St. Louis and talked briefly with the director of the whole area west of the Mississippi. They would do their best for the evacuated sharecroppers and tenants in Arkansas, he said. Some planters were cooperating and some the Red Cross looked on and listened to with a skeptic eye. But they would do their best . . . they were not there to solve the sharecropper problem or the race problem . . . just to give relief according to need, not according to loss.

Home again to Fifth avenue and Harlem, far from the flood area and yet so near to the flood victims. I can see some of them still. The shy youngster in Paducah who wanted to pose for his picture and yet hesitated. The resolute middle-aged farmer, looking me straight in the eye and saying he wasn't going back to Arkansas because he did not have anything to go back to. The little lad on Main street, Memphis, who said he was from Earle, Ark., but "I ain't on the Red Cross." The man and woman and nine children hanging to a dilapidated wagon hauled by briskly-trotting, bony mules, getting along the highway back home into Arkansas. Children, children everywhere. Patient, worried mothers trying to keep broods together. Grandmothers with their pipes, rocking; or folded up under a blanket, sleeping trouble away. Here and there a clear, soft voice—a school voice, college-bred, alert, seeing the whole picture and wondering what will come of it.

And the big man and the fat woman in the jim crow waiting room of the Memphis railroad station:

"Hit's God's work. When He want the water to come, it come, and they ain't no use of man making dikes and walls. Cain't stop God! Nuthin' to do but git yo' belongings and get out when God's water come."

It may have been God's work. I am not an authority on that point. But certain it is that the wildly-flowing waters of the Ohio did wash away, for the moment, some of the meanness, and pettiness and hatred in the hearts of men for their fellow men. We are a little ahead of where we were before the flood; a few gains have been registered in the never-ending battle for peace, respect and security.

John Davis □ A Black Inventory of the New Deal

In the fall of 1933, John Davis, a young Negro lawyer, organized the Joint Committee on National Recovery to rectify the inequities of the NRA. The following is his evaluation of Roosevelt's first two years in office.

It is highly important for the Negro citizen of America to take inventory of the gains and losses which have come to him under the "New Deal." The Roosevelt administration has now had two years in which to unfold itself. Its portents are reasonably clear to anyone who seriously studies the varied activities of its recovery program. We can now state with reasonable certainty what the "New Deal" means for the Negro.

At once the most striking and irrefutable indication of the effect of the New Deal on the Negro can be gleaned from relief figures furnished by the government itself. In October, 1933, six months after the present administration took office, 2,117,000 Negroes were in families receiving relief in the United States. These represented 17.8 per cent of the total Negro population as of the 1930 census. In January, 1935, after nearly two years of *recovery measures,* 3,500,000 Negroes were in families receiving relief, or 29 per cent of our 1930 population. Certainly only a slight portion of the large increase in the number of impoverished Negro families can be explained away by the charitable, on the grounds that relief administration has become more humane. As a matter of fact federal relief officials themselves

From John Davis, "A Black Inventory of the New Deal," *Crisis,* Vol 42–3 (1935), pp. 141–145. Reprinted with the permission of The Crisis Publishing Company.

admit that grave abuses exist in the administration of rural relief to Negroes. And this is reliably borne out by the disproportionate increase in the number of urban Negro families on relief to the number of rural Negro families on relief. Thus the increase in the number of Negroes in relief families is an accurate indication of the deepening of the economic crisis for black America.

The promise of NRA to bring higher wages and increased employment to industrial workers has glimmered away. In the code-making process occupational and geographical differentials at first were used as devices to exclude from the operation of minimum wages and maximum hours the bulk of the Negro workers. Later, clauses basing code wage rates on the previously existing wage differential between Negro and white workers tended to continue the inferior status of the Negro. For the particular firms, for whom none of these devices served as an effective means of keeping down Negro wages, there is an easy way out through the securing of an exemption specifically relating to the *Negro* worker in the plant. Such exemptions are becoming more numerous as time goes on. Thus from the beginning relatively few Negro workers were even theoretically covered by NRA labor provisions.

But employers did not have to rely on the code-making process. The Negro worker not already discriminated against through code provisions had many other gauntlets to run. The question of importance to him as to all workers was, "as a result of all of NRA's maneuvers will I be able to buy more?" The answer has been "No." A worker cannot eat a wage rate. To determine what this wage rate means to him we must determine a number of other factors. Thus rates for longshoremen seem relatively high. But when we realize that the average amount of work a longshoreman receives during the year is from ten to fifteen weeks, the wage rate loses much of its significance. When we add to that fact the increase in the cost of living—as high as 40 per cent in many cases—the wage rate becomes even more chimerical. For other groups of industrial workers increases in cost of living, coupled with the part time and irregular nature of the work, make the results of NRA negligible. In highly mechanized industries speed-up and stretch-out nullify the promised result of NRA to bring increased employment through shorter hours. For the workers are now producing more in their shorter work periods than in the longer periods before NRA. There is less employment. The first sufferer from fewer jobs is the Negro worker. Finally the complete break-down of compliance machinery in the South has cancelled the last minute advantage to Negro workers which NRA's enthusiasts may have claimed.

The Agricultural Adjustment Administration has used cruder methods in enforcing poverty on the Negro farm population. It has made violations of the rights of tenants under crop reduction contracts easy; it has rendered enforcement of these rights impossible. The reduction of the acreage under cultivation through the government rental agreement rendered unnecessary large numbers of tenants and farm laborers. Although the contract with the government provided that the land owner should not reduce the number of his tenants, he did so. The federal courts have now refused to allow tenants to enjoin such evictions. Faced with this Dred Scott decision against farm tenants, the AAA has remained discreetly silent. Farm laborers are now jobless by the hundreds of thousands, the conservative government estimate of the decline in agricultural employment for the year 1934 alone being a quarter of a million. The larger portion of these are unskilled Negro agricultural workers—now without income and unable to secure work or relief.

But the unemployment and tenant evictions occasioned by the crop reduction policies of the AAA is not all. For the tenants and sharecroppers who were retained on the plantations the government's agricultural program meant reduced income. Wholesale fraud on tenants in the payment of parity checks occurred. Tenants complaining to the Department of Agriculture in Washington have their letters referred back to the locality in which they live and trouble of serious nature often results. Even when this does not happen, the tenant fails to get his check. The remainder of the land he tills on shares with his landlord brings him only the most meagre necessities during the crop season varying from three to five months. The rest of the period for him and his family is one of "root hog or die."

The past year has seen an extension of poverty even to the small percentage (a little more than 20 per cent) of Negro farmers who own their own land. For them compulsory reduction of acreage for cotton and tobacco crops, with the quantum of such reduction controlled and regulated by local boards on which they have no representation, has meant drastic reduction of their already low income. Wholesale confiscation of the income of the Negro cotton and tobacco farmer is being made by prejudiced local boards in the South under the very nose of the federal government. In the wake of such confiscation has come a tremendous increase in land tenantry as a result of foreclosures on Negro-owned farm properties.

Nor has the vast public works program, designed to give increased employment to workers in the building trades, been free from prejudice. State officials in the South are in many cases in open rebellion against the ruling of PWA that the same wage scales must be paid to Negro and white labor. Compliance with this paper ruling is enforced in only rare cases. The majority of the instances of violation of this rule are unremedied. Only unskilled work is given Negroes on public works projects in most instances. And even here discrimination in employment is notorious. Such is bound to be the case when we realize that there are only a handful of investigators available to seek enforcement.

Recently a move has been made by Negro officials in the administration to effect larger employment of Negro skilled and unskilled workers on public works projects by specifying that failure of a contractor to pay a certain percentage of his payroll to Negro artisans will be evidence of racial discrimination. Without doubting the good intentions of the sponsors of this ingenious scheme, it must nevertheless be pointed out that it fails to meet the problem in a number of vital particulars. It has yet to face a test in the courts, even if one is willing to suppose that PWA high officials will bring it to a test. Percentages thus far experimented with are far too low and the number of such experiments far too few to make an effective dent in the unemployment conditions of Negro construction industry workers. Moreover the scheme gives aid and comfort to employer-advocates of strike-breaking and the open shop; and, while offering, perhaps, some temporary relief to a few hundred Negro workers, it establishes a dangerous precedent which throws back the labor movement and the organization of Negro workers to a considerable degree. The scheme, whatever its Negro sponsors may hope to contrary, becomes therefor only another excuse for their white superiors maintaining a "do-nothing" policy with regard to discrimination against Negroes in the Public Works Administration.

The Negro has no pleasanter outlook in the long term social planning ventures of the new administration. Planning for subsistence homesteads for industrially stranded workers has been muddled enough even without consideration of the problem of integrating Negroes into such plans. Subsistence Homesteads projects are overburdened with profiteering prices for the homesteads and foredoomed to failure by the lack of planning for adequate and permanent incomes for prospective homesteaders.

In callous disregard of the interdiction in the Constitution of the United States against use of federal funds for projects which discriminate against applicants solely on the ground of color, subsistence homesteads have been planned on a strictly "lily-white" basis. The more than 200 Negro applicants for the first project at Arthurdale, West Virginia were not even considered, Mr. Bushrod Grimes (then in charge of the project) announcing that the project was to be open only to "native white stock." As far north as Dayton, Ohio, where state laws prohibit any type of segregation against Negroes, the federal government has extended its "lily-white" policy. Recently it has established two Jim-Crow projects for Negroes. Thus the new administration seeks in its program of social planning to perpetuate ghettoes of Negroes for fifty years to come.

An even more blatant example of this policy of "lily-white" reconstruction is apparent in the planning of the model town of Norris, Tennessee, by the Tennessee Valley Authority. This town of 450 model homes is intended for the permanent workers on Norris Dam. The homes are rented by the federal government, which at all times maintains title to the land and dwellings and has complete control of the town management. Yet officials at TVA openly admit that no Negroes are allowed at Norris.

TVA has other objectionable features. While Negro employment now approaches an equitable proportion of total employment; the payroll of Negro workers remains disproportionately lower than that of whites. While the government has maintained a trade school to train workers on the project, no Negro trainees have been admitted. Nor have any meaningful plans matured for the future of the several thousand Negro workers who in another year or so will be left without employment, following completion of work on the dams being built by TVA.

None of the officials of TVA seems to have the remotest idea of how Negroes in the Tennessee Valley will be able to buy the cheap electricity which TVA is designed to produce. They admit that standards of living of the Negro population are low, that the introduction of industry into the Valley is at present only a nebulous dream, that even if this eventuates there is no assurance that Negro employment will result. The fairest summary that can be made of TVA is that for a year or so it has furnished bread to a few thousand Negro workers. Beyond that everything is conjecture which is most unpleasant because of the utter planlessness of those in charge of the project.

Recovery legislation of the present session of Congress reveals the same fatal flaws which have been noted in the operation of previous recovery ventures. Thus, for example, instead of genuine unemployment insurance we have the leaders of the administration proposing to exclude from their plans domestic and agricultural workers, in which classes are to be found 15 out of every 23 Negro workers. On every hand the New Deal has used slogans for the same raw deal.

The sharpening of the crisis for Negroes has not found them unresponsive. Two years of increasing hardship has seen strange movement among the masses. In Chicago, New York, Washington and Baltimore the struggle for jobs has given rise to action on the part of a number of groups seeking to boycott white employers who refuse to employ Negroes. "Don't Buy Where You Can't Work" campaigns are springing up everywhere. The crisis has furnished renewed vigor to the Garvey Movement. And proposals for a 49th State are being seriously considered by various groups.

In sharp contrast with these strictly racial approaches to the problem, have been a number of interracial approaches. Increasing numbers of unemployed groups have been organized under radical leadership and have picketed relief stations for bread. Sharecroppers unions, under Socialist leadership in Arkansas, have shaken America into a consciousness of the growing resentment of southern farm tenants and the joint determination of the Negro and white tenants to do something about their intolerable condition.

In every major strike in this country Negro union members have fought with their white fellow workers in a struggle for economic survival. The bodies of ten Negro strikers killed in such strike struggles offer mute testimony to this fact. Even the vicious policies of the leaders of the A. F. or L. in discrimination against Negro workers is breaking down under the pressure for solidarity from the ranks of whites.

This heightening of spirit among all elements of black America and the seriousness of the crisis for them make doubly necessary the consideration of the social and economic condition of the Negro at this time. It was a realization of these conditions which gave rise to the proposal to hold a national conference on the economic status of Negroes under the New Deal at Howard University in Washington, D.C., on May 18, 19 and 20. At this conference, sponsored by the Social Science Division of Howard University and the Joint Committee on National Recovery, a candid and intelligent survey of the social and economic condition of the Negro will be made. Unlike most conferences it will not be a talk-fest. For months nationally known economists and other technicians have been working on papers to be presented. Unlike other conferences it will not be a one-sided affair. Ample opportunity will be afforded for high government officials to present their views of the "New Deal." Others not connected with the government, including representatives of radical political parties, will also appear to present their conclusions. Not the least important phase will be the appearance on the platform of Negro workers and farmers themselves to offer their own experience under the New Deal. Out of such a conference can and will come a clear-cut analysis of the problems faced by Negroes and the nation.

But a word of caution ought to be expressed with regard to this significant conference. In the final analysis it cannot and does not claim to be representative of the mass opinion of Negro citizens in America. All it can claim for itself is that it will bring together on a non-representative basis well informed Negro and white technicians to discuss the momentous problem it has chosen as its topic. It can furnish a base for action for any organization which chooses to avail itself of the information developed by it. It cannot act itself.

Thus looking beyond such a conference one cannot fail to hope that it will furnish impetus to a national expression of black America demanding a tolerable solution to the economic evils which it suffers. Perhaps it is not too much to hope that public opinion may be moulded by this conference to such an extent that already existing church, civic, fraternal, professional and trade union organizations will see the necessity for concerted effort in forging a mighty arm of protest against injustice suffered by the Negro. It is not necessary that such organizations agree on every issue. On the problem of relief of Negroes from poverty there is little room for disagreement. The important thing is that throughout America as never before Negroes awake to the need for a unity of action on vital economic problems which perplex us.

Such a hope is not lacking in foundation upon solid ground. Such an instance as the All India Congress of British India furnishes an example of what repressed groups can do to better their social and economic status. Perhaps a *"National Negro Congress"* of delegates from thousands of Negro organizations (and white organizations willing to recognize their unity of interest) will furnish a vehicle for channeling public opinion of black America. One thing is certain: the Negro may stand still but the depression will not. And unless there is concerted action of Negroes throughout the nation the next two years will bring even greater misery to the millions of underprivileged Negro toilers in the nation.

Grant Reynolds □ What the Negro Thinks of this War

In 1944, the editors of *Crisis* dispatched Grant Reynolds, a former chaplain in the U.S. Army, to study the morale of Negro troops. Here he reports his findings, which indicate a considerable amount of frustration among Negro recruits.

For the past two years and ten months I have been a Chaplain on active duty with the United States Army. I have found Negro soldiers bitterly resentful of their lot in this war. My having served with Medical Troops in Virginia, Infantry Troops in Massachusetts, raw recruits at a reception center in Michigan, sick and wounded soldiers from both Negro Divisions at a hospital in Arizona, and the troops comprising a Station Complement in California, has given me a broad picture of the conditions which affect our men from coast to coast. In each instance, regardless of the geography, the net result has been the same . . . Negro soldiers are damned tired of the treatment they are getting. This dislike cannot be attributed to the natural antipathy of the majority of soldiers, white and black, developed out of their efforts to adjust themselves to the rigors and uncertainties of war. Now the Negro soldier is as easily adaptable as any other American soldier. I'd even go as far as to say that he is more adaptable. His lifetime of adjusting himself to the whims and inconsistencies of the American white man substantiates this claim. His resentment then goes much deeper than this. It grows out of the unamerican treatment which plagues his every day while at the same time having to listen to loud voices telling him what a great honor it is to die for his country.

From Grant Reynolds, "What the Negro Thinks of This War," *Crisis,* Vol 51 (September 1944), pp. 289–291, 299. Reprinted with the permission of The Crisis Publishing Company.

The Negro soldier needs no one to remind him that this is his country. He knows this. But he knows also that there is a lot of unfinished business about individual human decency that he would like to see cleared up before he becomes a corpse for *any* country. To deny him food when he is hungry, dignified transportation when he has to travel, a voice in choosing those who rule him, or just the most fundamental aspects or our proclaimed method of living, and then propagandize him daily into becoming a hero for democracy, is nauseating, to say the least. As one Negro soldier asked me in this respect: "Chaplain, do the white folks who are running this war think we are fools? Or, are they a pack of damned fools themselves? Excuse me, sir, for being profane, but this mess makes a man say a lot of nasty things."

My tour of active duty which began in Virginia and ended in California, after periods of service in Massachusetts, Michigan, Ohio, and Arizona, has provided me the opportunity not only of observing the Negro soldier under the varied JIM–CROW conditions which make life miserable for him, but because I am a Negro too I have lived under the same conditions and shared his resentment to them. Then too it must be remembered that a chaplain who tries to do a real job does more than sermonize on Sundays. His activities extend into areas concerned with the thoughts and lives of the thousands of men he serves.

How do I know what the Negro soldier thinks? Until a few days ago I was one myself. I have lived with him in his barracks because white officers in Virginia would not permit a colored officer to occupy quarters built by the War Department for its officers. Interesting, to say the least, is a personal experience which grew out of this insult. By a sudden jolt of fate I began my military career at Camp Lee, Virginia. There I immediately discovered the South more vigorously engaged in fighting the Civil War than in training soldiers to resist Hitler. And what was obvious, though nonetheless disturbing, this war was being won . . . as far as the Negro was concerned anyway. Because of the few officers needed with my small outfit less than fifty percent of the available rooms in the officers' barracks were occupied. But there was no room for me. I was therefore assigned quarters with the enlisted men in their barracks. What did it matter that such an assignment infringed upon the freedom of Negro soldiers during their leisure moments? What did it matter how this personal embarrassment and humiliation impaired my morale? My job, it seemed, was to *build* morale, not to *have* it. Anyhow, of what importance is the condition of the Negro soldier's morale to the proper performance of his duty? But of equal importance, what did it matter that army policy prohibiting officers and enlisted men from sharing common quarters except under field conditions was deliberately ignored? The Negro soldier has learned that army policy, binding upon whites, far too often relaxes to his disadvantage. This separation of officers and enlisted men is supported on the grounds that the familiarity involved is destructive to proper discipline. There are other methods of maintaining discipline among Negro soldiers, some of which make Gestapo Chief Himmler look like a rank amateur. What *did* matter in this situation was the doctrine of white supremacy which had to remain undefiled regardless of the cost. To assign a Negro officer quarters in an officers' barracks which housed white officers was unthinkable! Entirely ignored was the fact that this officer by virtue of his military status indicated the same willingness to die for American fair play . . . for democracy.

After some weeks of this humiliation, which the Negro soldiers resented as much as I did, I was called to meet with the Post Construction Officer. To my utter amazement he showed me the blue prints of plans for the construction of an officers' quarters for my exclusive use. As an added favor to me I was given the privilege of selecting the site where the quarters of the "untouchable" would be erected. But here I made my usual mistake, a mistake which was to plague the remainder of my military service. I did not say: "Thank you white folks for being so kind and generous to this nigger." Instead I summoned the effrontery to remark that this was an unnecessary waste of the taxpayers' money. For this I was immediately labelled as a Negro who not only did not "know his place," but one who was also a base ingrate.

I have been on occasion the only colored officer in the Negro soldier's outfit and therefore the one most likely to hear both his gripes and his legitimate complaints. I have marched with him in the heat of a southern sun, shivered with him in the wake of a New England blizzard, and with him I too have breathed the scorching dust of an Arizona desert. I have laughed with him in his moments of pleasure, heard his confession of the worthlessless of his former life as he embraced the Christian religion, sorrowed with him in the loss of loved ones, and suffered with him under the heel of the dehumanizing demon of American race prejudice. I know what the Negro soldier thinks, not only because he has told me, but because I know my own thoughts.

Not long ago Secretary of War Stimson revealed in no uncertain terms what the War Department thought about the Negro soldier. I propose to relate in like manner what the Negro soldier thinks about the War Department's War. In the next installment I shall relate what the Negro soldier thinks about the War Department itself. But a word about Mr. Stimson's insult. Negroes throughout the nation along with other decent Americans were scandalized and they were prompt in making their protests known. But let us not be too harsh on a man who is the victim of the "logic" of his own thinking. Anyone sharing the traditional American regard for the colored citizen, and being party to that regard as it daily segregated the Negro soldier and citizen, could not have reached any other conclusion. This is especially true if he had given ear to reports of Army Intelligence on the Negro Soldier.

Mr. Stimson must have been told that the Negro soldier is demoralized, that he does not want to fight—unless a second front is opened in Mississippi, Texas, Georgia, South Carolina, Louisiana, or just *anywhere* below the Mason and Dixon Line—that his heart is not in this war. Such a soldier cannot be depended upon to offer up his life against German or Japanese soldiers who know why they are fighting and demonstrate each day their willingness to die for their beliefs. Where are the American soliers, of any color, who would destroy their own lives rather than fall into the hands of a hated enemy. The Japs did this on Attu. Incidentally, the record of our forces at Anzio and Cassino for 4 months showed that American white troops with only one enemy to fight were hardly super men in face of their German opposition. We might just as well realize that the Negro soldier has two enemies to fight, one foreign and the other at home. Now since public opinion forced the Secretary of War to give some reason for the War Department's refusal to allow Negro soldiers to die for America in some appreciable manner other than in labor battalions and in the "highfalutin Engineers," which is a camouflaged term meaning practically the same thing, Mr. Stimson's hand was called. Those who expected the unvarnished truth about this matter were either dreamers or drunks. Who among our military authorities would admit that the nation's indecent treatment of the Negro soldier had rendered him unfit for combat with a foreign enemy? So following the traditional point of view, since this point of view led to the creation of the dilemma in the first place, the Negro soldier was promptly discredited. Not because he could not master the technique of modern weapons of war—this was the Secretary of War's claim—but because this is the logical stand that the traditional race haters were bound to use in defense of their hypocritical and infamous conduct. Talk about impeding the war effort! What *is* treason anyway?

Out on the Pacific Coast I found young Negroes holding key positions in the industries—the airplane industry to be exact—which produce the most difficult of weapons to master, the army bomber. Other young Negroes are now flying these planes. Still other young Negroes are now prepared to be their navigators. Now it is a commonly accepted fact among honest men and women that no racial group has cornered the market on either intelligence or native ability. This is what the celebrated pamphlet *The Races Of Mankind* would have told a few thousand army officers had it not been banned by stupid people who refuse to recognize the obvious. All Negro soldiers are not graduate engineers. Nor are all white soldiers. All Negro soldiers were not born in that section of the nation, which because it seeks to keep the Negro in the educational gutter, directs that white youth too must wallow in the pig sty of ignorance. But the Honorable Secretary of War has not claimed that white soldiers cannot master the techniques of modern weapons of war. His blanket statement about the Negro soldier's inability in this respect not only insults the thousands of intelligent Negro youth in our armed forces from all sections of the country, but by indirection it classifies them as morons incapable of attaining the intelligence level of the most ignorant southern cracker. What does the Negro soldier think about this? He considers it a vicious attack upon his manhood. And what is more he thinks that the Administration continues to insult him as long as such men are allowed to control his destiny in this war. The Negro soldier will not give his life for the perpetuation of this outright lynching of his ability, nor for the right of domestic nazis to make of him a military scapegoat.

Every factual pronouncement which falls from the lips of Anglo-Saxon war leaders in this conflict lays foundation for the Negro soldier's conviction that this is a war to maintain the white man's right to keep the colored man in social and economic bondage. The Negro soldier is not so dumb as far too many people in authority lead themselves to believe. He is asking a lot of questions. Does the Atlantic Charter apply to colored people now enslaved by the British, Dutch, Portuguese, and other imperialistic powers? Why is our ally Britain silent about the fate of Hong Kong and Singapore in the post-war world? Why are the great leaders of India, especially Nehru, kept in prison at the very moment when all India should be rallied against the Japanese invader? Why does our foreign policy fail to make clear America's stand in regard to spilling the blood of its sons to dictate the destiny of people who admittedly have a right to self-determination? But most important of all, the Negro soldier is asking how he can be expected to give his last full measure of devotion for his country when each day, while he wears the uniform of his country, he is insulted, humiliated, and even murdered for attempting to be an American?

My experience with Negro soldiers has led me to oppose the idea that the majority of them consider this a "race war." One must confess, however, that at times they are given strong evidence to the contrary. To say that all Negro soldiers share this or any one point of view is to engage in deliberate falsehood. Many of them think that this is a white man's war, "lock, stock, and barrel." This conclusion is reached in spite of Hitler's treatment of the people in the occupied countries and what the Chinese have suffered at the hands of the Japanese. Like countless thousands of whites this group has listened too intently to the expressed convictions of the "white supremacy boys." Responsibility for their conclusion can be traced to the ravings of such misrepresentatives of the nation as Bilbo, Rankin, "Cotton" Ed Smith and many others of the same litter. "But what about Russia?" you ask them. The immediate answer is that there are good betting odds that Russia will have to fight Britain and the United States before peace actually comes. This group knows too well what everyone willing to face reality knows—that there are far too many people in high places who love Russia less than they hate Nazi Germany. If Russia were not killing so many German soldiers and therefore the only hope at the moment for an Allied victory, the anti-Red voices in this country would be reaching a deafening crescendo. But Russia, these soldiers will tell you, is merely a tool to be used until it can be safely cast aside. Anglo-Saxon pride and a sense of imminent danger make strange bedfellows.

Much more strongly entrenched in the Negro soldier's thinking is the firm conviction that Soviet Russia's expulsion of the nazi race-haters from Russian soil and the herculean struggle of the Chinese people are evidence that something far more valuable than concepts of race is involved in this struggle. The freedom of millions of men and women, and countless generations which follow them, is involved . . . possibly his freedom too. The realization of this, however, does not lessen in any great degree his state of confusion and bewilderment. What man who has worn the shackles of slavery would not gladly strike a blow for freedom? The Negro soldier is prevented from striking that blow, at least with great enthusiasm, because freedom for his race during the past eighty years has not gibed with its definition in the dictionary. The march of daily events convince the Negro soldier that his efforts in the struggle for freedom might well result in solidifying the control with which the South now directs and determines the national welfare and vigorously thwarts every effort of scientific progress in the field of human relations. A struggle for freedom which materialized in such a goal would not be worth a single drop of sweat . . . to say nothing about a single drop of blood. As a result the Negro soldier sees himself a miserable pawn in the inexorable hands of a fate which has already stacked the cards against him. He will fight if ordered in contact with the enemy. But this will be a fight for personal survival, a fight for his own life. His fight will hardly be characterized by that spark of enthusiasm which in war raises men to the heights of glory and heroism to which normally they would not dare aspire. Yet who knows but that the absence of this mysterious, though highly essential quality, in the Negro soldier may some day explain the difference between defeat and victory for a potentially great nation? The Negro soldier deplores the existence of such a probability.

One of the great soldiers who has emerged from this war is Lt. Col. Evans F. Carlson, famous for his development of that group of supermarine fighters known as *Carlson's Raiders.* This man not only built this extraordinary fighting outfit but led it in the Makin Island raid which resulted in complete destruction of all enemy military emplacements and annihilation of more than eight hundred Japanese soldiers which constituted the island garrison. Only eighteen of Carlson's Raiders lost their lives. Col. Carlson borrowed the fighting slogan, GUNG HO, from the Chinese Red Army with which he spent many months as a military observer. This experience convinced him that men, although they were hungry, nondescript, and poorly equipped could by living the full meaning of this slogan become unconquerable in the face of overwhelming odds. When he was called upon to train a group of American soldiers in the technique of guerrilla warfare he not only made GUNG HO their battle cry but insisted that the deeper significance of this battle cry become the philosophy which undergirded every thought and action of every man. GUNG HO means: WORK TOGETHER . . .

The nation's utter lack of this essential spirit would seem to direct that it be made our national battle cry on both the military and home fronts. In fact GUNG HO could with great wisdom be extended to comprise the entire war effort of the United Nations. It would pay far greater dividends than the existing pattern of suspicion and dissension. Hats off then to a great soldier who was first a great man. The inspired feats of Carlson's Raiders have made military history, and with the passing of time will take on legendary dimensions. Said Col. Carlson: "My men, who are professionally competent, *know* why they are fighting."

The young Americans who followed this leader were not Negroes. How could they have been if honest answers were given to the following questions which Col. Carlson asked each man before accepting him: "Do you know why this war is being fought? What do you expect the world to be like after this war? Do you think the American dream of the postwar world is worth suffering for as much as you will probably have to suffer?" Can't you hear the Negro soldier ask the Colonel: "Sir, are you all right?" The answer contained in this contemporary colloquialism would not be a flippant answer. Negro soldiers want to be heroes just like their white comrades; they want to distinguish themselves for the land they love. But most of all they want to be given the opportunity to become *real soldiers;* they want to be able to find clarity out of the maze of confusion and contradiction from which this love for country grows.

In spite of his frustration the Negro soldier sees a New World A-Coming. But he hasn't read about it in anybody's book. He sees its light beginning to break across the dark and distant horizon of time and events. It won't dawn tomorrow, nor on any tomorrow for a long time to come. This knowledge makes him sad. But that light has begun to shine, dimly 'tis true, and the darkness of man's inhumanity will not prevail against it because it is the light of determined millions of men and women marching toward freedom. That light is burning in the hearts of Russia's intrepid millions and brightens the path of the victorious Red Army. That light has provided the spark of warm hope which has kept the valiant millions of Chinese from capitulating to a superior military power. That light is slowly penetrating the darkness of India's miserable millions, causing an unmistakable urge toward freedom that will ultimately destroy all opposition.

That light now burning weakly will on some not too far distant tomorrow burst into a consuming flame in the hearts of more than a billion darker people. Thus will be created a power for good so intense in our rapidly shrinking world that human debasement can no longer exist anywhere. The Negro soldier sees this light and it quickens his pulse . . . yes, in spite of little minds now wielding big clubs trying to hold back the dawn.

The Negro soldier thinks . . . !

Frank Horne □ Niggers Ought to Quit

For many Negroes, World War II was a painful anomaly. Supposedly the war was being fought for democratic goals and against the racist teachings of Hitler. At the same time, however, segregation and exploitation were still very much a part of American life. In the following poem, Frank Horne, an official with the U.S. Housing Authority, bitterly attacks the hypocrisy of this situation.

Niggers ought to stop
making suckers
out of white folks
Niggers ought to quit
showing white folks up . . .

White ideals—
 Haile Selassie
 whimpers
 to England and France
 of their perfidy—
 . . . Promises to a black man . . .!
 Who gives a damn
 about promises
 to a black man . . .?

From Frank Horne, "Niggers Ought To Quit," *Phylon,* (1941), pp. 360–361. Reprinted by permission of *Phylon,* The Atlanta University Review of Race and Culture.

Supremacy of race—
    Joe Louis ought to stop
    hammering white men
    to their knees—
    Aryans
    Romans
    Celts—
    Don't that slug know
    that white folks don't kneel
    or lie on the floor
    helpless
    before a black boy . . .?
    That fool ought to quit that stuff.

Land of the free and
Home of the brave . . .
    Nigger
    dangling in a Georgia tree—
    Long may he wave—

All men are created equal—
Life, liberty, and the pursuit
of happiness . . .
    Dangling nigger
    in a Georgia tree
    Maybe he looked
    at a white woman
    or kissed her
    or spit in a white man's eye.

Life, liberty and the pursuit
of happiness . . .
    Did the black fool
    really think
    they had made a

"For Colored" entrance
to the Constitution . . .?
What a sap!

Niggers ought to quit
making white folks look so bad . . .!
Jesus
stumbling up the way . . .
A sap named Simon
the Cyrenian
Some black fool
reached down
to bear the cross . . .
One thing a nigger
can certainly have
and that is the privilege
of Christ
to hang
nailed to a tree
twixt thieves . . .

A nigger ought to quit
being an everlasting
mockery
to this white man's world . . .
He just ought to quit!

Lester B. Granger □ Barriers to Negro War Employment

Just as there was no real equality in the military, so there was little on the home front, especially regarding the employment of Negro workers in defense plants. In 1941, President Roosevelt signed Executive Order 8802 which forbade defense plants from discriminating against any minority group seeking employment. Lester B. Granger, an executive in the Urban League, discusses the problems faced by Negroes in seeking employment in war industries.

On June 18, 1942 several thousand white Detroit workers, members of the United Automobile Workers, CIO, went on a wildcat strike shutting down 60 per cent of the Hudson Naval Ordnance Arsenal. The strike occurred because eight Negro employees, in accordance with their union senoirity rights, had been assigned to machines formerly operated by white men. Prompt action by R. J. Thomas, president of the union, ended the strike after seven hours. The strikers were told to return to work or be expelled from the union. The walkout was described by the UAW head as sabotage of our war effort that played into the hands of the enemies of our Nation. "Our constitution," declared Mr. Thomas, "provides for safeguarding the rights of all our members irrespective of their race or creed."

In New York City a group of Negro college graduates protested to the War Department and the President's Committee on Fair Employment Practice against what they charged was flagrant racial discrimination by the New York Office of the War Department in selection for employment of translators from a list of qualified candidates. Negroes were refused appointment no matter what their qualifications, stated these protests.

From Lester B. Granger, "Barriers to Negro War Employment," *Annals of the American Academy*, Vol. 222 (September 1942), pp. 72–80. Reprinted by permission of the American Academy of Political and Social Science.

In Atlanta, Georgia, a committee formed by the Urban League of Atlanta, and representing numerous Negro organizations of that city, vigorously attacked policies of the local educational authorities in denying training to Negro workers who wished employment at the Bell aircraft plant near Atlanta. Promises had been received from the Bell officials that Negroes would be employed if trained. Five thousand Negroes had registered to show their desire for training and employment. Instructions have been given to local educational officers to set up training classes for Negroes at once to match the fifteen classes already in operation for whites. But on June first, Atlanta officials were still refusing to move.

On June 18, 1942 the President's Committee on Fair Employment Practice cited two Chicago labor unions—Steamfitters' Protective Association Local 597 and Chicago Journeymen Plumbers' Union Local 130—as being guilty of racial discrimination in preventing Negro steamfitters and plumbers from working on defense projects. This discrimination, the Committee stated, violated Executive Order 8802 and constituted a hindrance to the war effort.

During September 1941 the United States Employment Service inquired of selected defense industries throughout the country how many jobs would be opened to qualified Negroes out of the new jobs that management expected to produce during the following six months. Out of 282, 245 prospective job openings, 144,583 or 51 per cent were absolutely barred to Negroes, the answers holding good for northern and southern states and for unskilled as well as skilled jobs. They showed how seriously Executive Order 8802 had failed of its purpose, which was to eliminate racial discrimination from defense employment.

The history of the Executive order is more than interesting. It throws a searching light on some of the difficulties standing in the way of solving one of America's most serious social problems—economic discrimination against minority groups, chiefly the Negro population.

At the very opening of the National Defense Program in 1940, it was apparent that employment discrimination against Negro workers, long a general policy of industrial management, was erecting formidable barriers against effective use of American industrial manpower. Thoughtful leadership instantly recognized that industry faced a production assignment far beyond the existing resources of skilled and semi-skilled labor; before the quotas tentatively set by Government could be reached, many more millions of workers would be employed than ever before in the Nation's industrial history.

For this reason, the Advisory Commission to the Council of National

Defense addressed special instructions to holders of defense contracts, calling their attention to the unprecedented drain on labor reserves that was anticipated, and urging full consideration of the training and employment of Negro workers in all occupations for which they could be made available. In the congressional bill that appropriated funds for vocational training of defense workers, there was a provision that the benefits of such training must not be denied to any worker because of his race, religion, or place of birth.

But not Government's urging nor even the threat of war could persuade many employers to drop old habits of thought. Persisting in ideas handed down from a plantation economy, employers still regarded Negroes as a wholly unskilled rural group. They ignored the fact that as early as 1930 there were over a million Negro workers experienced or trained in skilled and white-collar work; that in one year over fifty thousand young Negroes had completed trades and industrial courses in vocational and technical schools; and that nearly five thousand others were awarded college degrees in chemistry, engineering, other sciences, and the liberal arts.

Management officials usually shrewd in sizing up labor resources held onto old ideas because it was easier to retain an old mental error than to make the effort involved in a new outlook. Continuance of these attitudes produced a virus of discrimination that infected nearly every area of the Negro's living. Commercial employment offices and public employment services reflected the unwillingness of employers to use Negro workers by refusing to refer or even to register Negro applicants except in domestic or unskilled jobs. Vocational schools also took their cue from industry by discouraging or rejecting Negro youth seeking training for industrial occupations. White workers readily accepted their employers' designation of industry as an "economic white man's country" and regarded the employment of Negroes with hostility. Their labor unions frequently formalized this attitude by adopting constitutional clauses, ritualistic practices, or tacit policies barring the membership of Negro workers.

Here was the picture that had long been familiar to students of social problems. Nothing in the picture had been changed by the fall months of 1940 when industry began to recruit trained labor on a scale unprecedented in two decades. The recommendation of the Advisory Commission to the Council of National Defense had stirred not a ripple of interest among employers to whom it was addressed. Ominous portents of what was to come were seen when construction of army cantonments began all over the country. Contractors were frantically seeking skilled building trades workers; building trades unions were summoning delinquent members to reinstatement and re-employment; there were over seventy-five thousand Negroes experienced as carpenters, bricklayers, painters, electricians, plasterers, and cement workers. But when these dark-skinned craftsmen moved forward to take their places at the hiring gates, they were met with outright refusal by contractors who, in the same breath, continued to shout for more workers. Or they were referred to business agents of local unions, to be told in one way or another, "Sorry, no Negroes!" It was the exceptional construction job where employment could be found by the skilled Negro worker for the seeking.

Against this forming pattern of defense discrimination, Negro leadership bestirred itself, taking advantage of experiences suffered in the days of the last World War. The Negro public was forewarned by disappointments of those times, and had moreover received thorough training during the depression period in developing mass weight of public opinion. The national Negro press came out with one sustained roar of protest against the sin of racial discrimination in a country preparing to defend democracy. Organizations representing Negro welfare, such as the National Urban League, addressed memoranda to government agencies and held frequent conferences in Washington offices. Negro labor, church, medical, legal, dental, fraternal, and political groups swelled the volume of protest. Emergency committees in nearly every important Negro community gave the masses of people a chance to express themselves. A mass meeting called by the Urban League of Kansas City, Missouri, attracted five thousand persons, the largest protest meeting of Negroes in the history of that city. The more angry Negroes became, the longer grew the names of their "co-ordinating committees."

Careful surveys, as well as impromptu investigations, were made in various parts of the country so as to "get the goods" on discriminating employers. The Curtiss-Wright and Bell aircraft plants of Buffalo, New York, employed no Negroes at production jobs; Standard Steel of Kansas City, Missouri, declared, "We have never had a Negro worker in twenty-five years and don't intend to start now." North American aircraft of the same city stated that Negroes would be employed only in custodial jobs. Of all the companies manufacturing war planes, only the Douglass Corporation of California employed even a handful of Negro production workers. Similar reports of racial discrimination piled up regarding Sperry Gyroscope of New York; Pratt and Whitney of Harford, Connecticut; Budd Manufacturing of Philadelphia; New York Shipbuilding Corporation of Kearney, New Jersey; Buick, Chrysler, and Packard of Detroit and Flint, Michigan; Bethlehem Shipbuilding of Los Angeles; Stewart-Warner, Majestic Radio, Studebaker, and White Motors of Chicago; Julius Heil and A. O. Smith of Milwaukee; and hundreds of other large manufacturers in every part of the country.

The reasons given for the nonemployment of Negroes were of infinite variety, often mutually contradictory. Most common were the following: Negroes never applied; whites and blacks can't mix on the same job; haven't time or money to build separate toilets; no trained Negroes are available; they are racially unequipped for skilled work; the union won't have them; don't like Negroes and don't want them around; this is a rush job and we haven't time for experiments.

And so Negro spokesmen, realizing the futility of trying to break past employer resistance without heavier weapons, turned their attention to Washington again. Some defense agencies were now lumbering into motion on this matter, in response to the proddings of public opinion. The Labor Division of the National Defense Advisory Commission had already added to its staff an experienced Negro member, Dr. Robert C. Weaver, previously consultant on racial problems with the United States Housing Authority; but the small size of the staff assigned to him at first was an indication of how little the National Defense Advisory Commission realized the importance and magnitude of the job that had to be done.

But realization gradually came. The National Urban League brought to Washington in October 1940 a group of local league secretaries from different parts of the country to undertake the job of educating key defense officials. Over several days they sat in conference with staffs of the United States Office of Education, charged with carrying out much of the defense training program; the Bureau of Employment Security, responsible for public employment services; the Division of Defense Housing Coordination, entrusted with plans for housing defense workers; and the Labor Division of the National Defense Advisory Commission.

Other organizations made pilgrimages to Washington to lay their complaints directly before central authority. Waves of telegrams and letters of protest began again to sweep over defense officials, who now realized that they dealt with an aroused Negro population. When the Office of Production Management superseded the Defense Council, Sidney Hillman, as co-director, brought over the Weaver staff, bag and baggage, and enlarged it to establish a Negro Labor Training and Supply Branch of the Labor Division of OPM. It is true that William Knudsen, Hillman's fellow director, was never sympathetic to a program for increasing effective use of Negro labor, but one-half of the authority in this strategic government agency was in support of the Weaver program.

The Office of Education came in for sharp criticism over continued discrimination in defense training. State educational officers, through whom vocational training funds were disbursed, almost completely ignored the new law that stipulated equality of training opportunity. Negroes in southern states reported that training classes for whites were being set up in such trades as welding, sheet metal work, aviation mechanics, machine operation, and blueprint reading, while "defense" classes for Negroes were in nonindustrial occupations. In several states no provision at all was made for Negroes. The training-within-industry program of OPM followed the same pattern. Employers who were unwilling to employ Negroes at production jobs were doubly resistant against admitting them to training classes established in their plants. Even the Newport News Shipbuilding Company, 35 per cent of whose workers were Negroes, refused to train their dark-skinned labor for such jobs as electricians and machinists. Since OPM supervision for this program was recruited directly from industrial corporations, there was slight chance of serious pressure being brought to bear on such employers by government representatives.

Thus by the winter of 1940 the whole pattern of racial discrimination in defense industry lay clearly exposed. The employment gates of an estimated 75 per cent of defense industry were closed against all Negro labor. Exclusion of skilled Negro workers was even more widespread. Absence of any real defense training for Negroes in most southern cities and discrimination against Negro trainees in most northern cities reduced this group's chances to find jobs in the future.

State employment services either refused to register skilled Negro workers at their trades or failed to refer them to jobs when they were registered, or referred them only when employers clearly specified preference for Negroes. In only two states, New York and Illinois, did state employment services adopt constructive steps to induce employers to accept Negro labor, and these steps were usually tentative. In typical northern states, employment interviewers were instructed to fill job orders as they came in, without attempting to persuade employers to change discriminatory specifications. In all states, north or south, the fate of the Negro job applicant depended to a great extent upon the personal interest or prejudices of the interviewer regarding the Negro's "place" as an industrial worker.

The situation created by racial policies of labor unions was familiar to students of American social problems. Eighteen international unions, A.F. of L. and independent, still maintained constitutional or ritualistic restrictions against Negro membership. Most important among these in the defense field were the International Association of Machinists, holding closed shop contracts with twelve major aircraft companies; the Brotherhood of Boilermakers, Iron Shipbuilders and Helpers of America; and the railway unions. In addition, thousands of local unions openly excluded Negroes from jobs, whether in defiance or with the tacit consent of international officers. Practically none of the officials of these unions showed any indication that the threat of war had influenced their contemptuous attitude toward black labor. Aeronautical Mechanics Local No. 751 of Seattle, International Machinist Association, made a public issue of its refusal to admit Negroes to closed shop employment in the Boeing aircraft plant. The union's general organizer for that district declared to the press, "Organized labor has been called upon to make many sacrifices for defense and has made them gladly, but this [admission of Negroes] is asking too much." Thus was completed the vicious circle of defense discrimination against Negroes. No training and therefore no jobs; no jobs and therefore no union memberships; employer and union opposition and therefore no training.

Only one force could break this circle, and that was government action backed by enlightened public opinion. In developing such opinion and securing such action within a space of ten months, Negro leadership accomplished what will eventually be recognized as a feat of social statesmanship. The repeated protests of Negroes developed support from liberal white citizens. The daily press took notice and not only reported the opinions of Negroes but also presented strong editorials in their behalf. An interracial committee of 160 distinguished Americans, under the leadership of Dr. Anson Phelps Stokes, made public a signed protest against the intolerable evil of racial discrimination in a democracy preparing for defense. The Council for Democracy issued a special pamphlet on the subject. Governors in several states appointed committees to find some way of attacking the problem. State legislatures considered bills for banning racial bias in defense employment.

In some cases Federal officials welcomed this aroused public opinion; in most cases they responded to it. Sidney Hillman issued an emphatic memorandum on April 11, 1941 calling employers' attention to the wastefulness of importing labor from distant areas or raiding the employment rolls of competitive firms when unused Negro labor remained available at their plants' very doors.

The United States Employment Service adopted in its entirety a plan of reorganization offered by the National Urban League for improving services to Negro workers. An impractical "Division of Negro Employment" in the USES was eliminated. Experienced Negro employment service officials were placed in regional posts to advise on state service functions as they related to Negro labor. An able Negro economist, Dr. Ira De A. Reid, was appointed as assistant to the Director of the Bureau of Employment Security, of which the USES is part.

Now, under constant prodding, the United States Office of Education addressed another communication to state educational officers, instructing them to make defense training available to Negroes, either by their admission to existing classes or by setting up classes for them similar to those established for whites.

OPM had already conferred with heads of A.F. of L. and CIO unions in the building and shipbuilding trades so as to gain official trade union support for Negro employment on jobs in these fields. Results of these conferences, combined with the efforts of civic groups, were seen in a gradual increase of Negro building trades and shipbuilding workers on defense contracts in the South as well as the East and the Mid-west. The more progressive union leadership, especially in the CIO, secured the passage of resolutions at labor conventions demanding an end to the color line in defense industry. Several CIO unions, such as the United Automobile Workers, the United Electrical, Radio and Machine Workers, the National Maritime Union, and the Steel Workers' Organizing Committee, made equal job opportunity for Negroes a part of their agreements with management.

The next move came from the White House. The President, urged for months to take official cognizance of a serious national problem, broke silence on June 17, 1941 with a memorandum addressed to OPM directors Hillman and Knudsen. The President stated:

> . . . I place the full support of my office behind your statement that "all holders of defense contracts are urged to examine their employment and training policies at once to determine whether or not these policies make ample provision for the full utilization of available and competent Negro workers. . . ."

But this statement, well-directed as it was, proved insufficient to stem the tide of Negro resentment which had risen by now to truly formidable proportions. The White House found itself faced with immediate prospects of a mass demonstration by Negroes unparalleled in national history, scheduled for July 1. All over the country racial organizations were preparing for a march on Washington similar in size and scope to the Bonus Army demonstration of 1932. The movement was spontaneous in that numerous groups had been urging such a step for months; it was deliberately organized in that the prestige of A. Philip Randolph, president of the Brotherhood of Sleeping Car Porters, made it possible to put the idea into action. A March-on-Washington Committee was organized under Randolph's leadership, including many well-known Negro spokesmen. One hundred thousand Negroes prepared to "meet in Washington."

The administration emphatically did not desire this. It would have been notice to foreign critics of our domestic disunity at a time when a semblance of unity was most essential to national prestige. It is significant that arguments to this effect, addressed to Randolph, had no effect on his committee's plans. For possibly the first time in history, Negroes were willing to make an issue of their citizenship rights, even to the point of delaying plans for military and naval defense. A delayed start that is sound, they argued, is better in the long run than a hasty start based on the fatal error of racial discrimination.

The President summoned Randolph and members of his committee to Washington. Flanked by Cabinet members and other advisers, the President first requested cancellation of the march, then agreed to issue an Executive order forbidding racial discrimination in defense industry. The march was canceled; Executive Order No. 8802 was issued on June 25, 1941, stating, in part:

> . . . It is the duty of employers and labor organizations to provide for the full and equitable participation of all workers in the defense industries without discrimination. . . . All departments and agencies of the Government of the United States concerned with vocational and training programs for defense production shall take special measures appropriate to assure that such programs are administered without discrimination.
>
> All contracting agencies of the Government of the United States shall include in all defense contracts hereafter negotiated by them a provision obligating the contractor not to discriminate against any worker.
>
> There is established in the Office of Production Management a committee on fair employment practices, which shall consist of a chairman and four other members to be appointed by the President.

So ended the long fight of Negroes for direct action by the highest executive authority of the land. But they soon found that this action of itself did not solve their difficulties. The Committee on Fair Employment Practice was appointed, with Mark Ethridge, liberal Louisville newspaper publisher, as chairman. Its remaining membership consisted of William Green, president of the A.F. of L.; Philip Murray, head of the CIO; David Sarnoff, president of RCA; and two Negro members—Earl Dickerson, attorney from the city of Chicago, and Milton Webster, vice-president of the Brotherhood of Sleeping Car Porters. After several months of plan-making and preparation, the Committee began a series of investigations and public hearings on defense discrimination in Los Angeles, Chicago, New York, and Birmingham. On the basis of facts uncovered, firms found guilty of discrimination were cited, ordered to correct their practices, and in case of failure to comply were certified to the President as violating Executive Order 8802.

The record of the Committee on Fair Employment Practice is worthy of special study because it constitutes a new approach by the Government of the United States to an old problem. It is the first time since the Emancipation Proclamation that a Presidential Executive order has been issued especially in behalf of Negroes and similarly disadvantaged groups. This may be the first step toward a permanent body, empowered by congressional action, to act in the sphere of racial discrimination, just as the National Labor Relations Board does in the field of union discrimination.

It must be confessed that without such authority the role of the Committee on Fair Employment Practice must be largely exhortatory and persuasive. At present it must exert its punitive authority through the President. It can recommend cancellation of the contract of an offending employer; it cannot assess fines or apply other intermediate punishment. The "all-or-none" nature of its recommendations to the President exposes the Committee to a fatal weakness which employers have been quick to seize upon. They can persist in discrimination, possibly less openly, knowing that the administration will hesitate long before canceling any important contract for ships, planes, tanks, or guns. This is the policy that many employers have followed with impunity. But the net results of the Committee's work have been good, because the larger firms investigated have not desired the unfavorable publicity that comes from citation for racial discrimination at such a time as this. The pressure exerted on some of the larger industrial corporations has been reflected in relaxing discrimination by their smaller competitors.

Meanwhile, war's outbreak and the merger and reorganization of key agencies into efficient warmaking bodies brought important changes in the Federal race relations program. The War Production Board swallowed OPM. The War Manpower Commission took over the United States Employment Service as its recruiting agency. Robert Weaver was appointed a member of the War Manpower Commission as director of the Negro Manpower Service. The staff had been greatly enlarged with regional field representatives assigned throughout the country. Weekly reports poured in emphasizing the extent to which jobs were being opened for Negroes in war industry. The Curtiss-Wright plants now reported more than 3,000 Negro workers employed. Glenn L. Martin, North American Aviation, Consolidated, Brewster, Bell Aircraft, and Lockheed Vega plants were all using Negroes at production jobs. Thousands of Negroes were at work in ordnance plants throughout the country. The number of Negro shipbuilding workers at skilled and semiskilled jobs had doubled in one year, with over 14,000 employed in Navy yards and with more than 5,000 employed in the Newport News Shipbuilding Company alone. The Sun Shipbuilding Company of Chester, Pennsylvania, announced that it would open a new shipyard manned entirely by Negro workers at all skills. The Higgins Industries of New Orleans, applying the assembly line to shipbuilding, planned an all-Negro assembly line with skilled and semiskilled Negro workers. In the shipbuilding field Negroes were now employed in 37 different crafts, including first-class machinists. Auto plants converted to war industry, such as Kelly Heyes, Chrysler, Oldsmobile, Murray, and Briggs, were upgrading skilled and semiskilled Negro workers who had formerly been confined to unskilled and custodial work.

Activity of the Federal Government had been matched by similar special efforts in several states. In New York and Illinois, state laws had been passed forbidding racial discrimination on war contracts. In New York a special committee was appointed by the Governor as part of the State War Council to make this policy effective.

Refusal of public officials to train Negro workers for war production jobs remains a serious stumbling block. The United States Office of Education has been ineffective in handling the situation. Figures produced by this Federal agency show that in eighteen southern and border states, where 22 per cent of the total population are Negroes, only 3,215 Negroes, or 4 per cent of the total trainees, were enrolled last January in pre-employment and refresher training courses. Out of 4,630 training courses in southern states, only 194 were open to Negro trainees. In Florida, Negroes are 27 per cent of the state's population, but only .17 of 1 per cent of its trainees. In the state of Texas, where Negroes comprise 14.3 per cent of the population, only 206 Negroes were admitted to training courses out of 12,472 persons trained in defense production last February. This is a confession of almost complete failure by the Office of Education to enforce the provisions of the law that there shall be no racial discrimination in defense training.

When this barrier is cleared away, as it must be, the prospects for Negroes in war and postwar industry will be brighter than ever. The first World War brought about initial entrance on a large scale of Negroes into northern industry. The second World War is already providing them a chance to move up the occupational ladder. Whether this is a permanent advance or only a temporary perch "for the duration" will depend upon the efficiency that Negroes show in the jobs they are now doing, the extent to which they find and master training at skilled trades, and the readiness of employers to evaluate American workers on a basis not of their color but of their ability to do the job. It will depend, also, upon whether organized labor learns the lesson that labor in England has mastered too late—that white workers can never be free while their fellows are in chains.

A. Philip Randolph □ Why Should We March?

One of the Negro leaders responsible for Roosevelt's signing of Executive Order 8802 was A. Philip Randolph. Born in Crescent City, Florida in 1889, Randolph received his degree at City College of New York and organized the Brotherhood of Sleeping Car Porters in 1925. In 1940, he threatened to organize a march on Washington by thousands of Negroes unless the president promised to provide equal employment opportunities. In 1963, Randolph helped organize the march on Washington during which Dr. Martin Luther King, Jr. delivered his famous "I Have A Dream" oration.

Though I have found no Negroes who want to see the United Nations lose this war [World War II], I have found many who, before the war ends, want to see the stuffing knocked out of white supremacy and of empire over subject peoples. American Negroes, involved as we are in the general issues of the conflict, are confronted not with a choice but with the challenge both to win democracy for ourselves at home and to help win the war for democracy the world over.

There is no escape from the horns of this dilemma. There ought not to be escape. For if the war for democracy is not won abroad, the fight for democracy cannot be won at home. If this war cannot be won for the white peoples, it will not be won for the darker races.

Conversely, if freedom and equality are not vouchsafed the peoples of color, the war for democracy will not be won. Unless this double-

From A. Philip Randolph, "Why Should We March?" *Survey Graphic* (November 1942). pp. 488–489.

barreled thesis is accepted and applied, the darker races will never wholeheartedly fight for the victory of the United Nations. That is why those familiar with the thinking of the American Negro have sensed his lack of enthusiasm, whether among the educated or uneducated, rich or poor, professional or nonprofessional, religious or secular, rural or urban, North, South, East or West.

That is why questions are being raised by Negroes in church, labor union, and fraternal society; in poolroom, barbershop, schoolroom, hospital, hair-dressing parlor; on college campus, railroad, and bus. One can hear such questions asked as these: What have Negroes to fight for? What's the difference between Hitler and that "cracker" Talmadge of Georgia? Why has a man got to be Jim-Crowed to die for democracy? If you haven't got democracy yourself, how can you carry it to somebody else?

What are the reasons for this state of mind? The answer is: discrimination, segregation, Jim Crow. Witness the navy, the army, the air corps; and also government services at Washington. In many parts of the South, Negroes in Uncle Sam's uniform are being put upon, mobbed, sometimes even shot down by civilian and military police, and on occasion lynched. Vested political interests in race prejudice are so deeply entrenched that to them winning the war against Hitler is secondary to preventing Negroes from winning democracy for themselves. This is worth many divisions to Hitler and Hirohito. While labor, business, and farm are subjected to ceilings and doors and not allowed to carry on as usual, these interests trade in the dangerous business of race hate as usual.

When the defense program began and billions of the taxpayers' money were appropriated for guns, ships, tanks, and bombs, Negroes presented themselves for work only to be given the cold shoulder, North as well as South; and despite their qualifications, Negroes were denied skilled employment. Not until their wrath and indignation took the form of a proposed protest march on Washington, scheduled for July 1, 1941, did things begin to move in the form of defense jobs for Negroes. The march was postponed by the timely issuance (June 25, 1941) of the famous Executive Order No. 8802 by President Roosevelt. But this order and the President's Committee on Fair Employment Practice, established thereunder, have as yet only scratched the surface by way of eliminating discriminations on account of race or color in war industry. Both management and labor unions in too many places and in too many ways are still drawing the color line.

It is to meet this situation squarely with direct action that the March on Washington Movement launched its present program of protest mass meetings. Twenty thousand were in attendance at Madison Square Garden, June 16; sixteen thousand in the Coliseum in Chicago,

June 26; nine thousand in the City Auditorium of St. Louis, August 14. Meetings of such magnitude were unprecedented among Negroes. The vast throngs were drawn from all walks and levels of Negro life—businessmen, teachers, laundry workers, Pullman porters, waiters, and red caps; preachers, crapshooters, and social workers; jitterbugs and Ph.D.'s. They came and sat in silence, thinking, applauding only when they considered the truth was told, when they felt strongly that something was going to be done about it.

The March on Washington Movement is essentially a movement of the people. It is all Negro and pro-Negro, but not for that reason anti-white or anti-Semitic, or anti-Catholic, or anti-foreign, or anti-labor. Its major weapon is the nonviolent demonstration of Negro mass power. Negro leadership has united back of its drive for jobs and justice. "Whether Negroes should march on Washington, and if so, when?" will be the focus of a forthcoming national conference. For the plan of a protest march has not been abandoned. Its purpose would be to demonstrate that American Negroes are in deadly earnest, and all out for their full rights. No power on earth can cause them today to abandon their fight to wipe out every vestige of second class citizenship and the dual standards that plague them.

A community is democratic only when the humblest and weakest person can enjoy the highest civil, economic, and social rights that the biggest and most powerful possess. To trample on these rights of both Negroes and poor whites is such a commonplace in the South that it takes readily to anti-social, anti-labor, anti-Semitic, and anti-Catholic propaganda. It was because of laxness in enforcing the Weimar constitution in republican Germany that Nazism made headway. Oppression of the Negroes in the United States, like suppression of the Jews in Germany, may open the way for a fascist dictatorship.

By fighting for their rights now, American Negroes are helping to make America a moral and spiritual arsenal of democracy. Their fight against the poll tax, against lynch law, segregation, and Jim Crow, their fight for economic, political, and social equality, thus becomes part of the global war for freedom.

Program of the March on Washington Movement

1. We demand, in the interest of national unity, the abrogation of every law which makes a distinction in treatment between citizens based on religion, creed, color, or national origin. This means an end to Jim Crow in education, in housing, in transportation, and in every other social, economic, and political privilege; and especially, we demand, in the capital of the nation, an end to all segregation in public places and in public institutions.

2. We demand legislation to enforce the Fifth and Fourteenth Amendments guaranteeing that no person shall be deprived of life, liberty, or property without due process of law, so that the full weight of the national government may be used for the protection of life and thereby may end the disgrace of lynching.

3. We demand the enforcement of the Fourteenth and Fifteenth Amendments and the enactment of the Pepper Poll Tax bill so that all barriers in the exercise of the suffrage are eliminated.

4. We demand the abolition of segregation and discrimination in the army, navy, marine corps, air corps, and all other branches of national defense.

5. We demand an end to discrimination in jobs and job training. Further, we demand that the FEPC be made a permanent administrative agency of the U.S. Government and that it be given power to enforce its decisions based on its findings.

6. We demand that federal funds be withheld from any agency which practices discrimination in the use of such funds.

7. We demand colored and minority group representation on all administrative agencies so that these groups may have recognition of their democratic right to participate in formulating policies.

8. We demand representation for the colored and minority racial groups on all missions, political and technical, which will be sent to the peace conference so that the interests of all people everywhere may be fully recognized and justly provided for in the post-war settlement.

Thurgood Marshall □ The Gestapo in Detroit

Thurgood Marshall, a young lawyer for the NAACP, investigated the Detroit race riot of 1943. The outbreak was triggered by the federal government's vacillation regarding Negro occupancy of a public housing project which had been promised to them. When Negroes attempted to move in, white mobs attacked them, and a race riot ensued. Born in Baltimore in 1908, Marshall received his undergraduate degree at Lincoln University and a law degree at Howard. From 1938–1950, he was a special counsel for the NAACP. In 1961 he was appointed to a U.S. circuit judgeship, a position he occupied until his appointment to the U.S. Supreme Court.

Riots are usually the result of many underlying causes, yet no single factor is more important than the attitude and efficiency of the police. When disorder starts, it is either stopped quickly or permitted to spread into serious proportions, depending upon the actions of the local police.

Much of the blood spilled in the Detroit riot is on the hands of the Detroit police department. In the past the Detroit police have been guilty of both inefficiency and an attitude of prejudice against Negroes. Of course, there are several individual exceptions.

The citizens of Detroit, white and Negro, are familiar with the attitude of the police as demonstrated during the trouble in 1942 surrounding the Sojourner Truth housing project. At that time a mob of white persons armed with rocks, sticks and other weapons attacked

From Thurgood Marshall, "The Gestapo in Detroit," *Crisis,* Vol. 50 (August 1943), pp. 232–233. Reprinted with the permission of The Crisis Publishing Company.

Negro tenants who were attempting to move into the project. Police were called to the scene. Instead of dispersing the mob which was unlawfully on property belonging to the federal government and leased to Negroes, they directed their efforts toward dispersing the Negroes who were attempting to get into their own homes. All Negroes approaching the project were searched and their automobiles likewise searched. White people were neither searched nor disarmed by the police. This incident is typical of the one-sided law enforcement practiced by Detroit police. White hoodlums were justified in their belief that the police would act the same way in any further disturbances.

In the June riot of this year, the police ran true to form. The trouble reached riot proportions because the police once again enforced the law with an unequal hand. They used "persuasion" rather than firm action with white rioters, while against Negroes they used the ultimate in force: night sticks, revolvers, riot guns, sub-machine guns, and deer guns. As a result, 25 of the 34 persons killed were Negroes. Of the latter, 17 were killed by police.

The excuse of the police department for the disproportionate number of Negroes killed is that the majority of them were shot while committing felonies: namely, the looting of stores on Hasting street. On the other hand, the crimes of arson and felonious assaults are also felonies. It is true that some Negroes were looting stores and were shot while committing these crimes. It is equally true that white persons were turning over and burning automobiles on Woodward avenue. This is arson. Others were beating Negroes with iron pipes, clubs, and rocks. This is felonious assault. Several Negroes were stabbed. This is assault with intent to murder.

All these crimes are matters of record; Many were committed in the presence of police officers, several on the pavement around the City Hall. Yet the record remains: Negroes killed by police—17; white persons killed by police—none. The entire record, both of the riot killings and of previous disturbances, reads like the story of the Nazi Gestapo.

Evidence of tension in Detroit has been apparent for months. The *Detroit Free Press* sent a reporter to the police department. When Commissioner Witherspoon was asked how he was handling the situation he told the reporter: "We have given orders to handle it with kid gloves. The policemen have taken insults to keep trouble from breaking out. I doubt if you or I could have put up with it." This weak-kneed policy of the police commissioner coupled with the anti-Negro attitude of many members of the force helped to make a riot inevitable.

Belle Isle is a municipal recreation park where thousands of white and Negro war workers and their families go on Sundays for their outings. There had been isolated instances of racial friction in the past. On Sunday night, June 20, there was trouble between a group of white and Negro people. The disturbance was under control by midnight. During the time of the disturbance and after it was under control, the police searched the automobiles of all Negroes and searched the Negroes as well. They did not search the white people. One Negro who was to be inducted into the army the following week was arrested because another person in the car had a small pen knife. This youth was later sentenced to 90 days in jail before his family could locate him. Many Negroes were arrested during this period and rushed to local police stations. At the very beginning the police demonstrated that they would continue to handle racial disorders by searching, beating and arresting Negroes while using mere persuasion on white people.

A short time after midnight disorder broke out in a white neighborhood near the Roxy theatre on Woodward avenue. The Roxy is an all night theatre attended by white and Negro patrons. Several Negroes were beaten and others were forced to remain in the theatre for lack of police protection. The rumor spread among the white people that a Negro had raped a white woman on Belle Island and that the Negroes were rioting.

At about the same time a rumor spread around Hastings and Adams streets in the Negro area that white sailors had thrown a Negro woman and her baby into the lake at Belle Isle and that the police were beating Negroes. This rumor was also repeated by an unidentified Negro at one of the night spots. Some Negroes began to attack white persons in the area. The police immediately began to use their sticks and revolvers against them. The Negroes began to break out the windows of stores of white merchants on Hastings street.

The interesting thing is that when the windows in the stores on Hastings street were first broken, there was no looting. An officer of the Merchants' Association walked the length of Hastings street, starting 7 o'clock Monday morning and noticed that none of the stores with broken windows had been looted. It is thus clear that the original breaking of windows was not for the purpose of looting.

Throughout Monday the police, instead of placing men in front of the stores to protect them from looting, contented themselves with driving up and down Hastings street from time to time, stopping in front of the stores. The usual procedure was to jump out of the squad cars with drawn revolvers and riot guns to shoot whoever might be in the store. The policemen would then tell the Negro bystanders to "run and not look back." On several occasions, persons running were shot in the back. In other instances, bystanders were clubbed by police. To the police, all Negroes on Hastings street were "looters." This included war workers returning from work. There is no question that many Negroes were guilty of looting, just as there is always looting during earthquakes or as there was when English towns were bombed by the Germans.

Woodward avenue is one of the main thoroughfares of the city of Detroit. Small groups of white people began to rove up and down Woodward beating Negroes, stoning cars containing Negroes, stopping street cars and yanking Negroes from them, and stabbing and shooting Negroes. In no case did the police do more than try to "reason" with these mobs, many of which were, at this stage, quite small. The police did not draw their revolvers or riot guns, and never used any force to disperse these mobs. As a result of this, the mobs got larger and bolder and even attacked Negroes on the pavement of the City Hall in demonstration not only of their contempt for Negroes, but of their contempt for law and order as represented by the municipal government.

During this time, Mayor Jeffries was in his office in the City Hall with the door locked and the window shade drawn. The use of night sticks or the drawing of revolvers would have dispersed these white groups and saved the lives of many Negroes. It would not have been necessary to shoot, but it would have been sufficient to threaten to shoot into the white mobs. The use of a fire hose would have dispersed many of the groups. None of these things was done and the disorder took on the proportions of a major riot. The responsibility rests with the Detroit police.

At the height of the disorder on Woodward avenue, Negroes driving north on Brush street (a Negro street) were stopped at Vernor Highway by a policeman who forced them to detour to Woodward avenue. Many of these cars are automobiles which appeared in the pictures released by several newspapers showing them overturned and burned on Woodward avenue.

While investigating the riot, we obtained many affidavits from Negroes concerning police brutality during the riot. It is impossible to include the facts of all of these affidavits. However, typical instances may be cited. A Negro soldier in uniform who had recently been released from the army with a medical discharge, was on his way down Brush street Monday morning, toward a theatre on Woodward avenue. This soldier was not aware of the fact that the riot was still going on. While in the Negro neighborhood on Brush street, he reached a corner where a squad car drove up and discharged several policemen with drawn revolvers who announced to a small group on the corner to run and not look back. Several of the Negroes who did not move quite fast enough for the police were struck with night sticks and revolvers. The soldier was yanked from behind by one policeman and struck in the head with a blunt instrument and knocked to the ground, where he remained in a stupor. The police then returned to their squad car and drove off. A Negro woman in the block noticed the entire incident from her window, and she rushed out with a cold, damp towel to bind the soldier's head. She then hailed two Negro postal employees who carried the soldier to a hospital where his life was saved.

There are many additional affidavits of similar occurrences involving obviously innocent civilians throughout many Negro sections in Detroit where there had been no rioting at all. It was characteristic of these cases that the policemen would drive up to a corner, jump out with drawn revolvers, striking at Negroes indiscriminately, ofttimes shooting at them, and in all cases forcing them to run. At the same time on Woodward avenue, white civilians were seizing Negroes and telling them to "run, nigger, run." At least two Negroes, "shot while looting," were innocent persons who happened to be in the area at that time.

One Negro who had been an employee of a bank in Detroit for the past eighteen years was on his way to work on a Woodward avenue street car when he was seized by one of the white mobs. In the presence of at least four policemen, he was beaten and stabbed in the side. He also heard several shots fired from the back of the mob. He managed to run to two of the policemen who proceeded to "protect" him from the mob. The two policemen, followed by two mounted policemen, proceeded down Woodward avenue. While he was being escorted by these policemen, the man was struck in the face by at least eight of the mob, and at no time was any effort made to prevent him from being struck. After a short distance this man noticed a squad car parked on the other side of the street. In sheer desperation, he broke away from the two policemen who claimed to be protecting him and ran to the squad car, begging for protection. The officer in the squad car put him in the back seat and drove off, thereby saving his life.

During all this time, the fact that the man was either shot or stabbed was evident because of the fact that blood was spurting from his side. Despite this obvious felony, committed in the presence of at least four policemen, no effort was made at that time either to protect the victim or to arrest the persons guilty of the felony.

In addition to the many cases of one-sided enforcement of the law by the police, there are two glaring examples of criminal aggression against innocent Negro citizens and workers by members of the Michigan state police and Detroit police.

On the night of June 22 at about 10 o'clock, some of the residents of the St. Antoine Branch of the Y.M.C.A. were returning to the dormitory. Several were on their way home from the Y.W.C.A. across the street. State police were searching some other Negroes on the pavement of the Y.M.C.A. when two of the Y.M.C.A. residents were stopped and searched for weapons. After none was found they were allowed to proceed to the building. Just as the last of the Y.M.C.A. men was about to enter the building, he heard someone behind him yell what sounded to him like, "Hi, Ridley." (Ridley is also a resident of the Y.) Another resident said he heard someone yell what sounded to him like "Heil, Hitler."

A state policeman, Ted Anders, jumped from his car with his revolver drawn, ran to the steps of the Y.M.C.A., put one foot on the bottom step and fired through the outside door. Immediately after firing the shot he entered the building. Other officers followed. Julian Witherspoon, who had just entered the building, was lying on the floor, shot in the side by the bullet that was fired through the outside door. There had been no show of violence or weapons of any kind by anyone in or around the Y.M.C.A.

The officers with drawn revolvers ordered all those residents of the Y.M.C.A. who were in the lobby of their building, to raise their hands in the air and line up against the wall like criminals. During all this time these men were called "black b——— and monkeys," and other vile names by the officers. At least one man was struck, another was forced to throw his lunch on the floor. All the men in the lobby were searched.

The desk clerk was also forced to line up. The officers then went behind the desk and into the private offices and searched everything. The officers also made the clerk open all locked drawers, threatening to shoot him if he did not do so.

Witherspoon was later removed to the hospital and has subsequently been released.

On the night of June 21 at about eight o'clock, a Detroit policeman was shot in the two hundred block of Vernor Highway, and his assailant, who was in a vacant lot, was, in turn, killed by another policeman. State and city policemen then began to attack the apartment building at 290 E. Vernor Highway, which was fully occupied by tenants. Searchlights were thrown on the building and machine guns, revolvers, rifles, and deer guns were fired indiscriminately into all of the occupied apartments facing the outside. Tenants of the building were forced to fall to the floor and remain there in order to save their lives. Later slugs from machine guns, revolvers, rifles, and deer guns were dug from the inside walls of many of the apartments. Tear gas was shot into the building and all the tenants were forced out into the streets with their hands up in the air at the point of drawn guns.

State and city policemen went into the building and forced out all the tenants who were not driven out by tear gas. The tenants were all lined up against the walls, men and women alike, and forced to remain in this position for some time. The men were searched for weapons. During this time these people were called every type of vile name and men and women were cursed and threatened. Many men were struck by policemen.

While the tenants were lined up in the street, the apartments were forcibly entered. Locks and doors were broken. All the apartments were ransacked. Clothing and other articles were thrown around on the floor. All of these acts were committed by policemen. Most of the tenants reported that money, jewelry, whiskey, and other items of personal property were missing when they were permitted to return to their apartments after midnight. State and city police had been in possession of the building in the meantime.

Many of these apartments were visited shortly after these events. They resembled part of a battlefield. Affidavits from most of the tenants and lists of property destroyed and missing are available.

Although a white man was seen on the roof of an apartment house up the street from the Vernor apartments with a rifle in his hand, no effort was made to either search that building or its occupants. After the raid on the Vernor apartments, the police used as their excuse the statement that policeman Lawrence A. Adams had been shot by a sniper from the Vernor apartments, and that for that reason, they attacked the building and its occupants. However, in a story released by the police department on July 2 after the death of Patrolman Lawrence A. Adams, it was reported that "The shot that felled Adams was fired by Homer Edison, 28 years old, of 502 Montcalm, from the shadows of a parking lot. Edison, armed with a shot gun, was shot to death by Adams' partner." This is merely another example of the clumsy and obvious subterfuges used by the police department in an effort to cover up their total disregard for the rights of Negroes.

Justification for our belief that the Detroit police could have prevented the trouble from reaching riot proportions is evidenced in at least two recent instances. During the last month in the town of Atlanta, Georgia, several white youths organized a gang to beat up Negroes. They first encountered a young Negro boy on a bicycle and threw him to the ground. However, before they could beat this lone Negro, a squad car drove up. The police promptly arrested several of the white boys, and dispersed the group immediately, thus effectively forestalling and preventing what might have resulted in a riot. On the Sunday preceding the Detroit riots, Sheriff Baird, of Wayne County, Michigan, with jurisdiction over the area just outside Detroit, suppressed a potential riot in a nearby town. A large group of Negroes and a large group of white people were opposing each other and mob violence was threatened. The sheriff and his deputies got between the two groups and told them that in case of any violence, the guilty parties would be handled and that the law enforcement officers would do everything possible to prevent the riot. Because of this firm stand, the members of both groups dispersed.

If similar affirmative action had been taken by the Detroit police when the small groups were running up and down Woodward avenue beating, cutting and shooting Negroes, the trouble never would have reached the bloody and destructive magnitude which has shocked the nation.

This record by the Detroit police demonstrates once more what all Negroes know only too well: that nearly all police departments limit their conception of checking racial disorders to surrounding, arresting, maltreating, and shooting Negroes. Little attempt is made to check the activities of whites.

The certainty of Negroes that they will not be protected by police, but instead attacked by them is a contributing factor to racial tensions leading to overt acts. The first item on the agenda of any group seeking to prevent rioting would seem to be a critical study of the police department of the community, its record in handling Negroes, something of the background of its personnel, and the plans of its chief officers for meeting possible racial disorders.

Editorial from *Crisis* □ The Harlem Riot

The Harlem riot of 1943, like so many other disorders, began when a white policeman attempted to arrest a Negro. A black soldier intervened and was shot. Here the editors of *Crisis* evaluate the riot in terms of what it meant to the Negro community at large.

There were many sound, sensible editorial expressions on the Harlem riot from all sections of the country, but of the 346 daily newspaper editorials examined in this office, the one by the Richmond, Va., *Times Dispatch* easily ranks with the worst. To counteract the *Times Dispatch,* easily one of the best was from the neighboring Norfolk *Virginian-Pilot.* Louis I. Jaffe is still the scholarly and thoughtful editor of the Norfolk morning daily, while our old "friend," Virginius Dabney bosses the editorial page of the Richmond morning paper.

Dabney's diatribe entitled, "Dixie's Fault, Of Course," is unworthy of him, even considering his obsession with the idea that northern Negro agitators are responsible for all the racial tension in the country. Dabney sneers at the idea that mistreatment of Negro soldiers in the South could have had anything whatsoever to do with sparking the riot of August 1–2 in far-away Harlem. It is this type of thinking which has made riots possible, this failure to realize that there is widespread knowledge and resentment of the general treatment of the race and particularly of the Negro soldier.

A soldier in uniform was shot by a policeman in Harlem. The question of who was right and who was wrong at the moment did not

From "The Harlem Riot," *Crisis* (September 1943), p. 263. Reprinted with the permission of The Crisis Publishing Company.

interest the mob. Mobs, white or black, don't reason. The white Beaumont mob did not reason. A white woman had not been raped, but you could not tell them that—not that night. So, in Harlem the wildfire story was of the shooting of a Negro soldier in uniform by a civilian policeman.

Negro soldiers have been shot down by civilian police in Alexandria, La., in Little Rock, Ark., in Baltimore, Md., in Beaumont, Tex., and in a half dozen other places. They have been humiliated, manhandled, and beaten in countless instances.

The Harlem mob knew all this. It hated all this. It could not reach the Arkansas cop who fired a full magazine of his revolver into the prone body of a Negro sergeant, or any of the others, so it tore up Harlem. It was a wild, senseless, criminal action, the boiling over of people who felt they could not get the Dabneys, the Connallys, or even the Roosevelts, much less the War department, the governors, the mayors, the chiefs of police to listen and act.

For his own purposes Dabney has caricatured the picture. Harlem's riot was not exclusively and solely the fault of Dixie. It was New York City's riot and New York City must bear its share of blame. All the old problems are there; and New York is a part of America, in many ways very like Dixie. But the stimulant in this particular instance did come from below the Mason and Dixon line; every Negro feels that in his bones, and white men, in Richmond as in New York, should understand it. In the minds of Harlemites that Sunday night the gun in the hands of a good New York policeman doing his duty was the gun in the hands of Dixie cops shooting down men in the uniform, if you please, of the Army of Democracy. That's the fact, much too big and much too bitter to be laughed away.

4

The Modern Period: From Sit-In to Soul

Carl Rowan □ Go South to Sorrow

After the Supreme Court decision of 1954 invalidating segregation in the public schools, many Negroes, like Carl Rowan, felt that considerable racial progress would result. Born in 1926, Rowan graduated from the University of Minnesota and became a staff writer for the *Minneapolis Tribune* in 1950. Formerly Director of the U.S. Information Service, Rowan served for a time as ambassador to Finland in the Johnson administration.

So you talk to this livestock dealer, to this sharecropping old mayor, to hundreds more like them, and you sense a strange sympathy, even though you are black and they are white and between you there is a labyrinth of barriers—barriers that they have built. You wonder if you can ever fully understand their anguish, the mental and moral anxieties so aptly expressed by a young white newspaperman.

"We are a sick and miserable people, we southerners," he said to me. "We are in America, but not of it. We can see justice and recognize it at a distance, but we cannot embrace it. Men have always feared change, and sometimes I think we fear it as no collection of people ever have. We are supersensitive, overly defensive—we tell ourselves that we cannot look straight in the eye those countrymen of ours who are struggling to protect the nation's place in a world of turmoil. We are a miserable bunch of bastards—nice bastards, but without guts, or whatever it takes, to get off our backs the burdens and sins of our grandpappies."

So it was, in November, 1953, that I listened to white men and black men speak, some in anger, deceit, self-pity and despair, some with a sense of ominous foreboding, and I got a vision of men struggling against destiny—their own and that of their country.

Still—the Supreme Court was going to rule; rule because the turbulent world was on the move; rule because the Negro was restless; rule because a heavy feeling of guilt was weighing on the American conscience. So, in 1953, I anticipated that decision, knowing that it involved the hopes and dreams of millions of Negroes who had come to believe that all the social and economic ills that beset them stemmed directly from segregation. More and more, these Negroes had come to believe that there could be no justice, no equality of opportunity, under state-imposed segregation. But the court's answer also involved the deepest emotions of millions of white people who feared the results, real or imagined, of the end of legalized segregation. Feared new ways of life in employment, politics, social conditions, sex—the entire gamut of southern mores.

By the time I reached Clarendon County, a legal cornerstone in the court dispute, the issue was already woefully complicated—complicated because not all Negroes wanted to see an end to segregation, nor did all whites want to see it maintained. But there was general awareness among members of both races that the five cases before the court were the most momentous on the race question since the Dred Scott case of pre-Civil War days.

Then, even as I listened to the angry words of Negroes and whites, even as I watched an area of my country squirm and grope with its and the nation's gravest social problem, I had no reason to doubt that whatever the court's decision, it would be obeyed, that all over the South, white men and their Negro fellow Americans would sit down, though sometimes reluctantly, to forge a new social order that would do credit to themselves and to democratic institutions.

But that was 1953. Now I am not so sure of my countrymen, and my countrymen do not seem certain of themselves. Now the South is a bitter crossroads of racial hatred—and new pockets of racial harmony. From Delaware to Louisiana to New Mexico there is a turbulent pattern of change . . . of confusion . . . of defiance and even despair. All because the United States Supreme Court did rule, and it said that there is a new law in the land. . . .

I returned to my native South in 1956 with a colleague, Richard Kleeman, also of the Minneapolis *Tribune,* and what I saw made me feel our country had sadly miscalculated—had underestimated the ability of those few individuals so skilled in racial demagoguery that they could arouse the passions of insecure or greedy white men and herd them into angry, irresponsible mobs that resort even to murder to protect the status quo.

So today we face the nation's severest constitutional crisis since the Civil War, for from Virginia to Texas there is talk of "nullification" and "interposition," of a state's right to step between its people and the federal authorities and declare that the state is supreme. We have the very serious question of whether this country—all of it—is a land of law or whether portions of it are to be ruled by mobs. We have the crucial question of whether the Negro has been for forty years naïve in maintaining faith in democratic processes and the judicial system of America; that is, whether the Negro can achieve final justice only through the violence, obstruction, noncooperation and destruction that have marked the rise of underprivileged peoples in other portions of the world. Most important of all, we have the vital question of whether a nation is to sit meekly by, hoping Father Time will rush in like the U.S. Cavalry to rescue us, while a few ruthless men discredit the nation's judicial system, render meaningless its Constitution, trample roughshod over the basic liberties of the people.

In this book, I intend to show what has happened since that May day in 1954 when so many Americans beamed proudly over the Supreme Court ruling. I think the record will show that we have invited crisis after crisis by our cowardliness, by falling victim to a national sickness—for which the germ carriers are both Democrats and Republicans—that I can describe only as gutlessness in the name of "moderation." The record may even show that much of the press that exulted so loudly over the ruling, spawning great editorial phrases about freedom and justice, and those government officials who before the ruling expressed such alarm over our relations with the dark peoples abroad, have been the major forces lulling the nation into a slumber of meekness during which the agents of darkness have grabbed the initiative.

For all the noble words in its decision of May 17, 1954, the United States Supreme Court left a vacuum—a dangerous vacuum that represented a calculated gamble. The court was firm in its opinion, but it as much as confessed weakness as to how to secure the application of its ruling. It had to count on the American public for implementation. So the court left a "cooling-off period" of more than a year before issuing the final decree that was legally necessary to provoke any steps toward compliance in the areas affected. The justices obviously hoped that in the months between their dramatic ruling outlawing segregation and the final decree giving orders as to how and when the segregating areas would have to comply, responsible citizens of both races would sit together and chart a course of orderly change. But was the court's delay a practical move firmly founded on the belief that the cries of defiance would die out in time, or was it a needless and dangerous concession to hate peddlers who know no compromise? There were a few Americans who commented unhappily that "justice delayed is justice denied," who observed that those Negro plaintiffs who actually filed the suits asking for judicial relief from state-imposed segregation would finish school without receiving relief, without receiving the justice to which the court now said they were entitled. But at the time there was no great debate on this point, for even the most militant leaders of the NAACP appeared happy to win the legal principle. Negro leaders joined with the Supreme Court in hoping that time would show the South to be law-abiding and amenable to change.

But for the uncompromising racists, the court-ordered delay was a bonanza—a time in which to organize, to harangue, to frighten, to conduct a venomous racial campaign of a magnitude never before experienced by Americans, even in the heyday of the Ku Klux Klan. Thousands of pamphlets, booklets and handbills spewed from the sewers of the National Citizens Protective Association in St. Louis and from a handful of other "hate" organizations that had struggled along in near-obscurity during a decade when a few men of courage in high places were vigorously attacking the American cancer of racism. But many of these courageous men, who had helped produce the Supreme Court decision, fell silent after the ruling, or became absorbed in the cult of "moderation" and left the Supreme Court "holding the bag." The hate leaflets, attacking Negroes primarily, but also Jews and Catholics, flowed into the hands of Mississippi "rednecks," the rural "woolhats" of Georgia, the honky-tonk hoodlums and the still-in-the-hills thugs, but they also reached bankers, doctors, businessmen and the other leading citizens of thousands of communities. It was like poking narcotics into rodeo broncos. . . .

Dick Gregory □ Nigger

Dick Gregory, a native of St. Louis, is a Negro comedian deeply committed to the cause of racial justice. "I began taking more and more time off from being a funny man," he wrote, "to help our people." In the early 1960's Gregory joined other activists in aiding Mississippi Negroes. The following is an extract from his laconic autobiography, *Nigger*.

In November of 1962 I was sitting on the stage of a jam-packed auditorium in Jackson, Mississippi, with Roy Wilkins, waiting to go on. I was a little restless. I had flown in just for that night, and I wanted to make my speech and get out of town. And now I had to sit up there and wait while they were introducing some old Negro who had just gotten out of jail. I hardly listened. He had killed a man, they said, another Negro who had been sent by the whites to burn the old man's house down. The old man had been leading a voter registration drive. I should have listened carefully. But I had no way of knowing that old man was going to change my entire life.

The old man shuffled out to the microphone. I think he said he was seventy-eight years old. I'll never forget what he said next.

"I didn't mind going to jail for freedom, no, I wouldn't even mind being killed for freedom. But my wife and I was married a long time, and, well, you know I ain't never spent a night away from home. While I was in jail, my wife died."

That destroyed me. I sat there, and my stomach turned around, and I couldn't have stood up if I had to. Here's this little old Mississippi

Negro, the kind of big-lipped kinky-haired, black-faced verb-buster every other Negro in America looks down on. And this man bucked and rose up and fought the system for me, and he went to jail for me, and he lost his wife for me. He had gone out on the battle lines and demonstrated for a tomorrow he would never see, for jobs and rights he might not even be qualified to benefit from. A little old man from a country town who never spent a night away from his wife in his married life. And he went to jail for me and being away killed her.

After the old man finished speaking, I went to him and told him thanks. I told him that I hated to come to him with money after what had happened to him, but if he had a child or loved one anywhere in the world he wanted to see on Christmas, I wanted the privilege of sending him there. He said he had a son in California, and later I gave Medgar Evers a train ticket and a check for the old man.

I don't remember what I spoke about that night, I was so upset. As I came off the stage, Medgar introduced me to a woman named Leona Smith as if I should know her. When I didn't react, he said she was the mother of Clyde Kennard. That name didn't mean anything to me either. So Medgar told me a story that made me sick.

Clyde Kennard was thirty-five years old, and for the past three years he had been in jail. The charge was stealing five bags of chicken feed. But the real reason was that he had tried to enroll in Mississippi Southern College. Before I left Jackson that night, I promised Mrs. Smith that I would do everything in my power to get her son out of jail. When I got back to Chicago, Medgar started calling me about the case and sending me more information. I couldn't believe it.

Kennard was born in Mississippi, and he attended the University of Chicago. When he got out of the paratroopers after Korea, he bought his parents a farm in Mississippi. His stepfather got sick, and Clyde went down to run the farm. He wanted to finish his college education, so in 1959 he applied to the nearest school, Mississippi Southern. He was turned down and harassed by the police, and finally somebody planted five stolen bags of chicken feed on his farm. The price of feed was raised to make the charge a felony, and Kennard was sentenced to seven years at hard labor. When another Negro admitted stealing the feed, the white authorities told him to shut up.

On New Year's Eve, from the stage of Mister Kelley's in Chicago, I made a resolution for 1963: Get Kennard out of jail. I thought that if all the facts were dug up and printed in the newspapers, America would get Kennard out of jail. A white UPI reporter who came by to interview me was so upset by the story that he volunteered to go into Mississippi and gather more information. The first bit of information he dug up was that Clyde Kennard was dying of cancer.

Irv Kupcinet, the famous Chicago columnist, broke the Kennard story. My new researcher came up with Kennard's medical records, and gave them to the press. Kennard was transferred to the prison hospital. Then a Chicago millionaire called business connections in Mississippi, and Kennard was released from jail. He was thirty-five years old when we flew him to Chicago to start cancer treatments, but he looked eighty-five. And it was too late. He died six months later.

I met James Meredith that year, too—one of the most brilliant and courageous men in America, a man who gave dignity to every Negro in the country, who put every Negro in college, who played one of the biggest parts in setting up the revolution in the history of the American Negro struggle. Negroes looked a little different and acted a little different when James Meredith was graduated because they all were graduated with him, graduated from the derogatory stigma that all Negroes are ignorant, that all Negroes are lazy, that all Negroes stink.

I was different, too. An old man's wife had died. Two young men had tried to integrate schools that the biggest fools wouldn't want to go to. One had failed and died, and the other had succeeded and suffered. For the first time, I was involved. There was a battle going on, there was a war shaping up, and somehow writing checks and giving speeches didn't seem enough.

Made in the shade? Hell, as long as any man, white or black, isn't getting his rights in America I'm in danger. Sure I could stay in the night clubs and say clever things. But if America goes to war tomorrow would I stay home and satirize it at the Blue Angel? No, I'd go overseas and lay on some cold dirt, taking the chance of dying to guarantee a bunch of foreigners a better life than my own Momma got in America.

I wanted a piece of the action now, I wanted to get in this thing. I got my chance sooner than I expected.

Some people in Mississippi were having problems with food. A guy came by the night club one evening in Chicago and asked me to sign a fund-raising letter. I told him I never lend my name to anything. If it's an organization I can work with, I'll work. I told him I didn't get through at the night club until 4 A.M. but if he'd leave some literature under my apartment door I'd read it before I went to sleep. He did. I got another lesson on how dirty this situation was.

Leflore County in Mississippi had cut off its shipments of federal surplus foods, most of which went to Negroes. This was in retaliation for voter registration drives in Greenwood, the county seat. The white authorities claimed they couldn't afford the $37,000 a year it cost them to store and distribute the free food to the poor people. I endorsed the letter that morning and sent a check for $100.

Later that day, the fund-raisers called me and asked if I would come by for a press conference. I asked for more information so I could answer questions intelligently. And I sent my new researcher down to Greenwood. Then I went into the streets of Chicago. Daddy-O Dayley, the disc jockey, and I collected 14,000 pounds of food. I chartered a plane, and on February 11, 1963, we flew the food into Memphis. We loaded it into trucks there, and drove 134 miles to Clarksdale. From there it was taken to Greenwood. I was still afraid of the South, and I wanted to leave that night. That's why I picked February 11 to go to Mississippi. The next day was Lincoln's Birthday and President Kennedy had invited Lil and me and 800 other people to a celebration at the White House. So we handed out the food, and I promised the voter registration workers from SNCC—the Student Non-Violent Coordinating Committee—that I'd come back when the demonstrations began. Then I headed back to Memphis, flew to Chicago to pick up Lil, and flew on to Washington.

It was a wonderful affair. We shook hands with President Kennedy, and with Lyndon Johnson. Lil was almost nine months pregnant at the time and I was hoping she'd give birth right in the White House. Waited around as long as we could, but the party was over and she didn't even feel labor pains. So we went back to Chicago.

I started getting reports from my researcher. Through February and March there was violence in Greenwood. Cars were wrecked, a Negro registration worker was shot in the back of the neck, the SNCC headquarters was set on fire. Bullets were fired into Negro homes. SNCC workers were beaten up. When Negroes marched in protest, the police put the dogs on them. They arrested the eleven top registration workers. And I had promised to go down to Greenwood.

I was scared to death. Making speeches, giving money, even going down South for a night or two at a time—that was one thing. But getting out on those streets and marching against bullets and dogs and water hoses and cattle prods . . .

I knew they were laying for me down there. The Mississippi newspapers and public officials were on me for the food lift. They claimed that I hadn't brought down 14,000 pounds of food after all, that it had been much less. They said that if Dick Gregory was going to take care of their poor Negroes, let's send them all up to Chicago. They said I was just doing it for publicity.

And then the time came to make up my mind. The big push for voter registration was scheduled to start on April 1. Most of the SNCC people were in jail, and they needed leaders in Greenwood. And they needed a well-known name that would bring the situation national attention. On Sunday, March 31, I lay on a hotel bed in Philadelphia and changed my mind a hundred times. I thought of a lot of good reasons for not going.

They'll kill me down there, those rednecks, they'll call me an outside agitator and pull me into an alley and beat my head in, they'll shoot me down in the street. What's that going to prove? And what about Michele and Lynne and Lil, lying in a hospital right now with Dick, Jr., my son, who's going to grow up with nothing but some press clippings for a Daddy?

If Whitey down South doesn't kill me in Greenwood, then Whitey up North will kill me in show business. Everybody I talked to but Lil told me not to go. It would ruin me as a comic. Nobody's going to come to laugh at an entertainer who goes marching and demonstrating and getting himself arrested.

I had two airline tickets in my room, one for me and one for James Sanders, a brilliant young Negro comedy writer. I dropped them in the wastebasket. I'll call SNCC headquarters, tell them I'm sick, I've changed my mind, I can't break my contract and leave town. I called Lil instead, at the hospital. She told me not to worry about anything, to go down if I wanted to, and suddenly I was telling her about that Mississippi Negro, the man that other Negroes called nigger, that cotton-picker in his tarpaper shack who could rip this thing, who could give courage to every Negro in America, who could wake up the nation. I had faith then that when America saw what was happening in Greenwood, it would make sure that it never happened again, anywhere. I wanted to be a part of this thing, but I was scared.

Sure, I had made speeches that every door of racial prejudice I can kick down is one less door that my children have to kick down. But, hell, my kids don't have to worry. . . .

I lay there all that night, into the morning, going, not going, picking the tickets out of the wastebasket, throwing them back in, but never tearing them up. And as I lay there my own life started spinning around in my mind, and my stomach turned over, and I thought about St. Louis and Momma and Richard, running off to buy himself a dinner of a Twinkie Cupcake and a bottle of Pepsi-Cola, little Richard whose Daddy was so broken by the system that he ran away and came back just to take the rent money out of the jar in the kitchen. Goddamn, we're always running and hiding, and then I thought about an old man whose wife had died, and about Clyde Kennard, and about James Meredith, they didn't run away, and now it was almost dawn in Philadelphia and there was a familiar dry taste in my mouth, and that old hot water was seeping into a cold body and my room was the grandstand of the biggest stadium in the world—America—and the race was for survival and the monster said go.

The Autobiography of Malcolm X

Malcolm X, born Malcolm Little in Omaha in 1925, was the son of a Baptist minister who served as an organizer for Marcus Garvey's back-to-Africa movement of the 1920's. Converted to the black muslim creed, Malcolm X departed from the doctrine of separatism shortly before his death by assassins' bullets in 1965. In this chapter from his autobiography, he summarizes his career and foresees the possibility of an early death.

I must be honest. Negroes—Afro-Americans—showed no inclination to rush to the United Nations and demand justice for themselves here in America. I really had known in advance that they wouldn't. The American white man has so thoroughly brainwashed the black man to see himself as only a domestic "civil rights" problem that it will probably take longer than I live before the Negro sees that the struggle of the American black man is international.

And I had known, too, that Negroes would not rush to follow me into the orthodox Islam which had given me the insight and perspective to see that the black men and white men truly could be brothers. America's Negroes—especially older Negroes—are too indelibly soaked in Christianity's double standard of oppression.

So, in the "public invited" meetings which I began holding each Sunday afternoon or evening in Harlem's well-known Audubon Ballroom, as I addressed predominantly non-Muslim Negro audiences, I did not immediately attempt to press the Islamic religion, but instead to embrace all who sat before me:

"—not Muslim, nor Christian, Catholic, nor Protestant . . . Baptist nor Methodist, Democrat nor Republican, Mason nor Elk! I mean the

From Malcolm X with the assistance of Alex Haley, *The Autobiography of Malcolm X* (1965), chapter 19. Reprinted by permission of Grove Press, Inc.

black people of America—and the black people all over this earth! Because it is as this collective mass of black people that we have been deprived not only of our civil rights, but even of our human rights, the right to human dignity. . . ."

On the streets, after my speeches, in the faces and the voices of the people I met—even those who would pump my hands and want my autograph—I would feel the wait-and-see attitude. I would feel—and I understood—their uncertainty about where I stood. Since the Civil War's "freedom," the black man has gone down so many fruitless paths. His leaders, very largely, had failed him. The religion of Christianity had failed him. The black man was scarred, he was cautious, he was apprehensive.

I understood it better now than I had before. In the Holy World, away from America's race problem, was the first time I ever had been able to think clearly about the basic divisions of white people in America, and how their attitudes and their motives related to, and affected Negroes. In my thirty-nine years on this earth, the Holy City of Mecca had been the first time I had ever stood before the Creator of All and felt like a complete human being.

In that peace of the Holy World—in fact, the very night I have mentioned when I lay awake surrounded by snoring brother pilgrims—my mind took me back to personal memories I would have thought were gone forever . . . as far back, even, as when I was just a little boy, eight or nine years old. Out behind our house, out in the country from Lansing, Michigan, there was an old, grassy "Hector's Hill," we called it—which may still be there. I remembered there in the Holy World how I used to lie on the top of Hector's Hill, and look up at the sky, at the clouds moving over me, and daydream, all kinds of things. And then, in a funny contrast of recollections, I remembered how years later, when I was in prison, I used to lie on my cell bunk—this would be especially when I was in solitary: what we convicts called "The Hole"—and I would picture myself talking to large crowds. I don't have any idea why such previsions came to me. But they did. To tell that to anyone then would have sounded crazy. Even I didn't have, myself, the slightest inkling. . . .

In Mecca, too, I had played back for myself the twelve years I had spent with Elijah Muhammad as if it were a motion picture. I guess it would be impossible for anyone ever to realize fully how complete was my belief in Elijah Muhammad. I believed in him not only as a leader in the ordinary *human* sense, but also I believed in him as a *divine* leader. I believed he had no human weaknesses of faults, and that, therefore, he could make no mistakes and that he could do no wrong. There on a Holy World hilltop, I realized how very dangerous it is for people to hold any human being in such esteem, especially to consider anyone some sort of "divinely guided" and "protected" person.

My thinking had been opened up wide in Mecca. In the long letters I wrote to friends, I tried to convey to them my new insights into the American black man's struggle and his problems, as well as the depths of my search for truth and justice.

"I've had enough of someone else's propaganda," I had written to these friends. "I'm for truth, no matter who tells it. I'm for justice, no matter who it is for or against. I'm a human being first and foremost, and as such I'm for whoever and whatever benefits humanity *as a whole*."

Largely, the American white man's press refused to convey that I was now attempting to teach Negroes a new direction. With the 1964 "long, hot summer" steadily producing new incidents, I was constantly accused of "stirring up Negroes." Every time I had another radio or television microphone at my mouth, when I was asked about "stirring up Negroes" or "inciting violence," I'd get hot.

"It takes no one to stir up the sociological dynamite that stems from the unemployment, bad housing, and inferior education already in the ghettoes. This explosively criminal condition has existed for so long, it needs no fuse; it fuses itself; it spontaneously combusts from within itself. . . ."

They called me "the angriest Negro in America." I wouldn't deny that charge. I spoke exactly as I felt. "I *believe* in anger. The Bible says there is a *time* for anger." They called me "a teacher, a fomentor of violence." I would say point blank, "That is a lie. I'm not for wanton violence, I'm for justice. I feel that if white people were attacked by Negroes—if the forces of law prove unable, or inadequate, or reluctant to protect those whites from those Negroes—then those white people should protect and defend themselves from those Negroes, using arms if necessary. And I feel that when the law fails to protect Negroes from whites' attack, then those Negroes should use arms, if necessary, to defend themselves."

"Malcolm X Advocates Armed Negroes!"

What was wrong with that? I'll tell you what was wrong. I was a black man talking about physical defense against the white man. The white man can lynch and burn and bomb and beat Negroes—that's all right: "Have patience" . . . "The customs are entrenched" . . . "Things are getting better."

Well, I believe it's a crime for anyone who is being brutalized to continue to accept that brutality without doing something to defend himself. If that's how "Christian" philosophy is interpreted, if that's what Gandhian philosophy teaches, well, then, I will call them criminal philosophies.

I tried in every speech I made to clarify my new position regarding white people—"I don't speak against the sincere, well-meaning, good white people. I have learned that there *are* some. I have learned that not all white people are racists. I am speaking against and my fight is against the white *racists*. I firmly believe that Negroes have the right to fight against these racists, by any means that are necessary."

But the white reporters kept wanting me linked with that word "violence." I doubt if I had one interview without having to deal with that accusation.

"I *am* for violence if non-violence means we continue postponing a solution to the American black man's problem—just to *avoid* violence. I don't go for non-violence if it also means a delayed solution. To me a delayed solution is a non-solution. Or I'll say it another way. If it must take violence to get the black man his human rights in this country, I'm *for* violence exactly as you know the Irish, the Poles, or Jews would be if they were flagrantly discriminated against. I am just as they would be in that case, and they would be for violence—no matter what the consequences, no matter who was hurt by the violence."

White society *hates* to hear anybody, especially a black man, talk about the crime the white man has perpetrated on the black man. I have always understood that's why I have been so frequently called "a revolutionist." It sounds as if *I* have done some crime! Well, it may be the American black man does need to become involved in a *real* revolution. The word for "revolution" in German is *Umwälzung*. What it means is a complete overturn—a complete change. The overthrow of King Farouk in Egypt and the succession of President Nasser is an example of a true revolution. It means the destroying of an old system, and its replacement with a new system. Another example is the Algerian revolution, led by Ben Bella; they threw out the French who had been there over 100 years. So how does anybody sound talking about the Negro in America waging some "revolution"? Yes, he is condemning a system—but he's not trying to overturn the system, or to destroy it. The Negro's so-called "revolt" is merely an asking to be *accepted* into the existing system! A *true* Negro revolt might entail, for instance, fighting for separate black states within this country—which several groups and individuals have advocated, long before Elijah Muhammad came along.

When the white man came into this country, he certainly wasn't demonstrating any "non-violence." In fact, the very man whose name symbolizes non-violence here today has stated:

"Our nation was born in genocide when it embraced the doctrine that the original American, the Indian, was an inferior race. Even before there were large numbers of Negroes on our shores, the scar of racial hatred had already disfigured colonial society. From the sixteenth century forward, blood flowed in battles over racial supremacy. We are perhaps the only nation which tried as a matter of national policy to wipe out its indigenous population. Moreover, we elevated that tragic experience into a noble crusade. Indeed, even today we have not permitted ourselves to reject or to feel remorse for this shameful episode. Our literature, our films, our drama, our folklore all exalt it. Our children are still taught to respect the violence which reduced a red-skinned people of an earlier culture into a few fragmented groups herded into impoverished reservations."

"Peaceful coexistence!" That's another one the white man has always been quick to cry. Fine! But what have been the deeds of the white man? During his entire advance through history, he has been waving the banner of Christianity . . . and carrying in his other hand the sword and the flintlock.

You can go right back to the very beginning of Christianity. Catholicism, the genesis of Christianity as we know it to be presently constituted, with its hierarchy, was conceived in Africa—by those whom the Christian church calls "The Desert Fathers." The Christian church became infected with racism when it entered white Europe. The Christian church returned to Africa under the banner of the Cross —conquering, killing, exploiting, pillaging, raping, bullying, beating—and teaching white supremacy. This is how the white man thrust himself into the position of leadership of the world—through the use of naked physical power. And he was totally inadequate spiritually. Mankind's history has proved from one era to another that the true criterion of leadership is spiritual. Men are attracted by spirit. By power, men are *forced.* Love is engendered by spirit. By power, anxieties are created.

I am in agreement one hundred per cent with those racists who say that no government laws ever can *force* brotherhood. The only true world solution today is governments guided by true religion—of the spirit. Here in race-torn America, I am convinced that the Islam religion is desperately needed, particularly by the American black man. The black man needs to reflect that he has been America's most fervent Christian—and where has it gotten him? In fact, in the white man's hands, in the white man's interpretation . . . where has Christianity brought this world?

It has brought the non-white two-thirds of the human population to rebellion. Two-thirds of the human population today is telling the one-third minority white man, "Get out!" And the white man is leaving. And as he leaves, we see the non-white peoples returning in a rush to their original religions, which had been labeled "pagan" by the conquering white man. Only one religion—Islam—had the power to stand

and fight the white man's Christianity for a *thousand years*! Only Islam could keep white Christianity at bay.

The Africans are returning to Islam and other indigenous religions. The Asians are returning to being Hindus, Buddhists and Muslims.

As the Christian Crusade once went East, now the Islamic Crusade is going West. With the East—Asia—closed to Christianity, with Africa rapidly being converted to Islam, with Europe rapidly becoming un-Christian, generally today it is accepted that the "Christian" civilization of America—which is propping up the white race around the world—is Christianity's remaining strongest bastion.

Well, if *this* is so—if the so-called "Christianity" now being practiced in America displays the best that world Christianity has left to offer—no one in his right mind should need any much greater proof that very close at hand is the *end* of Christianity.

Are you aware that some Protestant theologians, in their writings, are using the phrase "post-Christian era"—and they mean *now*?

And what is the greatest single reason for this Christian church's failure? It is its failure to combat racism. It is the old "You sow, you reap" story. The Christian church sowed racism—blasphemously; now it reaps racism.

Sunday mornings in this year of grace 1965, imagine the "Christian conscience" of congregations guarded by deacons barring the door to black would-be worshipers, telling them "You can't enter *this* House of God!"

Tell me, if you can, a sadder irony than that St. Augustine, Florida —a city named for the black African saint who saved Catholicism from heresy—was recently the scene of bloody race riots.

I believe that God now is giving the world's so-called "Christian" white society its last opportunity to repent and atone for the crimes of exploiting and enslaving the world's non-white peoples. It is exactly as when God gave Pharaoh a chance to repent. But Pharaoh persisted in his refusal to give justice to those whom he oppressed. And, we know, God finally destroyed Pharaoh.

Is white America really sorry for her crimes against the black people? Does white America have the capacity to repent—and to atone? Does the capacity to repent, to atone, exist in a majority, in one-half, in even one-third of American white society?

Many black men, the victims—in fact most black men—would like to be able to forgive, to forget, the crimes.

But most American white people seem not to have it in them to make any serious atonement—to do justice to the black man.

Indeed, how *can* white society atone for enslaving, for raping, for unmanning, for otherwise brutalizing *millions* of human beings, for centuries? What atonement would the God of Justice demand for the robbery of the black people's labor, their lives, their true identities, their culture, their history—and even their human dignity?

A desegregated cup of coffee, a theater, public toilets—the whole range of hypocritical "integration"—these are not atonements.

After a while in America, I returned abroad—and this time, I spent eighteen weeks in the Middle East and Africa.

The world leaders with whom I had private audiences this time included President Gamal Abdel Nasser, of Egypt; President Julius K. Nyerere, of Tanzania; President Nnamoi Azikiwe, of Nigeria; Osagyefo Dr. Kwame Nkrumah, of Ghana; President Sekou Touré, of Guinea; President Jomo Kenyatta, of Kenya; and Prime Minister Dr. Milton Obote, of Uganda.

I also met with religious leaders—African, Arab, Asian, Muslim, and non-Muslim. And in all of these countries, I talked with Afro-Americans and whites of many professions and backgrounds.

An American white ambassador in one African country was Africa's most respected American ambassador: I'm glad to say that this was told to me by one ranking African leader. We talked for an entire afternoon. Based on what I had heard of him, I had to believe him when he told me that as long as he was on the African continent, he never thought in terms of race, that he dealt with human beings, never noticing their color. He said he was more aware of language differences than of color differences. He said that only when he returned to America would he become aware of color differences.

I told him, "What you are telling me is that it isn't the American white *man* who is a racist, but it's the American political, economic, and social *atmosphere* that automatically nourishes a racist psychology in the white man." He agreed.

We both agreed that American society makes it next to impossible for humans to meet in America and not be conscious of their color differences. And we both agreed that if racism could be removed, America could offer a society where rich and poor could truly live like human beings.

That discussion with the ambassador gave me a new insight—one which I like: that the white man is *not* inherently evil, but America's racist society influences him to act evilly. The society has produced and nourishes a psychology which brings out the lowest, most base part of human beings.

I had a totally different kind of talk with another white man I met in Africa—who, to me, personified exactly what the ambassador and I had discussed. Throughout my trip, I was of course aware that I was under constant surveillance. The agent was a particularly obvious and obnoxious one; I am not sure for what agency, as he never identified it, or I would say it. Anyway, this one finally got under my skin when I found I couldn't seem to eat a meal in the hotel without seeing him somewhere around watching me. You would have thought I was John Dillinger or somebody.

I just got up from my breakfast one morning and walked over to where he was and I told him I knew he was following me, and if he wanted to know anything, why didn't he ask me. He started to give me one of those too-lofty-to-descend-to-you attitudes. I told him then right to his face he was a fool, that he didn't know me, or what I stood for, so that made him one of those people who let somebody else do their thinking; and that no matter what job a man had, at least he ought to be able to think for himself. That stung him; he let me have it.

I was, to hear him tell it, anti-American, un-American, seditious, subversive, and probably Communist. I told him that what he said only proved how little he understood about me. I told him that the only thing the F.B.I., the C.I.A., or anybody else could ever find me guilty of, was being open-minded. I said I was seeking for the truth, and I was trying to weigh—objectively—everything on its own merit. I said what I was against was strait-jacketed thinking, and strait-jacketed societies. I said I respected every man's right to believe whatever his intelligence tells him is intellectually sound, and I expect everyone else to respect my right to believe likewise.

This super-sleuth then got off on my "Black Muslim" religious beliefs. I asked him hadn't his headquarters bothered to brief him—that my attitudes and beliefs were changed? I told him that the Islam I believed in now was the Islam which was taught in Mecca—that there was no God but Allah, and that Muhammad ibn Abdullah who lived in the Holy City of Mecca fourteen hundred years ago was the Last Messenger of Allah.

Almost from the first I had been guessing about something; and I took a chance—and I really shook up that "super-sleuth." From the consistent subjectivity in just about every thing he asked and said, I had deduced something, and I told him, "You know, I think you're a Jew with an Anglicized name." His involuntary expression told me I'd hit the button. He asked me how I knew. I told him I'd had so much experience with how Jews would attack me that I usually could identify them. I told him all I held against the Jew was that so many Jews actually were hypocrites in their claim to be friends of the American black man, and it burned me up to be so often called "anti-Semitic" when I spoke things I knew to be the absolute truth about Jews. I told him that, yes, I gave the Jew credit for being among all other whites the most active, and the most vocal, financier, "leader" and "liberal" in the Negro civil rights movement. But I said at the same time I knew that the Jew played these roles for a very careful strategic reason: the more prejudice in America could be focused upon the Negro, then the more the white Gentiles' prejudice would keep diverted off the Jew. I said that to me, one proof that all the civil rights posturing of so many Jews wasn't sincere was that so often in the North the quickest segregationists were Jews themselves. Look at practically everything the black man is trying to "integrate" into for instance; if Jews are not the actual owners, or are not in controlling positions, then they have major stockholdings or they are otherwise in powerful leverage positions—and do they really sincerely exert these influences? No!

And an even clearer proof for me of how Jews truly regard Negroes, I said, was what invariably happened wherever a Negro moved into any white residential neighborhood that was thickly Jewish. Who would always lead the whites' exodus? The Jews! Generally in these situations, some whites stay put—you just notice who they are: they're Irish Catholics, they're Italians; they're rarely ever any Jews. And, ironically, the Jews themselves often still have trouble being "accepted."

Saying this, I know I'll hear "anti-Semitic" from every direction again. Oh, yes! But truth is truth.

Politics dominated the American scene while I was traveling abroad this time. In Cairo and again in Accra, the American press wire services reached me with trans-Atlantic calls, asking whom did I favor, Johnson—or Goldwater?

I said I felt that as far as the American black man was concerned they were both just about the same. I felt that it was for the black man only a question of Johnson, the fox, or Goldwater, the wolf.

"Conservatism" in America's politics means "Let's keep the niggers in their place." And "liberalism" means "Let's keep the *knee*-grows in their place—but tell them we'll treat them a little better; let's fool them more, with more promises." With these choices, I felt that the American black man only needed to choose which one to be eaten by, the "liberal" fox or the "conservative" wolf—because both of them would eat him.

I didn't go for Goldwater any more than for Johnson—except that in a wolf's den, I'd always know exactly where I stood; I'd watch the dangerous wolf closer than I would the smooth, sly fox. The wolf's very growling would keep me alert and fighting him to survive, whereas I *might* be lulled and fooled by the tricky fox. I'll give you an illustration of the fox. When the assassination in Dallas made Johnson President, who was the first person he called for? It was for his best friend, "Dicky"—Richard Russell of Georgia. Civil rights was "a moral issue," Johnson was declaring to everybody—while his best friend was the Southern racist who *led* the civil rights opposition. How would some sheriff sound, declaring himself so against bank robbery —and Jesse James his best friend?

Goldwater as a man, I respected for speaking out his true convictions—something rarely done in politics today. He wasn't whispering to racists and smiling at integrationists. I felt Goldwater wouldn't have risked his unpopular stand without conviction. He flatly told black men he wasn't for them—and there is this to consider: always, the black people have advanced further when they have seen they had to rise up against a system that they clearly saw was outright against them. Under the steady lullabys sung by foxy liberals, the Northern Negro became a beggar. But the Southern Negro, facing the honestly snarling white man, rose up to battle that white man for his freedom—long before it happened in the North.

Anyway, I didn't feel that Goldwater was any better for black men than Johnson, or vice-versa. I wasn't in the United States at election time, but if I had been, I wouldn't have put myself in the position of voting for either candidate for the Presidency, or of recommending to any black man to do so. It has turned out that it's Johnson in the White House—and black votes were a major factor in his winning as decisively as he wanted to. If it had been Goldwater, all I am saying is that the black people would at least have known they were dealing with an honestly growling wolf, rather than a fox who could have them half-digested before they even knew what was happening.

I kept having all kinds of troubles trying to develop the kind of Black Nationalist organization I wanted to build for the American Negro. Why Black Nationalism? Well, in the competitive American society, how can there ever be any white-black solidarity before there is first some black solidarity? If you will remember, in my childhood I had been exposed to the Black Nationalist teachings of Marcus Garvey —which, in fact, I had been told had led to my father's murder. Even when I was a follower of Elijah Muhammad, I had been strongly aware of how the Black Nationalist political, economic and social philosophies had the ability to instill within black men the racial dignity, the incentive, and the confidence that the black race needs today to get up off its knees, and to get on its feet, and get rid of its scars, and to take a stand for itself.

One of the major troubles that I was having in building the organization that I wanted—an all-black organization whose ultimate objective was to help create a society in which there could exist honest white-black brotherhood—was that my earlier public image, my old so-called "Black Muslim" image, kept blocking me. I was trying to gradually reshape that image. I was trying to turn a corner, into a new regard by the public, especially Negroes; I was no less angry than I had been, but at the same time the true brotherhood I had seen in the Holy World had influenced me to recognize that anger can blind human vision.

Every free moment I could find, I did a lot of talking to key people whom I knew around Harlem, and I made a lot of speeches, saying: "True Islam taught me that it takes *all* of the religious, political, economic, psychological, and racial ingredients, or characteristics, to make the Human Family and the Human Society complete.

"Since I learned the *truth* in Mecca, my dearest friends have come to include *all* kinds—some Christians, Jews, Buddhists, Hindus, agnostics, and even atheists! I have friends who are called capitalists, Socialists, and Communists! Some of my friends are moderates, conservatives, extremists—some are even Uncle Toms! My friends today are black, brown, red, yellow, and *white*!"

I said to Harlem street audiences that only when mankind would submit to the One God who created all—only then would mankind even approach the "peace" of which so much *talk* could be heard . . . but toward which so little *action* was seen.

I said that on the American racial level, we had to approach the black man's struggle against the white man's racism as a human problem, that we had to forget hypocritical politics and propaganda. I said that both races, as human beings, had the obligation, the responsibility, of helping to correct America's human problem. The well-meaning white people, I said, had to combat, actively and directly, the racism in other white people. And the black people had to build within themselves much greater awareness that along with equal rights there had to be the bearing of equal responsibilities.

I knew, better than most Negroes, how many white people truly wanted to see American racial problems solved. I knew that many whites were as frustrated as Negroes. I'll bet I got fifty letters some days from white people. The white people in meeting audiences would throng around me, asking me, after I had addressed them somewhere, "What *can* a sincere white person do?"

When I say that here now, it makes me think about that little co-ed I told you about, the one who flew from her New England college down to New York and came up to me in the Nation of Islam's restaurant in Harlem, and I told her that there was "nothing" she could do. I regret that I told her that. I wish that now I knew her name, or where I could telephone her, or write to her, and tell her what I tell white people now when they present themselves as being sincere, and ask me, one way or another, the same thing that she asked.

The first thing I tell them is that at least where my own particular Black Nationalist organization, the Organization of Afro-American

Unity, is concerned, they can't *join* us. I have these very deep feelings that white people who want to join black organizations are really just taking the escapist way to salve their consciences. By visibly hovering near us, they are "proving" that they are "with us." But the hard truth is this *isn't* helping to solve America's racist problem. The Negroes aren't the racists. Where the really sincere white people have got to do their "proving" of themselves is not among the black *victims*, but out on the battle lines of where America's racism really *is*—and that's in their own home communities; America's racism is among their own fellow whites. That's where the sincere whites who really mean to accomplish something have got to work.

Aside from that, I mean nothing against any sincere whites when I say that as members of black organizations, generally whites' very presence subtly renders the black organization automatically less effective. Even the best white members will slow down the Negroes' discovery of what they need to do, and particularly of what they can do—for themselves, working by themselves, among their own kind, in their own communities.

I sure don't want to hurt anybody's feelings, but in fact I'll even go so far as to say that I never really trust the kind of white people who are always so anxious to hang around Negroes, or to hang around in Negro communities. I don't trust the kind of whites who love having Negroes always hanging around them. I don't know—this feeling may be a throwback to the years when I was hustling in Harlem and all of those red-faced, drunk whites in the afterhours clubs were always grabbing hold of some Negroes and talking about "I just want you to know you're just as good as I am—" And then they got back in their taxicabs and black black limousines and went back downtown to the places where they lived and worked, where no blacks except servants had better get caught. But, anyway, I know that every time that whites join a black organization, you watch, pretty soon the blacks will be leaning on the whites to support it, and before you know it a black may be up front with a title, but the whites, because of their money, are the real controllers.

I tell sincere white people, "Work in conjunction with us—each of us working among our own kind." Let sincere white individuals find all other white people they can who feel as they do—and let them form their own all-white groups, to work trying to convert other white people who are thinking and acting so racist. Let sincere whites go and teach non-violence to white people!

We will completely respect our white co-workers. They will deserve every credit. We will give them every credit. We will meanwhile be working among our own kind, in our own black communities—showing and teaching black men in ways that only other black men can—that the black man has got to help himself. Working separately, the sincere white people and sincere black people actually will be working together.

In our mutual sincerity we might be able to show a road to the salvation of America's very soul. It can only be salvaged if human rights and dignity, in full, are extended to black men. Only such real, meaningful actions as those which are sincerely motivated from a deep sense of humanism and moral responsibility can get at the basic causes that produce the racial explosions in America today. Otherwise, the racial explosions are only going to grow worse. Certainly nothing is ever going to be solved by throwing upon me and other so-called black "extremists" and "demagogues" the blame for the racism that is in America.

Sometimes, I have dared to dream to myself that one day, history may even say that my voice—which disturbed the white man's smugness, and his arrogance, and his complacency—that my voice helped to save America from a grave, possibly even a fatal catastrophe.

The goal has always been the same, with the approaches to it as different as mine and Dr. Martin Luther King's non-violent marching, that dramatizes the brutality and the evil of the white man against defenseless blacks. And in the racial climate of this country today, it is anybody's guess which of the "extremes" in approach to the black man's problems might *personally* meet a fatal catastrophe first—"non-violent" Dr. King, or so-called "violent" me.

Anything I do today, I regard as urgent. No man is given but so much time to accomplish whatever is his life's work. My life in particular never has stayed fixed in one position for very long. You have seen how throughout my life, I have often known unexpected drastic changes.

I am only facing the facts when I know that any moment of any day, or any night, could bring me death. This is particularly true since the last trip that I made abroad. I have seen the nature of things that are happening, and I have heard things from sources which are reliable.

To speculate about dying doesn't disturb me as it might some people. I never have felt that I would live to become an old man. Even before I was a Muslim—when I was a hustler in the ghetto jungle, and then a criminal in prison, it always stayed on my mind that I would die a violent death. In fact, it runs in my family. My father and most of his brothers died by violence—my father because of what he believed in. To come right down to it, if I take the kind of things in which I believe, then add to that the kind of temperament that I have, plus the one hundred per cent dedication I have to whatever I believe in—these are ingredients which make it just about impossible for me to die of old age.

I have given to this book so much of whatever time I have because I feel, and I hope, that if I honestly and fully tell my life's account, read objectively it might prove to be a testimony of some social value.

I think that an objective reader may see how in the society to which I was exposed as a black youth here in America, for me to wind up in a prison was really just about inevitable. It happens to so many thousands of black youth.

I think that an objective reader may see how when I heard "The white man is the devil," when I played back what had been my own experiences, it was inevitable that I would respond positively; then the next twelve years of my life were devoted and dedicated to propagating that phrase among the black people.

I think, I hope, that the objective reader, in following my life—the life of only one ghetto-created Negro—may gain a better picture and understanding than he has previously had of the black ghettoes which are shaping the lives and the thinking of almost all of the 22 million Negroes who live in America.

Thicker each year in these ghettoes is the kind of teen-ager that I was—with the wrong kinds of heroes, and the wrong kinds of influences. I am not saying that all of them become the kind of parasite that I was. Fortunately, by far most do not. But still, the small fraction who do add up to an annual total of more and more costly, dangerous youthful criminals. The F.B.I. not long ago released a report of a shocking rise in crime each successive year since the end of World War II—ten to twelve per cent each year. The report did not say so in so many words, but I am saying that the majority of that crime increase is annually spawned in the black ghettoes which the American racist society permits to exist. In the 1964 "long, hot summer" riots in major cities across the United States, the socially disinherited black ghetto youth were always at the forefront.

In this year, 1965, I am certain that more—and worse—riots are going to erupt, in yet more cities, in spite of the conscience-salving Civil Rights Bill. The reason is that the *cause* of these riots, the racist malignancy in America, has been too long unattended.

I believe that it would be almost impossible to find anywhere in America a black man who has lived further down in the mud of human society than I have; or a black man who has been any more ignorant than I have been; or a black man who has suffered more anguish during his life than I have. But it is only after the deepest darkness that the greatest joy can come; it is only after slavery and prison that the sweetest appreciation of freedom can come.

For the freedom of my 22 million black brothers and sisters here in America, I do believe that I have fought the best that I knew how, and the best that I could, with the shortcomings that I have had. I know that my shortcomings are many.

My greatest lack has been, I believe, that I don't have the kind of academic education I wish I had been able to get—to have been a lawyer, perhaps. I do believe that I might have made a good lawyer. I have always loved verbal battle, and challenge. You can believe me that if I had the time right now, I would not be one bit ashamed to go back into any New York City public school and start where I left off at the ninth grade, and go on through a degree. Because I don't begin to be academically equipped for so many of the interests that I have. For instance, I love languages. I wish I were an accomplished linguist. I don't know anything more frustrating than to be around people talking something you can't understand. Especially when they are people who look just like you. In Africa, I heard original mother tongues, such as Hausa, and Swahili, being spoken, and there I was standing like some little boy, waiting for someone to tell me what had been said; I never will forget how ignorant I felt.

Aside from the basic African dialects, I would try to learn Chinese, because it looks as if Chinese will be the most powerful political language of the future. And already I have begun studying Arabic, which I think is going to be the most powerful spiritual language of the future.

I would just like to *study*. I mean ranging study, because I have a wide-open mind. I'm interested in almost any subject you can mention. I know this is the reason I have come to really like, as individuals, some of the hosts of radio or television panel programs I have been on, and to respect their minds—because even if they have been almost steadily in disagreement with me on the race issue, they still have kept their minds open and objective about the truths of things happening in this world. Irv Kupcinet in Chicago, and Barry Farber, Barry Gray and Mike Wallace in New York—people like them. They also let me see that they respected my mind—in a way I know they never realized. The way I knew was that often they would invite my opinion on subjects off the race issue. Sometimes, after the programs, we would sit around and talk about all kinds of things, current events and other things, for an hour or more. You see, most whites, even when they credit a Negro with some intelligence, will still feel that all he can talk about is the race issue; most whites never feel that Negroes can contribute anything to other areas of thought, and ideas. You just notice how rarely you will ever hear whites asking any Negroes what they think about the problem of world health, or the space race to land men on the moon.

Every morning when I wake up, now, I regard it as having another borrowed day. In any city, wherever I go, making speeches, holding meetings of my organization, or attending to other business, black men are watching every move I make, awaiting their chance to kill me. I have said publicly many times that I know that they have their orders. Anyone who chooses not to believe what I am saying doesn't know the Muslims in the Nation of Islam.

But I am also blessed with faithful followers who are, I believe, as dedicated to me as I once was to Mr. Elijah Muhammad. Those who would hunt a man need to remember that a jungle also contains those who hunt the hunters.

I know, too, that I could suddenly die at the hands of some white racists. Or I could die at the hands of some Negro hired by the white man. Or it could be some brainwashed Negro acting on his own idea that by eliminating me he would be helping out the white man, because I talk about the white man the way I do.

Anyway, now, each day I live as if I am already dead, and I tell you what I would like for you to do. When I *am* dead—I say it that way because from the things I *know,* I do not expect to live long enough to read this book in its finished form—I want you to just watch and see if I'm not right in what I say: that the white man, in his press, is going to identify me with "hate."

He will make use of me dead, as he has made use of me alive, as a convenient symbol of "hatred"—and that will help him to escape facing the truth that all I have been doing is holding up a mirror to reflect, to show, the history of unspeakable crimes that his race has committed against my race.

You watch. I will be labeled as, at best, an "irresponsible" black man. I have always felt about this accusation that the black "leader" whom white men consider to be "responsible" is invariably the black "leader" who never gets any results. You only get action as a black man if you are regarded by the white man as "irresponsible." In fact, this much I had learned when I was just a little boy. And since I have been some kind of a "leader" of black people here in the racist society of America, I have been more reassured each time the white man resisted me, or attacked me harder—because each time made me more certain that I was on the right track in the American black man's best interests. The racist white man's opposition automatically made me know that I did offer the black man something worthwhile.

Yes, I have cherished my "demagogue" role. I know that societies often have killed the people who have helped to change those societies. And if I can die having brought any light, having exposed any meaningful truth that will help to destroy the racist cancer that is malignant in the body of America—then, all of the credit is due to Allah. Only the mistakes have been mine.

Ben Bagdikan □ The Black Immigrants

The problem of the Negro migrant, one that began in the 1880's, continues today as thousands of blacks pour into northern cities every year. In this article, Ben Bagdikan shows just how difficult the move can become.

At 6:40 on the evening of March 4, 1967, Walter Austin, who had lived for almost half a century within 60 miles of the Mississippi, actually saw the river for the first time. Still wearing his four dollar overalls, he was sitting in the back seat of an automobile, jammed in with four other members of his family, crossing a high bridge. His eyes were red with the fatigue of the last 38 sleepless hours. But he stared down through the dusk at the aluminum reflection of the greatest body of water he had ever seen, and he said the same thing that rose out of him earlier when someone told him that in New York City there is a building 102 stories high: a low, slow, "Good gracious!" The car moved across the bridge, its occupants turning to keep in sight the massive river that had been the source of life and of suffering for five generations of Austin families. And then the river was gone, and they turned forward again to look uncertainly into the darkness ahead.

It was the most momentous crossing of their lives. From that time on their experiences would be like nothing they or their ancestors had ever known. That morning they had been just another impoverished

Negro family working the fields on a remote Mississippi plantation. But at noon, with hardly a backward glance, they had slammed the doors of the two cars driven by a relative and a friend and headed north for a new life in the city. They carried all they could from the last hog they would ever butcher—the salted jaw, a slab of salt pork, two hams, 100 pounds of lard—stashed in the car like sacred objects. Riding with them as well was a new and confusing collection of hopes and fears.

That day the Austins—father, mother, five children aged 17 to 6, and one grandchild—added their eight lives to a flow of Americans that is one of the great unsung sagas of human history. It is an uprooting of more people in a shorter period of time than almost any peacetime migration known to man, a vast transfer that is changing America.

In a wicked moment Franklin Roosevelt once put a chill on a convention of the Daughters of the American Revolution by greeting them, "My fellow immigrants," and it is true enough that one thing all Americans share is a background of migration. The American Indians were immigrants, probably from Asia; the forebears of most white Americans came from Europe in the largest intercontinental human movement in history; the ancestors of most American Negroes were the 400,000 Africans brought into the South as slaves between 1619 and 1808. Now the descendants of these Negro immigrants are making another mass move, this time within the United States.

In this generation, some four million Negroes have left the South, most of them for six states: California, Illinois, Michigan, New York, Ohio and Pennsylvania. Where 50 years ago three quarters of Negro Americans were in rural areas, today three quarters are in cities. And the tide still runs strong. In 1960 there were four American cities that were 40 percent Negro; by 1970 there will be 14, and practically every city of any size will have a core of migrant Negroes, piling up, desperate. Like previous migrants, they are truly aliens, used to different customs, a different climate, essentially a different language, different everything. Their ghettos are countries within countries, in which nearly every inhabitant feels foreign to what surrounds him. But what surrounds the city Negroes is more hostile than anything any white alien has ever encountered. For them the ghetto perimeters are closed as tightly as foreign borders.

This exodus of southern Negroes is one of the most dramatic demographic events of the mid-century, yet it is a clandestine operation. When the Negro goes, he goes suddenly and secretly, because he is afraid of the white man. Generally, the Negro is a sharecropper, living in a feudal, noncash economy—his plantation owner provides him land and credit. When the harvest is over, the plantation owner announces that, after deducting the cost of food, fuel, seed, fertilizer and other things the sharecropper has obtained on credit, the sharecropper's profit is such and such. Or, much more likely, the owner tells him he owes the plantation as much as $100 or $500.

To the Negro this kind of debt is so astronomical that no one, laborer or landlord, expects that it will ever be paid off in cash. Only by working off the debt can the Negro family be clear. As manual farm work gives way to huge machines, the means of paying back the debt disappears. When that happens, most plantation owners are resigned to seeing their tenants leave.

Even so, there is often a question of who gets the paid-for television or kitchen range, in light of the debt, the landlord or the departing family's friends and relatives? And the rural Negro has been taught in the harshest way never to make an important decision without the approval of his landlord. So when he moves North, the Negro usually goes unannounced, a final gesture of rebellion and fear.

The families themselves seldom know when they will go until the moment comes. Moving vans are unknown to the dirt roads of the rural South, and departure frequently depends on the car of a visiting relative. Thus the times of greatest population loss in the South are the holidays—Christmas, New Year's, Memorial Day, July 4, Labor Day, any long weekend when city relatives can make the long trip down from the North. And at funerals. The South loses more than the dead at funerals. A brother from Chicago who comes down for the ceremony, having driven the 12 hours since work let out on Friday, arrives Saturday morning before dawn, and suddenly some of the youngsters, or the whole family, decide to go back with him.

Sometimes the mail arrives with the awaited passport: bus tickets sent by older children in the city. The next day the younger children drop out of school, and after dark that night the family heads for the station, carrying in their hands everything with which they will start their new life.

Or a mother takes the youngest children to "visit my sick aunty in the city," where she gets a job and sends the tickets back for her husband and the older children, and the next Saturday night the husband pays a neighbor $1.50 to drive him and his children and their suitcases to the station. Morning on the plantation finds the shack abandoned, and another rural family has entered the central mass of an American metropolis.

The decision to abandon a way of life, even one you love, can seem very simple.

"Christmas morning, last Christmas morning," Walter Austin said in his deep and vibrant voice, "I got up and I cried." Weeping did not seem to go with the dark, weather-beaten face. Austin is 48, has black hair without gray and a black moustache, and wears rugged-looking overalls and rubber boots clotted with mud. "I cried, and then I thanked the Lord to be living, because I could have been gone, and I was glad to be here, and all my children well. And the children had food. It put me in debt, but they had food, special Christmas food. For Christmas I saw to it that they had fresh apples and oranges."

Over and over he returned to the subject of moving to the city where, he knew, it takes even more money than in the country.

"Yes, yes, but you need *some* money here. You need *some* money here. I can't sit here with eight children"—he kept referring to eight children, though his two oldest sons had left for the city within the last two months—"I can't have my children around me and nothing to give them to eat. I feel bad in the morning. I feel *bad* in the morning, hearing the kids get up crying because they want something to eat and I can't find enough for them to eat. Then I feel bad. Then I feel like crying."

So the easy decision is really whether to eat or not. But there is a harder question for older people who know only their rural life and who love it. Walter Austin and his wife, Bessie, who is also 48, were born in Holmes County, Miss., but 10 years ago moved the 50 miles to Merigold, Miss., in Bolivar County.

"I don't want to leave Mississippi," Austin said. "I never been out of Mississippi except one time in my whole life, and that was only one week. Tell you the truth, up to the sixteenth day of March, 19 and 57, I never been out of Holmes County. I never been in no kind of trouble, never paid a fine, never been to court. I'll peck on wood"—he reached over the torn leatherette arm of the chair in his living room and rapped the bare wood floor of the shack with his knuckles—"I've been just plain Walter all my life."

We had spent hours talking country-versus-city, and there wasn't much doubt where he stood, given a free choice and enough food.

"I likes to farm. I loves it. I can raise my chickens, raise my hog, I have my garden with peas and beans and potatoes and squash and cucumbers and onions and greens. You can't do that in town. You can't raise a hog in town. I'm just a home child. I just don't want to leave home unless I have to. I'll be frank with you, I like the country."

He lifted his leather cap and scratched his hair.

"I know in the city you's supposed to have an education. If you got me a job in the morning and I was supposed to separate the salt from the sugar, I couldn't do it, not if they was in the same kind of bag, I couldn't do it, Cap'n, because I can't read."

His wife, with a soft face drawn with worry, and a blurry right eye blinded by a stroke seven years ago, told about a visit she made once to Chicago.

"I stayed with my husband's brother. I didn't even walk on the outside. That's all I know, what I saw from his place. I just couldn't stand that noise.

"I'd be satisfied working right here. If we had work. If I had enough to live on and be comfortable. Oh, I'd stay. I'd stay."

What did she mean, "comfortable"?

"Nothing extra. You come into this world with nothing, and when you leave you can't carry anything away. I need some covers—quilts, you know—comfortable mattresses, some beds don't need to be propped up. I would like some clothes."

She thought for a moment and then worried that I might misunderstand her desire for clothes. She didn't mean for herself (she bought her last dress in 1956, her husband had never bought a suit and limited his new clothes to a four-dollar pair of overalls each year).

"I mean for the children. And nothing fancy, just not all sewed up. Not half-priced or leftovers but good common clothes, you know? Not eight-dollar dresses, just good three-dollar dresses. What I need most is extra underclothes and socks. We have enough outerclothes so the kids can wear clean things to school, but the children have to wash their underwear and socks every night so they'll be clean in the morning. If they had extra sets they wouldn't have to wash them every night."

Walter Austin looked in mock severity at the apple of his eye, his 10-year-old daughter, Bessie.

"I gets up at four o'clock every morning. At four o'clock I'm up, Sunday, Saturday, rain, sleet or snow. I put on my clothes, wash my face, go out and feed my hog, feed my chickens, and then I come back in and see if the kids has washed their clothes before they went to bed, and if they didn't, then I gets them up early so they can do it before schooltime and give their underclothes and socks a chance to dry in time. Ain't that so, Bessie?"

Bessie obviously was the most recent transgressor, and she smiled sheepishly and said to her father, "Suh?" By "early," Austin explained, he meant the backsliding child rose at 5 A.M. instead of the usual 6.

To Mrs. Austin the prospect of the city held out the deadly danger that the children would learn to drink. Walter Austin would miss his farming and would no longer experience the pride of running and repairing a large combine. But the children had different thoughts. Frances, 17, whose formal, bland expression masked a quick and taunting wit, was fatalistic—"I think things would be just the same whether I go or stay"—but she looked excited when she described how well-dressed her girl friends and relatives were when they returned from the city. David, 14, also wore an outer mask of solemnity, but his black-cloth visor cap worn at a rakish angle hinted at the adolescent itch. "I just don't want to farm. No, suh. I just don't want to be a farmer." Hearing about the city, Bessie simply glowed wordlessly. Her younger sister, Zettie Mae, 8, and brother, Wendell, 6, looked bewildered and polite.

But their parents kept reminding themselves how much better off they are now than they were in their youth. Neither of them had ever lived in so good a house as this one. It had a tight roof, the five rooms were lined with wallboard. There was a cold-water faucet in the kitchen and a privy out back (some plantation shacks lack even a privy). Three open gas grates heated the place in winter, and they had some chairs, bedsteads, and from a few good years in the early 1960's a television set and a freezer, all paid for.

"My mother's house back in Holmes County," Walter Austin said, "you could see the chickens through the floor and the blue sky through the roof. And when I was a kid, what I had to eat for the whole day was one slice of hog jaw and corn bread with flour gravy, sometimes not even that.

"Now here's David here, fourteen years old and he's in—what grade is it? Eighth—yes, the eighth grade. When I was seven years old I was trying to go to school but, Lordy, I just had to work. When I was seven years old I had to walk three miles before sunup, get a mule and feed it and then work that mule in the fields until dark, all of that for only eight dollars a month.

"I married Bessie, here, the only wife I've ever known, when we were both seventeen, and the day we got married we ate corn bread and flour gravy. We started with an old wood stove, a bed, a pig and a calf my mother-in-law give me."

The family worked for 20 years on a plantation in Holmes County. At the end of that time, Austin was driving a tractor for $4.50 a day, during the season and when weather was good. Mrs. Austin and the children did sharecropping for the same plantation, planting, chopping (weeding) and picking a cotton crop. They provided the labor and the landlord provided the land and their rent-free house. The landlord also gave them credit for their share of the cost of their seed and fertilizer and lent then $40 a month for food until the crop was harvested and sold.

"The four kids and I," Mrs. Austin said, "that last year, did twenty-six bales. We had to keep the kids out of school to do it. But I got tired, just tired going with the crops, weighing my own cotton, tromping it, putting it on the trailer. I got so tired. As a woman, I couldn't farm no more." At that time she had seven living children, ages 19 to 4, the older ones working in the field, the younger ones brought out in boxes to play all day near the cotton rows. Two infants died early, and a daughter later died of leukemia at the age of 16. "And all we got for that year and twenty-six bales of cotton was a hundred and fifty dollars. The four kids and I, from May to October. When I told the boss man I just couldn't sharecrop with the four kids no more, he told us we'd have to move. That's when we come down here."

(The average price farmers received for cotton in 1956 was $152 a bale, so the Austins' half share apparently was $1,976, minus $480 lent for food and their share of seed and fertilizer; neither they nor anyone they knew ever saw an accounting.)

Walter's brother heard of an empty house in Bolivar County, and they moved, and though they loved Holmes County better than anyplace else on earth, they considered themselves much improved. People had a little bit more. In Holmes, median income for the rural Negro family was $895 a year; in Bolivar it was $1,198. The Austins didn't know that, but they sensed it, and they sensed that their new plantation owner and agent were more benign. And the house was better.

Life was not easy, of course. They had more children. Their daughter, Jean, had leukemia and spent the last six weeks of her life in University Hospital in Jackson, 100 miles away, where her father lived, penniless, in a chair in her room, fed by compassionate nurses. After she died, he returned home to find that his daughter, Bessie, had been born, and his wife was back in another hospital with the shock that blinded her right eye. But, then, life had never been easy, and their family kept its strong bonds and Walter Austin his mastery within the family.

The world of the Austins in Mississippi was simultaneously enormous and tiny. Their little home was a dot in the Mississippi delta, a flat ocean of land made from the silt of centuries of flooding, land as rich as any on earth. Square mile after square mile of cotton fields stretch out, in the winter a rusty sea with here and there a scrap of windblown paper snagged on a dry stalk like a whitecap. The huge landscape is punctuated by an occasional small town, a cotton gin, a stand of oaks, and the clusters of Negro shacks in the fields. Like most southern rural Negroes, the Austins lived on a dirt road without a name, in a house without a number. But though the view seems endless, their neighbors were few, their life concentrated around their own family.

"Watch for a burned-out house on the highway," a relative instructed me, "turn left and go in three miles and look for a brown house with a tan 1959 Chevy that's broke down."

I was lucky to have met the Austins before they decided to move and to be with them when they changed their minds, for their experience told much about the thoughts and emotions of families facing the great migration. Before he knew he would go, Walter Austin had uppermost in his mind the improvements he had seen since his youth and all the things he liked in the country and feared in the city. He was genuinely undecided. The plantation owner had told him there would be no guaranteed work the next year because their cotton acreage was being rented to a big agricultural operator. But the owner held out the possibility of a job in a machine shop in a nearby town, or, at least, some days of casual labor in the fields.

The pressure increased, especially during the winter, when work ceases in the delta fields. Merchants knew at once that Austin had been put in the doubtful category. Where credit for food, bottled gas and doctors had once been immediate, everyone wanted cash. Families around them were going away. Ten years earlier 50 families worked and the skies of the delta now were regularly streaked with smoke from empty shanties being burned down to clear the ground for growing. The smoke got thicker after a one-dollar-an-hour wages-and-hours law for agricultural workers began last winter. When motorists stopped one day to watch a spectacular fire consuming a plantation shack, the agent in charge called out, "Wages and hours got that one."

Yet the Austins hung on. He was a good worker. His plantation agent, within limits of feudalistic white supremacy, was a decent man. Each day Austin rose at 4, went to the plantation headquarters at 7. If there was work, he returned after dark, $10-minus-debts the richer. If there was no work, as was most often the case, he went home and worked in his yard and garden.

Mrs. Austin rose at 5:30 to start breakfast of sausage and corn bread, if they had it. The children rose at 6 and got ready for the 7:20 school bus, if they all had shoes. After school they played with the children of the few remaining neighbors, did homework, had supper of greens and salt pork, and were in bed around 8.

The end of the week was different. On a typical Saturday, David lighted a fire in the backyard under an ancient iron pot and heated water for the washing. Frances did the wash in a round, wringer-style washing machine on the back stoop and hung it on the "clothesline"—two strands, one old electrical cable, the other old barbed wire. David helped his father clean up the backyard. The hog grunted, and Walter Austin rubbed its head with his glove—"Baby, you want your breakfast?"—and told David to fetch the slops. Instantly at the trough were the pig, three puppies, two cats, four kittens and two roosters.

The three younger children, bundled in bright donated clothes, played hopscotch on packed earth at the end of some cotton rows, tiny scarlet figures under a huge sky, chased by their puppies, Frisco, Fuzzy and Alaska.

In the evening they look at television. "I cain't read," Walter Austin explained, "so I have to get the news and weather on the TV."

And they sang, Bessie leading and her mother and the others following. They coaxed David to do his imitation of a local preacher. His father called gaily to his children in the living room, using the private names he dreams up at their birth, and he alone uses: "Preacher" for Wendell, "Chicken" for Zettie Mae, "Barbie" for Bessie, "Ben" for David, and "Root" for Frances.

"Ben," he said, "Let's hear the one, 'Your God and My Love.'"

During the singing, the three youngest children played school with the most magnificent Christmas gift any Austin ever got, a plastic-and-chrome children's table-and-chair set from two years ago. As always, Bessie was the teacher, sitting at the table, facing Zettie Mae and Wendell in chairs.

"Wendell," she said imperiously, "spell . . ." and she said what sounded like, "gown."

Wendell, puzzled: "Gown?"

Bessie, impatiently, "Yes, 'gown.'"

Wendell, timidly, "Like, 'machine gown'?"

Bessie, outraged, "No, Wendell, no! Like, 'Yesterday they went. Now they is gown.'"

Everyone laughed, though teachers know that this kind of misunderstanding is significant in explaining the difficulties in reading and learning among children whose natural tongue is not standard English.

Later there were baths, in a galvanized washtub put in Frances's room, the most private one, with a heater.

During the evenings the Austins constantly churned over their view of the future. "I wants to stay, I wants to stay," Walter Austin said. "If I could just get that machine-shop job or work in the boss man's pig farm where they works rain or shine. But how in the world am I going to feed eight kids on fifteen dollars a week?"

Periodically he'd resign himself to moving. "But after the snow is off up there. I is naked here, and up north I'm going to freeze."

None of us was prepared for what happened. One Sunday, photographer Matt Herron and I decided to visit the Austins' small church in the fields. Eight years ago 70 people would attend but now, with the migration, only 20. As we drove we were surprised to see Walter Austin and David out on the road, flagging us down. Walter Austin looked grave, his face gray with tension.

"They don't want you to go to the church because they's afraid it'll get burned down. The deacons, they ask would you please not go."

He explained that the day before, the plantation agent announced that Austin would have to move, telling him angrily, "Those white men kept coming and coming and coming to your place, and that's more than I can take. I know what they're doing. They're down here organizing a union. The state's full of them. So you better leave." Austin could take some time, the agent said, but he had to go.

The concern in Walter Austin's face was justified: To fall out of favor, angrily and catastrophically, with the boss man, especially for unauthorized dealings with outsiders, implied peril to life and limb.

The nearest public phone was six miles away. We drove to it, and Austin called a married daughter in Springfield. Ill. She was alarmed. She urged her father to come that night "before something happens, please, Daddy." But Austin's voice was calm as he spoke on the phone. "No, baby, I need a week to sell my freezer and my hog and take care of things."

We drove Walter and David Austin back to their home and went to see the plantation agent, a round-faced man in his 60's. He and his wife, the plantation bookkeeper, were civil though they were often angry. They recited our movements in the state for the last week; it is not difficult for plantation operators in Mississippi to keep track of suspicious strangers. They told us they knew we were stirring up "our people" and forming a union. Furthermore, we had violated common rules of courtesy. "You can drive down that road," he said, "and you can maybe stop at a house once. But to keep coming and coming and coming and staying after dark—that's too much."

After about an hour we persuaded him we were not organizers, and we parted in a friendly way. In a sense, this was unusual, but what the agent did was even more so. The next day he went to Walter Austin and apologized for falsely accusing him and said he could stay. Austin says he thanked the agent, but he had decided to move, and so he told the agent that he was going through with it. "Boss Man, you was dissatisfied with Walter, so Walter's going to move.

The agent told him he didn't have to sneak off like all the others. And Walter Austin didn't.

The next Saturday morning the Austin place looked like the center of a carnival. A total of 23 neighbors and friends were in and out of the house, up on the roof dismantling the motorized television antenna (bought for $149 four years ago and now sold for $5), carrying out the freezer (bought for $400 and now sold for $50). There was gaiety and almost no sentimentality.

Walter Austin, quietly, calmly, and with humor, left no doubt who was in charge. At 7 he had gone to the agent's house, returned a ladder, a set of wrenches, and paid back $7 the agent had lent him last fall so David could have shoes for school. Neither one said anything, but they both knew Walter Austin was leaving that day.

Austin quietly directed his son-in-law and his oldest son, who had driven down in the night from Springfield. Wandering through the yard was Walter's 29-year-old brother, who worked on the same plantation, and toward the end he said almost to himself, "I'm the only one left." When the time came, Walter and his brother looked at each other briefly, and Walter said, "Good-bye, son."

Frances and her boyfriend talked constantly, arms linked. An old parlor chair, the one with the torn leatherette covering, couldn't be taken, and they gave it to Frances's boyfriend, who carried it out. Walter said, "You get to keep the chair, Robert, but you'd like to keep Frances."

A recent plantation acquaintance tried too often to engage Walter's attention, and finally in exasperation Walter said to him politely, "Well, good-bye and come see me."

"How will I know where you'll be?" the acquaintance said too eagerly. "I don't even know where you're going."

Austin: "I'm going yonder."

Acquaintance: "Where's yonder?"

Austin, nodding northward: "Up."

Finally, Walter Austin walked through his stripped house. Gone from the living-room walls were the photographs of his children and some of his 15 grandchildren; the shadowbox of Jesus with the burned-out electric bulb; the pink plastic cross with the chrome crucifix; the small window frame containing postcards of Cherokee Indians and a table of decimal equivalents; and the too-bright picture of a romantic thatched-roof cottage surrounded by seed-catalogue flowers with the legend, GOD SHALL SUPPLY ALL YOUR NEEDS.

Walter Austin looked around and saw one remaining artifact on the faded blue wall—a calendar of the "Delta Burial Corporation, Seldom Equaled, Never Excelled," the society to which they paid $3.75 a month to guarantee them a decent Mississippi funeral. He hesitated a moment, then lifted the calendar off its nail and handed it to Bessie. "Barbie, in the green car."

In the kitchen he looked at the stove he had just bought on time but not made any payments on, at two lamps he had long paid for, the wringer washing machine for which he paid $200 and owed only $95 more, all left behind to be picked up by the dealer in town. Asked why he was leaving behind the lamps and the half-paid-for machine, he said, "I'm not looking for trouble. I'm just looking for a little peace and a little love."

And then he left, and when the car engines were started, Walter Austin never looked back.

As the cars moved rapidly northward, one could almost feel the arguments for staying sinking out of sight and the ones for going coming to the top. Before, the need for food and money had dominated conversation. Now, deeper things, long repressed, came to the surface. I asked if he had any fear of facing the strange life in the city at his age.

"Well, I guess so. But it had to come. It had to come. Back in Mississippi I was forty-eight years old, but I was still like a child. I needed the white man for protection. If the colored man had that he could keep out of lots of trouble. He could get credit. He could do lots of things, lots of things. But he just had to have that protection. If you didn't have that protection all kinds of things could happen, all *kinds* of things, just like could happen to a child without a daddy."

His eyes were red and tired, but he talked on.

"You'd get up every morning, and you'd ask the boss man what to do, and every morning he'd tell you, just like you was a child. When you got your pay, he'd take out of it what he wanted for what you owned. He didn't ask you. Now I had a good boss man, for Mississippi, and if I had something special now and then, I could ask him to let me have all my pay, and he'd let me have it. But usual thing, he'd take out what he wanted. He handled most of your bills.

"Now I figure in the North one man pays you, and then you got to take care of your bills yourself. I know a man can get into a mess of trouble handling his own bills, but I reckon that ought to be up to him, to learn and decide himself. But not on a Mississippi plantation. They figured I was a child."

He described the tensions and treacheries on a plantation where all are struggling for approval and survival, and helped explain the too-eager acquaintance that morning. "You always had to watch those other boys on the plantation and be careful who you trusted and who you didn't.

You knew Walter Austin had not been caught up in the civil-rights movement because he still referred to Negroes in the white supremacists' term, "boys," and called all white men "boss man" or "captain."

"If the boss man was always giving the easy jobs to a boy, and he and The Man always had their heads together, then you better be careful with that boy, 'cause he's probably telling the boss everything he knows about you. So on the plantation you learn to be careful what you say, what you do, and who you speaks to. And if the boss man asks you about somebody else, and you don't want to be telling him no lies, you got to tell him you just don't know nothing."

The cars were still in Mississippi, but in Walter Austin's mind already "here" was North.

"Here you can be with who you wants and ride with who you wants."

The Sunday before, while we rode to the phone booth, we had to stop for gas. It was what is known in Mississippi as an "integrated car," and the white gas-station proprietor had a common reaction: He fixed a menacing, unblinking stare at Walter Austin and kept it on him as he deliberately and slowly wiped every window of the car. To a Negro this stare, whether in an integrated car or behind a voting table, is a serious threat.

As the landscape streamed by, it caught different eyes at different times. Walter Austin would turn whenever we passed a small farm on its own plot of land. When we began to pass large used-car lots, a small smile leaked onto David's solemn face. Frances watched the increasingly large neighborhoods of ranch houses with their lawns. the largest number of middle-class houses she had ever seen, and the first not associated with the plantation hierarchy. "I'd like a house like that," she said once, "with one of those checkerboard tiles on the floor." Did she think she'd ever live in one? She thought about it seriously and then said, "Yes, I think I will."

Walter Austin and I joked a little over his calling me "Captain," which I had asked him not to do. At the time, two weeks earlier, he had said, "I know, but it's hard to stop. Up north you say, 'yas suh,' and they looks at you like you was crazy. But when you're brought up from the time you can talk, and your mammy makes you go back and say it every time you forgets to say 'yas suh,' then it's hard to stop all of a sudden."

Periodically, he would lapse into "captain" or "boss man" when we talked. But after we crossed the Mississippi River, he never did it again.

The cars went into the foggy night toward Springfield, Ill., with a homing instinct that affects almost every migrant. It was common during the foreign immigrations to have whole villages—from Sicily, Russia, Poland, Germany, Ireland—be transplanted to some particular American city. The same thing now happens within the country. There are counties in West Virginia from which most departing people go to Cincinnati, others from which they go to Cleveland. In Chicago there are two blocks made up largely of Holmes County Mississippians. The compass of the migrating poor is seldom fixed by a job already arranged and waiting, but by the presence of close relatives and friends.

In his youth, Walter Austin cut wood with a friend in Holmes County. During World War II the friend got a job on the Illinois Central Railroad, and took a room in Springfield. Later he bought a couple of rooming houses there and retired. From time to time the railroad man would return to Holmes County. Once he came to attend a wedding of his cousin with Walter Austin's cousin. When the cousins were evicted from their plantation, they moved to Springfield into a flat owned by the railroad man. In 1956 Austin's sister was told by her plantation owner that her family had to move, so the sister went to Springfield where she stayed with her cousin and got a job in Kennedy's Laundry. Four years later Austin's oldest daughter, Etoyre, decided there was no future in Mississippi, so when her aunt came from Springfield for a funeral, the daughter took her older children and rode back to Springfield. She also got a job in Kennedy's Laundry and found a flat, saved some money and sent bus tickets to her husband. They both saved some more money and sent tickets for their remaining small children and a full-fare ticket for the next oldest daughter, Mae Jessie, to accompany them. So Mae Jessie did this, taking her own daughter, an infant (no fare), and leaving her other children behind with her mother. She, too, got a job in Kennedy's Laundry, found a flat, and sent down tickets for her children and one for her mother to accompany them and visit.

Last winter Mae Jessie drove down for a New Year's visit, and the oldest Austin son, Walter Jr., decided to ride back with her. Walter Jr., unmarried, got a job sorting hides. A month later, Etoyre, the other married daughter in Springfield, drove down for a visit with her parents. Walter Austin's second oldest son, Jimmy Lee, who was married and had three children, was telling his parents he just didn't see how he could get enough work to support his family in Mississippi when the sister's car unexpectedly drew up in front. Jimmy Lee rushed to the window, saw who it was and said, "Daddy, I'm gone." He drove back to Springfield and got a job washing dishes, staying with his sister. A week later he drove down with his brother-in-law and fetched his wife and children. His wife got a job in Kennedy's Laundry.

Like an endless chain, whole tribes go link by link to some city where a base has been established. When the crisis came to Walter Austin, there was never any doubt where he would go, and when he got there, there were suddenly a total of 36 Austins within a scant half mile.

It was a scene of joy and relief, at 2 o'clock of a Sunday morning, when the two cars finally arrived at their destination, and the Austins of Merigold, Miss., became the Austins of Springfield, Ill., sharecroppers no longer but city dwellers now. Standing wearily on the sidewalk, they looked up with awe at Jimmy Lee's house, a neat, white clapboard with five spacious rooms and its own bathtub and toilet. Waiting inside were the older daughters who had come North earlier, and they helped sort the newcomers and send them to nearby homes to sleep the remaining hours of the night.

That day Walter Austin's family made the rounds of the relatives' homes. At Walter's sister's there were guitars, singing and joshing. The older women put on their wigs and urged Frances to try one. Bashfully, she put one on and imitated the modeling she had seen on television. Suddenly she was changed. One moment she was the shy country girl, the next a poised young woman. She lifted off the wig and said quietly. "I'm going to get one."

The next morning Jimmy Lee's wife took Frances with her to Kennedy's Laundry and introduced her to the boss, George Boehmer. He said, "I like to hire Mississippi people. They're good workers." So 29 hours after her arrival in the city, Frances Austin, working beside white women, was feeding flatwork into a presser and earning more than her father ever did in his 41 years of labor.

That same morning Mrs. Austin and her older daughter went out looking for a flat. In Jimmy Lee's house there were seven preschool children, crying, running, fighting, all tended by a new baby sitter, Walter Austin. He was no longer in overalls. Someone had lent him a white shirt, a pair of slacks and a too-large suit jacket. He stood in the middle of the kitchen with an open carton of milk. He cried out. "Hush, child," to one girl, and tried to restrain another one who was pounding a nail file into the linoleum with a hairbrush. "Soon as they find a place for us to stay, I'm hoping to find a job. Some kind of a job." Then, milk carton still in hand, he looked with bewilderment at the children. "This is one job I do not like."

The Austins had a small start. Four days later they found a pinched five-room flat for $65, where the whole family sleeps in just three beds and the beds are the only furniture in the place. The day after that, Walter Austin got a job that his son Jimmy Lee first had when he moved—mopping floors and washing dishes in a restaurant at $40 a week. His 17-year-old daughter earns $5 more than he does.

The Austins are in real need. They require medical attention, furniture, city clothes, and Walter Austin needs a job that will buy these things. But in some ways they are luckier than many migrants. For one thing, almost by chance, they followed the newer, less hopeless migratory routes from the rural South—more and more to the West and more and more to the medium-size cities. In the smaller cities the rate of growth is often better than in the huge ones, the Negro districts are distinct but lack the oppressiveness of square miles of squalor, and in a smaller community it is easier to match available men with available jobs.

Walter Austin had just left Merigold, Miss., which has a population of 602. When he heard that his new home, Springfield, had 86,000 people, of whom 5,000 are Negroes, he opened his eyes wide and said, "Good gracious!"

In Chicago there are a million Negroes.

The fact that migrants move means they hope for something better. The hope lasts remarkably long, so long that it seems a miracle in such places as the ghettos of cities like Chicago. Alice Perkins has been there almost two years now; she is wiser to the struggle than the Austins, harder to the squalor, but she still hopes for something better, hopes in the diminishing optimism that time and the ghetto steadily wear away.

She is a statuesque woman of 27 with a husky voice and a sardonic expression, and she lives in a second-floor flat on Van Buren Street in the middle of Chicago's West Side ghetto. Official statistics show that in 1960, eighty percent of all dwellings in her block were substandard and 30 percent lacked normal plumbing, but you don't need statistics to get the message: rubble and garbage is spread in vacant lots, the stairways are dark and dirty. Her door is untypically painted a fresh green, and on it her husband has used gay, red Christmas tape to letter out most of his name: HARRY PERKI—. But the door, typically, is locked several different ways and shows wounds from having been forced open several different ways. Inside there are rats the size of cats, and the children sleep crossways, usually four to a bed. The younger ones are normally barefoot and half bare-bodied so that the three older children can be properly dressed for school. Yet Alice Perkins and her husband have no doubt about the decision she made in the middle of a cotton field two years ago.

That day in August, 1965, she had, as usual, got up at 5:30 in their three-room shack, washed her face in a pail in the kitchen and, without breakfast, gone out to get on the back of a truck. In the field a mile away she dragged a bag nine feet long, putting in cotton balls, the ones a machine left behind. Early in the day the plantation agent started yelling that the cotton she and the others had picked was full of burrs and sticks. At noon she walked a half mile to a store and ate 10 Saltines, five pieces of baloney and a soda pop. Back in the field, The Man kept after them. "You-all are pullin' this goddamn cotton. I'm paying you to pick it, and you're just pullin' the goddamn stuff."

Toward the end of the afternoon he was still at it, and Alice Perkins said, "I don't have to take this no more. I'm going." She said it to herself.

She got back home that night at 6 o'clock. She had picked 84 pounds and made $2.10 minus lunch, for 11 hours. She cooked turnip greens and a pound of salt pork for her five children and her husband, who came home after dark from driving a tractor at $6 a day. The children went to bed, the oldest one, Beatrice, then 7, in a cot in their front room, the infant in the double bed she and her husband used, also in the front room. Her husband and two neighbors played a game of cards, pit-a-pat, also in the front room.

Without telling Harry about it, she found two pieces of lined paper and a short pencil, and she wrote a letter to her aunt in Chicago. "I can't stand it no more," she wrote, "please, Aunty, send me a ticket." She walked in the dark across the dirt road to a neighbor's house where she got an envelope and put the letter and a nickel in her rural mailbox. This was a Wednesday. Tuesday the tickets arrived. Then she told her husband she wanted to take their three youngest children and go. If she found no job in two weeks she would return. He listened quietly and said, "OK, baby."

So Alice Perkins joined the silent tide that goes by car, by bus, and still by that old reliable carrier of the cotton Negro, the Illinois Central Railroad.

On the platforms of the South they are there every day. The toothless old Negro woman in men's trousers, rubbers over slippers, a ragged coat, scarf over her head, a cardboard box tied with twine, the last tenacious root of a family gone earlier.

The neatly dressed woman in her 30's comforting her weeping teenage daughter, "Don't cry, baby. Take care of Daddy and the kids and I'll be back when I find a place."

The young woman in her 20's, so like Alice Perkins, with three wide-eyed preschool children, hugging older people on the platform and then, as the locomotive sounds its mournful southern cry, mounting the steps with her children, her eyes moist.

The old Negro porter watches the flat countryside stream monotonously by, as he has for 32 years on this run.

"It started in 1947. This train went through the delta, and there was nothing but black faces, for years and years and years. I used to wonder, 'Where are they coming from? How can there be anybody left? My God, they must be coming right out of the ground. They got to stop sometime.'

"Well, couple of years ago it seemed to slack off. You begin to see some whites now. Used to be twenty-thirty Negroes for every white on this train. Now it's more like three-to-one."

But there are still Negroes. At Durant, the station stop nearest the heart of the delta, more country people get on with boxes and old suitcases. As the train pulls out, it leaves others behind. Through the rain-splattered window you see the lonely Negro shack with three tiny children frozen in place, one boy hanging clothes on a line, his hand stopped in the act as he stares, another boy with a water pail in his hand, and at the pump a skinny-legged girl, her arm high on the motionless pump handle as the water shrivels to a trickle—all watching the speeding persimmon-and-brown cars with the big picture windows bearing dry, warm people holding passports.

The passport is a yellow ticket one-and-a-half-inches long that reads, "Illinois Central R.R. Co., coach ticket, Durant, Miss., to CHICAGO, ILL. Good in coaches only, for one passage. . . ." It costs $23.65 for adults, $11.83 for young children, and for the people who got on in Durant with a typical family, if they earned average Negro wages, it took every cent they earned for six weeks. To collect that much money, when food is scarce, and to decide to migrate is a decision that has torn millions of families in this generation.

Alice Perkins took that other mode of the Underground Railroad—the bus. On a Wednesday before the Christmas holidays, Harry Perkins got a letter from Alice in Chicago. He had to quit school in the fifth grade and can't read (Alice went through ninth grade), so he paid a neighbor 50 cents to drive him the two miles to his mother-in-law's house where she read the letter. Tickets for him and the two older children were inside. The next day the children turned in their school books. Saturday morning Harry went to work as usual. That night he got his week's pay, $36 minus $10 taken out toward his debts. By now it was dark. He walked home, pulled out a footlocker he had quietly bought in Clarksdale for $7.95 two weeks ago, put in two bedspreads, one quilt, two sheets, three pairs of pants, two shirts and three hats for the children. He paid the neighbor 50 cents again to drive him and the children to his mother-in-law's, where her son drove them to the 9:30 night bus from Clarksdale.

The children had never been to Clarksdale (population, 21,000), and when they saw it Harry Jr., 6, said, "Daddy, is this Chicago?"

On the bus was a man named Willie, brother of a friend, returning after a visit. Willie lived in Chicago and worked in a barrel factory where he thought there was an opening. Three days later Harry Perkins was stacking steel rings for $1.55 an hour, and three days after that he was running an automatic welder. He now makes $2.00 an hour with six or seven hours' overtime for about $100 a week.

Harry Perkins is a boyish, handsome, open-faced man who can't read but knows letters and remembers street signs and bus routes. At Christmas time he used the holiday tape to make letters on the wall over the double bed where he and his wife and their new infant sleep: ALICE.

Both of them insist on an unrelieved list of advantages Chicago has over their old life: Now they eat together at the same table because they have enough dinner plates; they have milk and fresh fruits and meats they never ate before; instead of a cold-water tub and washboard she gets the week's laundry delivered for $9; the school doctor and dentist examine their children regularly; instead of paying a neighbor $1 to take them shopping she can walk to a local market or take the rapid transit for 30 cents downtown; there the children often stayed out of school for lack of clothes but never here; down there Christmas meant at best a piece of simple clothing for each child, but here they have turkey and fur-lined jackets and guitars for the children.

"Look," Harry Perkins said as he sat in his tiny blue-and-pink kitchen, "for the first time in my life I own an innerspring mattress, three of them, a gas oven, a dinette, a TV, a stereo set. They treat me like a grown man. Down there the police killed colored men, two I knew just in the last couple of years we were there."

Alice Perkins shook her head slowly. "There ain't nothing I miss down there."

He nodded, "That goes for me."

Did that mean they would be happy to continue just as they are?

Alice Perkins looked surprised and said, "No, of course not."

And then she and her husband began a new recital that told the story of why families who move hopefully into the big cities then turn bitter and apathetic. Compared to the desperate poverty and endemic violence of the rural South, the city is obviously better in pay, in food, in material goods. But as the years go by, it becomes plain that the city makes demands the family never before had to meet: more education to get ahead, better clothes to enter the better world, participation in the vague and remote territory outside the ghetto in order to succeed. Food and a tight roof are no longer the focus of life. Simple survival is no longer enough; they must meet the requirements of high-speed urban life. Typically, the families enter eager and striving and then in three or four years get stalled. The Perkinses were still ambitious.

Now, the children want a bicycle, a piano, some new clothes like the ones they see on TV in *American Bandstand.* Harry Perkins would like to get a car. Mrs. Perkins has fallen in love with sectional couches. But she then described what they want more than anything else. With her husband's solemn nod of approval, she said softly, "A better house with no rats, in a better neighborhood, you know, some space for the kids to play in their own yard, with some grass in the back and in the front."

A nice house in a nice neighborhood is the conventional American family dream, but it has a special meaning in the ghetto, where most families are enclosed in a triple prison. The first is their own home. Slum-tenement doors are locked. The knock is answered, if at all, by a voice, "Who's there? What you want?" Unless the voice is familiar and the message safe, that may be the last communication from the other side. Young children are forbidden to go out alone, and hundreds of thousands of them spend all their time, except for a few hours a week, locked inside their rooms, often with the harshest discipline to quell their restlessness. Only when they go to school is there freedom. When the three Perkins school-children go, they run like rabbits released from cages. The fear is real, for outside there is the second prison: the neighborhood.

The range of movement of most slum dwellers is measured in yards and, at most, a few blocks. The density is enormous, the possibilities for play and relaxation almost nil. A 50-by-100-foot playground operated by the Marillac settlement house near the Perkinses' flat is the only one available to 4,000 children. One result of this merciless compaction is the teen-age gang, which follows a territorial imperative that includes murder of teen-agers who intrude from other neighborhoods. For all of them are trapped in the larger prison, the ghetto itself.

In Chicago the ghetto is divided in two territories, the West Side, with more than 300,000 Negroes, and the South Side, with more than 600,000. Each is a vast black island surrounded by whites. In 1950 there were only 500,000 Negroes in the city, in about five smaller islands interspersed among white neighborhoods. But now the spaces between the islands have been abandoned by whites who moved to the suburbs. So now the West Side is almost 9 square miles of black territory, the South Side, 30 square miles. On the South Side there remain a few white ethnic neighborhoods, resentful and belligerent, and some middle- and even upper-income blocks. But the mass is black and poor, the former rows of white homes partitioned and bringing in as much as 200 per cent of their old rents. In 1950 it was possible in any given ghetto to walk five blocks to a white neighborhood; now on the South Side a man can walk ten miles almost in a straight line, and never pass a home occupied by whites.

Inside the ghetto the schools are wretched, the unemployment rate three times the outside rate, the municipal services minimal, the landscape demoralizing. The uneducated parents get stalled in their climb up the work ladder, trapped in their ghetto. They produce new generations of the defeated.

So Alice Perkins, her large brown eyes longing, says, "I want a house of my own. Out in the suburbs. Like Maywood. A friend of mine drove me out there once and, oh, I want to move to a place like Maywood."

Maywood is about nine miles out on the expressway that goes by the Perkinses' flat, an "industrial suburb" in the metropolitan sprawl. It has its own character, a pleasant place of 27,000 working-class people with small one-family houses with small lawns front and back, children on swings in the yard or skipping rope on the sidewalks. There are 5,000 Negroes in Maywood, and they average $1,500 a year more than Negroes in the central city.

What are the odds of the Perkinses, or any ghetto family, making it out to a Maywood? About 1-in-11. In 1960 Chicago had 813,000 Negroes in its central city, the ghetto, and only 77,000 in the suburbs. In 1950 the ratio was about the same.

Elijah is a child of migrants, a child of the ghetto. He is Negro, thin, 126 pounds, five-foot-four, narrow-headed with slicked-down black hair, and he walks slightly stooped. If you didn't look closely you wouldn't pay attention to him in a group of six. But he is now 18, and has shot a few people. He has been involved in more burglaries and robberies than is wise to recall, and has had two personal friends murdered and countless others badly wounded. He has recently emerged from jail, where he was sent for shooting another boy in the stomach.

Elijah isn't his real name, though he insisted that his real name be used.

"Listen, I want people to understand, I want people to believe that these things happen, really, man, not just to a few oddballs but every kid I knew, every kid I grew up with on the South Side of Chicago. I don't mean they all went to jail. Two kids I knew well got killed. But some never went to jail, even. But this is what they grew up with. I want to help my people, and I want other people to know what's going on."

But it would be unfair to him, to his family and to his pregnant girlfriend to use real names. They are all struggling to repair their lives.

His parents came from Mississippi in 1952, but his mother came briefly to Chicago in 1949 for Elijah to be born. So since the age of three he has been in the ghetto. His training ground has been the tenement and the massive public-housing project.

The tenements are typified by one building in the ghetto, a grimy red-brick three-story place with three carved granite archways that tell you this was once a respectable neighborhood. Today there are 18 families in the building, and except for one that arrived last year from Texas, all have been in Chicago seven years or more. There are large signs all over the outside of the building, ordering trash to be thrown in barrels. Under the signs are glaciers and foothills of garbage that harbor huge rats. The children play among them with easy familiarity. (Landlords, by law, are required to provide private trash collections, but few of them ever bother; if an intense campaign by tenants and the settlement houses puts pressure on them, some will bribe city trash crews to collect the accumulation.) The tenement hallways are uriniferous, the walls covered with badly spelled obscenities ("thomas muther is a hoe"). In one corridor there is loose garbage, some feces in a corner and a raw egg broken on the floor. Out of one flat come two children less than four years old, one wearing only a dirty diaper, the other only a tiny T-shirt. Behind them comes a very old woman flailing at them with a leather strap. The children laugh and run down the corridor, one stepping in the egg, the other in the feces.

Ten of the 18 families are on welfare. Only five of the 18 families have a man as head of the household. There are 123 human beings who live in the old wreck of a building, of whom 98 are dependent children, 73 of them without a father at home. Eight of the households, despite great poverty, illness and other difficulties, have a tidy flat and a complete family. The landlord is considered better than average; the building has a market value of $25,000, and his gross rents are $24,000 a year.

Elijah spent the first part of his life growing up in such a building, and the rest in the other kind of ghetto dwelling, the large public-housing project. For most tenement residents, the project is a highly desired escape from what they have. Rents are lower—in Chicago they run from $40 to $90 a month for modern, well-equipped flats, with space enough to avoid having children of different sexes sleeping in the same beds and the same rooms. There are no rats. So just as the old tenements are better than the leaky three-room shacks of the South, "the projects" are deliverance from the chaos and squalor of the tenements. But after a few years in the projects their tenants begin to suffer their drawbacks, and many pray harder than ever for deliverance to the suburbs, or any place that is clean and airy and not packed with an incredible density of human beings.

Cities like Chicago turned to high-rise projects to house as many families as cheaply as possible as quickly as possible and, in many cases, to keep Negroes within the bounds of the ghetto. On a strip of land two blocks wide and less than four miles long, the Chicago Public Housing Authority built 65 buildings, 38 of them 16 stories or higher. In these buildings, in less than half a square mile, live 42,800 people. Little was done in surrounding areas to provide for the cliff-dwellers when they came out of the project. Boredom and noise are constant. In the summer the young who are still innocent wait for the event of the night—the turning on of the outside lights of the stairwells, and as each building does it a great soft wind seems to blow through the projects as thousands of watching children go, "Ah."

It is not surprising that territorial warfare and delinquency grow in such places. One wonders what would happen if a place of the same population, like Rapid City, S. Dak., instead of having its slightly more than 42,000 citizens spread over its present 16 square miles, had them all—including the sturdy, hard-working, middle-class folk—jammed into one quarter of a square mile. The people of Rapid City live 2,701 to the square mile; the project dwellers in Chicago's South Side live 170,000 to the square mile.

Elijah is the unhappy product, first of the horizontal and then of the vertical ghetto.

He is the oldest of 10 children, and he remembers that when his family came from Mississippi his father worked in the stockyards. The children kept coming, but work at the stockyards got scarcer. First there was no more lunch money, then no breakfasts. His father spent more days at home, then began to drink. When Elijah was 7, his father disappeared.

At the age of 11, Elijah joined the Cobras; a street gang that dominated his neighborhood. They fought rival gangs who intruded in their territory, or tried to date their girls, or uttered real or imagined insults. Avenging honor and protecting territory were the motivations for gang fights, the justifications for maiming and murder. Looking back and explaining it, Elijah often uses the word, "recognition."

"The poor people were the dumbest people because they didn't have any backing, they didn't push, nobody gave them any recognition. So most of us started gang fighting because of that. With the knowledge I've acquired since then it seems like I would never dream of going back to a life like that. But before I got the knowledge, it seemed fine, it seemed right, it was an art. The things you did you didn't mind telling about because you were trying to get more recognition with the bunch. You would meet girls, girls you never could have otherwise, the ones who dressed nice and looked nice. When your name was mentioned, everyone's eyes and ears opened."

After he joined the gang he began skipping school, attending parties in empty flats, drinking wine, having girls, smoking marijuana. He thinks his father's absence made a difference. "When your father is there, there are things you wouldn't dare bring into the house because your father would give you a whipping. I could do lots of things I could get by with, things my father would know about because he's a man and I'm a man, stealing, drinking, girls, smoking reefers."

As he moved into his teens, Elijah became more violent. "I could see I wasn't going to become anybody. All this was hitting me at the same time as the gang fighting, and it made me even harder because I knew this, I knew I wasn't going to become anybody, and I hated the whole world then.

"I began to use the gun more frequently, and in a gang fight I'd be the first to swing, the first to shoot. I hated conditions. I hated everything. I hated people around me because they had more than I had. I hated it when the kids were supposed to go to school and only had torn or dirty pants, and after you got to school there wasn't any lunch money, and you stood outside and got laughed at, and when you got home there was hardly anything to eat there, either."

Three things made a difference in Elijah's life. He went to jail for shooting a boy and read a book whose dust jacket in the prison library caught his eye: "I Dare You to Explore the Powers of Your Mind." With the help of a prison worker he began to read and to look into his own emotions.

He got five years' probation and came out to discover that his father had returned home, dried out, and was working at a good job in construction.

And he met Jim Taylor, a Y.M.C.A. street-gang worker who lives and works with teen-agers in the tougher neighborhoods, a schoolteacher who realized he wasn't reaching his students and quit to go where they lived. With Taylor's help Elijah signed up for a Y.M.C.A. study program where he works half a day and goes to school, combining the last years of high school and the first two years of college.

This will take until 1971. His work during that time will be with street gangs. "You've got to have something for these kids to do," Elijah said. "You've got to have someone who cares about them. Not just spending a few hours like most schoolteachers and then, zip, out of the neighborhood. But really caring, man.

"And you need new prizes, new rewards. Now it's the kid who fights the hardest, drinks the most, has the most girls, kills best. I'd like to make the big man, the one who's top of his class, and give him a special prize, a real good prize that would make people open up their eyes and ears. It would help. I know it would."

Elijah speaks with a combination of the soft Mississippi accent of his parents and the hip talk of the ghetto. He has studied and thought a great deal lately about the Negro American in the ghetto.

"When the Negro is born in the South, he grows up with hatred for the white man, but in the South they kill him if he shows it. So he comes to Chicago, and he lives here on the South Side, and he takes out his hatred on other Negroes. You get born with hatred because you see the white man in his Cadillac, and you see your father walking. The hate is in you, and when someone attacks you, the hate is going to come out, no matter if it comes out against your own people."

Elijah and his fellow migrants are mysteries. In the face of endless defeat, first on the farms and now in the ghetto, they have recurring hope. It is often expressed in riots and demonstrations, but it is there. The newest arrivals continue to work hard at the lowest pay in the expectation that it will lead to something better. The history books claim that the American genius has been to collect ethnic minorities at the bottom and then let them disperse up through the surrounding society. But the American Negro continues to be more densely packed, more hemmed in, and more confined to the bottom than any other migrant minority. And yet he continues to hope.

Elijah had been standing at a window through which I could hear the level roar of boisterous children, their sounds echoing between the 16-story buildings. He turned around, his brow wrinkled with concentration, and said with passion:

"The thing is that you grow up and, you *know,* you *know,* man . . ." He paused and said slowly and quietly, "*No-body cares!* Mothers are screaming at babies, there's no father, teachers are screaming at the students, and when the bell rings they leave the building before the kids do. And when you're dropping out of school, you know very well that they're really glad to see you go. You're glad to go, too, but you remember afterward that they were glad to see you go."

Elijah sat down, and after a time he spoke again.

"Nobody cares. Nobody. That's what you grow up with. The people on the outside, they have their own immediate problems, so they got no time for our problems. The ones here who get anywhere, they don't care about anybody else once they get up on their pedestal. They look down on their own people, and they say, 'They're fools' and then go on about their business."

And then the incredible hope and resilience:

"My kids someday, are going to finish school—a *good* school. They're going to have a set of goals, to think ahead, to make sense. But most of all, they got to have environment."

Environment?

"Live in a good house in a nice neighborhood with a real school. Out of . . ." and he pointed out the window to the tenements, the projects, the street with the squeal of the police siren receding. "Out of here. Period."

Claude Brown □ The Language of Soul

The language of subcultures—from Beatniks to Hippies—intrigues the so-called straight world, and so does the vocabulary of the ghetto Negro. Currently no term is more widely used than "Soul," a word that has many nuances according to novelist Claude Brown. Born in 1937, Brown studied at Howard University and has written plays performed by the American Afro-Negro Theater Guild. In 1965, he published *Manchild In The Promised Land,* an autobiographical novel.

Perhaps the most soulful word in the world is "nigger." Despite its very definite fundamental meaning (the Negro man), and disregarding the deprecatory connotation of the term, "nigger" has a multiplicity of nuances when used by soul people. Dictionaries define the term as being synonymous with Negro, and they generally point out that it is regarded as a vulgar expression. Nevertheless, to those of chitlins-and-neck-bones background the word nigger is neither a synonym for Negro nor an obscene expression.

"Nigger" has virtually as many shades of meaning in Colored English as the demonstrative pronoun "that," prior to application to a noun. To some Americans of African ancestry (I avoid using the term Negro whenever feasible, for fear of offending the Brothers X, a pressure group to be reckoned with), nigger seems preferable to Negro and has a unique kind of sentiment attached to it. This is exemplified in the frequent—and perhaps even excessive—usage of the term to denote either fondness or hostility.

It is probable that numerous transitional niggers and even established ex-soul brothers can—with pangs of nostalgia—reflect upon a day in the lollipop epoch of lives when an adorable lady named Mama bemoaned her spouse's fastidiousness with the strictly secular utterance: "Lord, how can one nigger be so hard to please?" Others are likely to recall a time when that drastically lovable colored woman, who was forever wiping our noses and darning our clothing, bellowed in a moment of exasperation: "Nigger, you gonna be the death o' me." And some of the brethren who have had the precarious fortune to be raised up, wised up, thrown up or simply left alone to get up as best they could, on one of the nation's South Streets or Lenox Avenues, might remember having affectionately referred to a best friend as "My nigger."

The vast majority of "back-door Americans" are apt to agree with Webster—a nigger is simply a Negro or black man. But the really profound contemporary thinkers of this distinguished ethnic group—Dick Gregory, Redd Foxx, Moms Mabley, Slappy White, etc.—are likely to differ with Mr. Webster and define nigger as "something else"—a soulful "something else." The major difference between the nigger and the Negro, who have many traits in common, is that the nigger is the more soulful.

Certain foods, customs and artistic expressions are associated almost solely with the nigger: collard greens, neck bones, hog maws, black-eyed peas, pigs' feet, etc. A nigger has no desire to conceal or disavow any of these favorite dishes or restrain other behavioral practices such as bobbing his head, patting his feet to funky jazz, and shouting and jumping in church. This is not to be construed that all niggers eat chitlins and shout in church, nor that only niggers eat the aforementioned dishes and exhibit this type of behavior. It is to say, however, that the soulful usage of the term nigger implies all of the foregoing and considerably more.

The Language of Soul—or, as it might also be called, Spoken Soul or Colored English—is simply an honest vocal portrayal of black America. The roots of it are more than three hundred years old.

Before the Civil War there were numerous restrictions placed on the speech of slaves. The newly arrived Africans had the problem of learning to speak a new language, but also there were inhibitions placed on the topics of the slaves' conversation by slave masters and overseers. The slaves made up songs to inform one another of, say, the underground railroads' activity. When they sang *Steal Away* they were planning to steal away to the North, not to heaven. Slaves who dared to speak of rebellion or even freedom usually were severely punished. Consequently, Negro slaves were compelled to create a semi-clandestine vernacular in the way that the criminal underworld had historically created words to confound law-enforcement agents. It is said that numerous Negro spirituals were inspired by the hardships of slavery, and that what later became songs were initially moanings and coded cotton-field lyrics. To hear these songs sung today by a talented soul brother or sister or by a group is to be reminded of an historical spiritual bond that cannot be satisfactorily described by the mere spoken word.

The American Negro, for virtually all of his history, has constituted a vastly disproportionate number of the country's illiterates. Illiteracy has a way of showing itself in all attempts at vocal expression by the uneducated. With the aid of colloquialisms, malapropisms, battered and fractured grammar, and a considerable amount of creativity, Colored English, the sound of soul, evolved.

The progress has been cyclical. Often terms that have been discarded from the soul people's vocabulary for one reason or another are reaccepted years later, but usually with completely different meaning. In the Thirties and Forties "stuff" was used to mean vagina. In the middle Fifties it was revived and used to refer to heroin. Why certain expressions are thus reactivated is practically an indeterminable question. But it is not difficult to see why certain terms are dropped from the soul language. Whenever a soul term becomes popular with whites it is common practice for the soul folks to relinquish it. The reasoning is that "if white people can use it, it isn't hip enough for me." To many soul brothers there is just no such creatures as a genuinely hip white person. And there is nothing more detrimental to anything hip than to have it fall into the square hands of the hopelessly unhip.

White Americans wrecked the expression "something else." It was bad enough that they couldn't say "sump'n else," but they weren't even able to get out "somethin' else." They had to go around saying *something else* with perfect or nearly perfect enunciation. The white folks invariably fail to perceive the soul sound in soulful terms. They get hung up in diction and grammar, and when they vocalize the expression it's no longer a soulful thing. In fact, it can be asserted that spoken soul is more of a sound than a language. It generally possesses a pronounced lyrical quality which is frequently incompatible to any music other than that ceaseless and relentlessly driving rhythm that flows from poignantly spent lives. Spoken soul has a way of coming out metered without the intention of the speaker to invoke it. There are specific phonetic traits. To the soulless ear the vast majority of these sounds are dismissed as incorrect usage of the English language and, not infrequently, as speech impediments. To those so blessed as to have had bestowed upon them at birth the lifetime gift of soul, these are the most communicative and meaningful sounds ever to fall upon human ears: the familiar "mah" instead of "my," "gonna" for "going to," "yo" for "your." "Ain't" is pronounced "ain'";

"bread" and "bed," "bray-ud" and "bay-ud"; "baby" is never "bay-bee" but "bay-buh"; Sammy Davis Jr. is not "Sammee" but a kind of "Sam-eh"; the same goes for "Eddeh" Jefferson. No matter how many "man's" you put into your talk, it isn't soulful unless the word has the proper plaintive, nasal "maee-yun."

Spoken soul is distinguished from slang primarily by the fact that the former lends itself easily to conventional English, and the latter is diametrically opposed to adaptations within the realm of conventional English. Police (pronounced pō'lice) is a soul term, whereas "The Man" is merely slang for the same thing. Negroes seldom adopt slang terms from the white world and when they do the terms are usually given a different meaning. Such was the case with the term "bag." White racketeers used it in the Thirties to refer to the graft that was paid to the police. For the past five years soul people have used it when referring to a person's vocation, hobby, fancy, etc. And once the appropriate term is given the treatment (soul vocalization) it becomes soulful.

However, borrowings from spoken soul by white men's slang—particularly teen-age slang—are plentiful. Perhaps because soul is probably the most graphic language of modern times, everybody who is excluded from Soulville wants to usurp it, ignoring the formidable fettering to the soul folks that has brought the language about. Consider "uptight," "strung-out," "cop," "boss," "kill 'em," all now widely used outside Soulville. Soul people never question the origin of a slang term; they either dig it and make it a part of their vocabulary or don't and forget it. The expression "uptight," which meant being in financial straits, appeared on the soul scene in the general vicinity of 1953. Junkies were very fond of the word and used it literally to describe what was a perpetual condition with them. The word was pictorial and pointed; therefore it caught on quickly in Soulville across the country. In the early Sixties when "uptight" was on the move, a younger generation of soul people in the black urban communities along the Eastern Seaboard regenerated it with a new meaning: "everything is cool, under control, going my way." At present the term has the former meaning for the older generation and the latter construction for those under thirty years of age.

It is difficult to ascertain if the term "strung-out" was coined by junkies or just applied to them and accepted without protest. Like the term "uptight" in its initial interpretation, "strung-out" aptly described the constant plight of the junkie. "Strung-out" had a connotation of hopeless finality about it. "Uptight" implied a temporary situation and lacked the overwhelming despair of "strung-out."

The term "cop," (meaning "to get"), is an abbreviation of the word "copulation." "Cop," as originally used by soulful teen-agers in the early Fifties, was deciphered to mean sexual coition, nothing more. By 1955 "cop" was being uttered throughout national Soulville as a synonym for the verb "to get," especially in reference to illegal purchases, drugs, pot, hot goods, pistols, etc. ("Man, where can I cop now?") But by 1955 the meaning was all-encompassing. Anything that could be obtained could be "copped."

The word "boss," denoting something extraordinarily good or great, was a redefined term that had been popular in Soulville during the Forties and Fifties as a complimentary remark from one soul brother to another. Later it was replaced by several terms such as "groovy," "tough," "beautiful" and, most recently, "out of sight." This last expression is an outgrowth of the former term "way out," the meaning of which was equivocal. "Way out" had an ad hoc hickish ring to it which made it intolerably unsoulful and consequently it was soon replaced by "out of sight," which is also likely to experience a relatively brief period of popular usage. "Out of sight" is better than "way out," but it has some of the same negative, childish taint of its predecessor.

The expression, "kill 'em," has neither a violent nor a malicious interpretation. It means "good luck," "give 'em hell," or "I'm pulling for you," and originated in Harlem from six to nine years ago.

There are certain classic soul terms which, no matter how often borrowed, remain in the canon and are reactivated every so often, just as standard jazz tunes are continuously experiencing renaissances. Among the classical expressions are: "solid," "cool," "jive" (generally as a noun), "stuff," "thing," "swing" (or "swinging"), "pimp," "dirt," "freak," "heat," "larceny," "busted," "okee doke," "piece," "sheet" (a jail record), "squat," "square," "stash," "lay," "sting," "mire," "gone," "smooth," "joint," "blow," "play," "shot," and there are many more.

Soul language can be heard in practically all communities throughout the country, but for pure, undiluted spoken soul one must go to Soul Street. There are several. Soul is located at Seventh and "T" in Washington, D.C., on One Two Five Street in New York City; on Springfield Avenue in Newark; on South Street in Philadelphia; on Tremont Street in Boston; on Forty-seventh Street in Chicago, on Fillmore in San Francisco, and dozens of similar locations in dozens of other cities.

As increasingly more Negroes desert Soulville for honorary membership in the Establishment clique, they experience a metamorphosis, the repercussions of which have a marked influence on the young and impressionable citizens of Soulville. The expatriates of Soulville are often greatly admired by the youth of soulville, who emulate the behavior of such expatriates as Nancy Wilson, Ella Fitzgerald, Eartha Kitt, Lena Horne, Diahann Carroll, Billy Daniels, or

Leslie Uggams. The result—more often than not—is a trend away from spoken soul among the young soul folks. This abandonment of the soul language is facilitated by the fact that more Negro youngsters than ever are acquiring college educations (which, incidentally, is not the best treatment for the continued good health and growth of soul); integration and television, too, are contributing significantly to the gradual demise of spoken soul.

Perhaps colleges in America should commence to teach a course in spoken soul. It could be entitled the Vocal History of Black America, or simply Spoken Soul. Undoubtedly there would be no difficulty finding teachers. There are literally thousands of these experts throughout the country whose talents lie idle while they await the call to duty.

Meanwhile the picture looks dark for soul. The two extremities in the Negro spectrum—the conservative and the militant—are both trying diligently to relinquish and repudiate whatever vestige they may still possess of soul. The semi-Negro—the soul brother intent on gaining admission to the Establishment even on an honorary basis—is anxiously embracing and assuming conventional English. The other extremity, the Ultra-Blacks, are frantically adopting everything from a Western version of Islam that would shock the Caliph right out of his snugly fitting shintiyan to anything that vaguely hints of that big, beautiful, bountiful black bitch lying in the arms of the Indian and Atlantic Oceans and crowned by the majestic Mediterranean Sea. Whatever the Ultra-Black is after, it's anything but soulful.

John Hope Franklin □ The New Negro History

John Hope Franklin, professor of History at the University of Chicago, is one of the most respected Negro scholars in America. His works include *From Slavery to Freedom,* the standard text in Negro history, *The Militant South,* and *Reconstruction After The Civil War.* In this essay, he argues that Negroes must make new attempts to recapture their past.

During the last two decades some significant changes have taken place in the writing, teaching, and study of the history of the Negro in the United States. On almost every side there has been a remarkable growth of interest in the history of the Negro. Of equal importance has been the modification of the approaches of those who have participated in writing the history. It is not necessary to evaluate precisely the impact of these developments to state, at the outset, that they have great relevance to any understanding of the rapidly unfolding developments in human relations in the United States.

In discussing the history of a people one must distinguish between what has *actually* happened and what those who have written the history have *said* has happened. So far as the *actual* history of the American Negro is concerned, there is nothing particularly new about it. It is an exciting story, a remarkable story. It is the story of slavery and freedom, humanity and inhumanity, democracy and its denial. It is tragedy and triumph, suffering and compassion, sadness and joy. The *actual* history of the Negro is David Walker in 1828 calling on his people to throw off the shackles of slavery by any means at

From John Hope Franklin, "The New Negro History," *Journal of Negro History,* XLIII (April 1957), pp. 89–97. Reprinted by permission of The Association for The Study of Negro Life and History, Inc.

their command. It is Robert Smalls in 1863 delivering a Confederate vessel into the hands of United States forces. It is Booker T. Washington electrifying a Southern audience and hammering out a program of accommodation and adjustment in a section inflamed by racial intolerance. It is W. E. B. DuBois providing intellectual inspiration to a despairing people and charting the course for the future. It is Thurgood Marshall calling on the Supreme Court to strike down the pernicious and un-American doctrine of "separate but equal." It is all these things and more, emblazoned on the national record to be seen by all who would care to look.

But Negro history is more than the exertions of Negroes in their behalf. It is Governor Hammond of South Carolina declaring that slavery is the best thing that has ever happened to the Negro people. It is Roger B. Taney denying freedom to Dred Scott. It is Abraham Lincoln issuing the Emancipation Proclamation. It is Joel and Arthur Springarn working to organize the National Association for the Advancement of Colored People. It is the United States Supreme Court striking down segregated public schools. It is White Citizens Councils, aptly called the "uptown Ku Klux Klan," stoning Autherine Lucy at the University of Alabama. It is Walter George, President Eisenhower's special representative to the NATO countries, leading the Senate fight to discredit the Supreme Court decision. Thus, Negro history is more than the overt actions of Negroes. It is also America's treatment of the Negro. It is the impact of forces and events affecting the lives of Negroes in countless ways.

These things are and have been; and no amount of dishonesty in the writing of history, no amount of specious propaganda designed to distort and misrepresent, can ever change them. These things do not constitute the New Negro history. They are new only in the sense that today's events are different from yesterday's; and every passing era during the past three centuries has witnessed a new stage in the struggle for freedom and human equality in the United States.

But it is all too clear that what has actually happened is one thing, and what has been described by writers of history as having happened is quite another thing. The changes that have occurred in the writing of the history of the Negro are as significant and, in some ways, even more dramatic than the very events themselves that the writers have sought to describe.

A century ago one of the South's most distinguished scientists, in discussing diseases peculiar to the Negro, wrote a lengthy treatise on dreptomania, a malady that gave Negroes a compulsion to run away. He showed, to the apparent satisfaction of his many readers, that whenever Negroes disappeared from the plantation it was not because they were unhappy or dissatisfied but because they were afflicted with a dread disease that forced them to run away. This was, he argued, a historical fact, running back into the history of the Negroes for centuries. This and many similar unsupported and fantastic claims became a part of the *written* history of the Negro in the United States. At about the same time and, indeed, for many ensuing decades, a host of writers described Negroes as happy with their lot as slaves; and they claimed that to emancipate them would not only be a tragedy but unChristian as well. In the generation following the Civil War several historians expressed the greatest grief that Negroes had been emancipated, for, they argued, it would only be a matter of time—a few decades at the most—and all Negroes would disappear. History, they claimed, clearly demonstrated that Negroes could not survive as free men.

Even the so-called scientific historians showed little inclination to use the materials of history for any purpose other than to support their own predilections, prejudices, and earlier commitments. Thus, they wrote at length about the childish nature of Negroes as displayed during slavery, their cowardice and ineffectiveness during the Civil War, and their barbarity and prodigality after emancipation. Even in the present century and *even in our own time* they have, with remarkable effectiveness, described the Negro as a beast, have worked assiduously to justify and even to glorify. Negro slavery, and have described the period since emancipation as one of unmitigated woe for Negroes and of inconvenience for whites.

The effect of this kind of written history has not only been far-reaching but deadly. It has provided the historical justification for the whole complex of mischievous and pernicious laws designed to create and maintain an unbridgeable gulf between Negroes and whites. It was the basis for a query put to a Negro by a white woman, "refined and educated," in Montgomery, Alabama, a few years ago. When she asked in all seriousness, if it were possible for a Negro with no admixture of white blood to learn anything in college, the Negro was reminded of the child who had horrible nightmares because he had seen too many murder mysteries on television. He began his reply by suggesting that she had been reading too many fairy stories parading under the guise of "authentic histories." And the deadly effects of such propaganda have been spread in all directions, pervading Northern communities and even countries abroad. The effects could be seen a few months ago in Heidelberg when a German was moved to observe that the American denazification program in his country not only permitted American white supremacy doctrines to flourish but, in some instances, encouraged such doctrines.

Negroes generally have not had any illusions about the distortions of their history, and they have not been unduly influenced by them.

Those who have been articulate have consistently and bitterly resented the systematic efforts to misrepresent their role in history or to deny them membership in the human family, to say nothing of first-class American citizenship. When John Russwurm issued the first Negro newspaper in 1827 he touched on this point when he said, "We wish to plead for our cause. Too long have others spoken for us. Too long has the public been deceived by misrepresentations, in things which concern us dearly. . . . We form a spoke in the human wheel, and it is necessary that we should understand our dependence on the different parts, and theirs on us, in order to perform our part with propriety." In 1851, when William C. Nell brought out his history of Negroes in the Revolution and the war of 1812, he declared, "I yield to no one in appreciating the propriety and pertinency of every *effort*, on the part of colored Americans, in *all* pursuits, which, as members of the human family, it becomes them to share in. . . ."

The baleful effects of the propaganda of history on the one hand and what one historian has aptly called "the conspiracy of silence" on the other were deeply understood by George W. Williams who devoted many years to research and writing and published in 1883 the first serious history of the Negro in the United States. "Not as a blind panegyrist of my race," he asserted, "nor as a partisan apologist, but for a love for *'the truth of history'* I have striven to record the truth. . . . My whole aim has been to write a thoroughly trustworthy history; and what I have written, if it have no other merit, is reliable." Williams was painfully aware that too many of the histories published in his own day fell far short of reliability where Negroes were concerned. And he knew all too well the uses to which distorted history and irresponsible propaganda were put in the establishment of second-class citizenship for Negroes. He was determined to combat them with weapons of indisputable truth. His success for the period in which he worked was nothing short of phenomenal.

It was an appreciation such as Nell and Williams had that caused Dr. Carter G. Woodson to found the Association for the Study of Negro Life and History more than forty years ago. The work of Dr. Woodson and the Association in those early years may be regarded as launching the era of "The New Negro History." Dr. Woodson and his associates went about the task of exploding the myths of Negro history and of putting the Negro in his rightful place in the history of this country. And they did it with as much precision and system as those who sought to tear the Negro out of any meaningful context of American history. This was no small undertaking. By the time Dr. Woodson began his work, the system of second-class citizenship, with its trappings of segregation and disfranchisement, was functioning effectively. It had, moreover, been buttressed by the sanctions of respectable religious and political institutions. And it had received the blessings of a great body of intellectual rationalizations.

The story of the work of Dr. Woodson and the Association is well known and does not need to be recounted here. It should be recalled, however, that the problem of restoring the Negro to his proper place in the nation's history was attacked on a wide front. Recognizing the indisputable fact that the distortion of Negro history prevailed at every level of society and in almost every facet of American life, Woodson proceeded to correct the defects at these numerous points. His own scholarly books and monographs and the works of several others, including W. E. B. DuBois, provided the grist for the Negro history mill. *The Journal of Negro History* projected the new approach to every part of the world where history was seriously studied. The Association and its branches proceeded to carry out a campaign at the grass-roots to revise the role of Negro history in the minds of the most ordinary laymen of the community. The *Negro History Bulletin* extended the new Negro history into the lower grades in the schools. Negro History Week popularized Negro history in a variety of ways.

This was, perhaps, the most far-reaching and ambitious effort to rewrite history that has ever been attempted in this country. But it was more than an attempt to rewrite history. It was a remarkable attempt to rehabilitate a whole people—to explode racial myths, to establish a secure and respectable place for the Negro in the evolution of the American social order, to develop self-respect and self-esteem among those who had been subjected to the greatest indignities known in the Western world. Finally, it was a valiant attempt to force America to keep faith with herself, to remind her that truth is more praiseworthy than power, and that justice and equality, long the state policy of this nation, should apply to all its citizens and *even* to the writing of history.

But the most significant intellectual result of the work of Dr. Woodson and the movement he founded lies in the impact on the writing of American history in general and on the writing of the history of the Negro in particular. Within the last two decades there has been a most profound and salutary change in the whole approach to the history of human relations in the United States. In the process the New Negro History has indeed come into its own.

It would be foolhardy to the point of creating a new myth to suggest that the Woodson movement enjoys exclusive responsibility for the new Negro history. This is a phenomenon caused by many factors among which Dr. Woodson and the work of the Association for the Study of Negro Life and History are significant and primary. The legal and political drive for first-class citizenship is another factor. The remarkable changes in the economic and social conditions among

Negroes are another. The work in the other social sciences in exploding numerous racial myths is another. Then, one must recognize the powerful effect of two world wars and the significant improvement in the status of peoples of color throughout the world. There is, also, the sense of guilt shared by many white Americans for three centuries of injustice and inhumanity in their treatment of Negroes. Finally, there is the factor of time. The passing of the years has removed the people of this country from the period when the race question was dealt with in the bloodiest terms; and these years have given Americans a new perspective from which to view the Negro and his role in American history. These and perhaps many other factors have brought forth this new Negro history.

Stimulated by the numerous forces that have been at work over the past generation, the writing of the history of the Negro in the United States has come into its own. In quantitative terms alone the results have been most impressive. White and Negro historians, Northern and Southern historians, Japanese and Dutch historians have turned their attention to the study of the history of the Negro in the United States. And they have produced an enormous quantity of studies of various aspects of Negro life. In books, monographs, learned journals, popular magazines, and newspapers they have shared with the world their findings regarding the American Negro's past. Within the past decade no less than a half dozen general histories of the Negro have appeared, compared with only one during the preceding twenty-five years. Every major historical association in this country in the past ten years has given considerable attention to subjects related to Negro history at its annual meetings. Newspapers, North and South, run feature stories on some phase of the history of the Negro, and several of the mass circulation magazines have featured the history of the Negro in recent years.

For the first time in the history of the United States, there is a striking resemblance between what historians are writing and what has actually happened in the history of the American Negro. A Northern white historian has laid bare the sordid details of slavery and has described it as the barbaric institution that is actually was. Another has described with telling effectiveness the numerous revolts of Negroes against slavery. A Southern white historian, after making due public apology for having once called Negroes "darkies," has proceeded to prove that during the Civil War slaves did everything possible to betray their masters and destroy the institution of slavery. Another has written with remarkable understanding and insight and has produced perhaps the best account in print of the Negro during the Reconstruction of a Southern state. One Negro historian has proved conclusively that Negroes did not have their freedom handed to them but fought for it with blood, sweat, and tears. Another, writing about the late nineteenth century, has described with vivid detail how even in the North there was no real desire to promote freedom and equality and how even the respectable elements of society joined in the general program of degrading the Negro. Historians of both races and both sections have contributed to establishing the fact that avarice and vice, honesty and virtue, and other human qualities are bi-racial; and that far from being men of unsullied virtue, those who have inveighed against the Negro have themselves frequently been villainous and hypocritical.

The new Negro history, then, is the literary and intellectual movement that seeks to achieve the same justice in history that is sought in other spheres. Moreover, it gives strength and support to the other efforts that today seek equality and freedom. To be sure, it has had to continue to struggle against those who persist in distorting history, for these latter elements have by no means given up their fight. But the new Negro history says to America that its rich heritage is the result of the struggles of all its peoples, playing the roles that conditions and circumstances have permitted them to play. These roles cannot be evaluated in terms of race. Rather, they must be judged in terms of their effect on the realization of the great American dream. In this context the role of the Negro in America is not only significant in itself but central in the task of fulfilling the nation's true destiny. This is the message of the new Negro history, and it is being carried forth with great effectiveness by an increasing number of able messengers.

No one can properly evaluate the influence of history on the minds of men. But one can say that through the ages history has been an important instrument in shaping the course of human affairs. It gave to Prussians that appreciation for the military prowess by which they were known for centuries. It has given to Americans a deep appreciation for the historic foundations of democratic principles. It has given to Negroes a sense of self-esteem and self-respect that has sustained them in their darkest hours. The future function of the new Negro history is even more important. It can and, in time, will provide *all America* with a lesson in the wastefulness, nay, the wickedness of human exploitation and injustice that have characterized too much of this nation's past. This is a lesson that must be learned if we are to survive and if we are to win the respect and admiration of the other peoples of the world. The new Negro history also provides all America with an inspiring lesson in human potentialities and a profound basis on which to build a better America. It is to be hoped that neither this great lesson nor this great inspiration will be lost in the years that lie ahead.

George S. Schuyler □ Teaching Negro History Is Questionable

Many American universities and colleges are introducing courses in Negro history. Despite this new interest, there is some disagreement as to the functions and purposes of such courses. George S. Schuyler voices his disagreement in characteristically strong terms.

To the ever-extending educationist smorgasbord, is now being added courses with credits in Negro history, languages and culture, thus yielding to the belligerent demands of black militants and assorted prospective teachers of these arcana.

The new courses seem to have the double purpose of flattering frustrated Negro youth (whose parents failed to do their homework) while at the same time brainwashing white students to facilitate racial equality—whatever that means.

As a by-product of this indoctrination in black racial mythology and largely aprocryphal folklore is doubtless the goal of ultimately establishing as national heroes such agitators as the late Martin Luther King Jr. and Malcolm X. Apparently we are to have open housing in the Pantheon.

This newest dish in the pedagogic cafeteria will add less to education than to propaganda. Already the booming textbook market which has kept pace with the population explosion is flooded with fat tomes bulging with wishful thinking and dubious interpretations on the subject. How these new courses will improve the Negro's lot here and now is unclear but certainly the book publishers will profit. The col-

From George S. Schuyler, "Teaching Negro History Is Questionable," *Globe Democrat*, (August 13, 1968, 6A). Reprinted by permission of the author.

ored will perhaps eventually learn that society everywhere pays off on performance, not on palaver about the past or future.

What actually happened in man's past is exceedingly difficult to know. Thomas Carlyle called history "a distillation of rumor." Napoleon Bonaparte asked "What is history but a fable agreed upon?"

Sir Robert Walpole said bluntly, "All history is a lie," while Henry Ford simply called it "bunk."

Nevertheless, we have to teach it because man habitually pants to know from whence he came and where he is going. The libraries overflow with books on why Rome declined, on the origins of World War I on the Bolshevik Revolution—with little agreement among the historians.

The question is, should history—elusive as it is—be further complicated by teaching it from a Negro point of view? If so, should World War II be taught, for the benefit of our German-Americans, from a German point of view? Do we teach the Irish one version of the Easter Uprising and the English another? And, for the benefit of our other minorities, do we clutter our high school curricula with courses on Polish literature, Ukrainian history, Japanese art and Jewish music? Would that our students thirst were so unquenchable.

Our overworked teachers cannot improperly impart the bare bones of an education as it is, especially since those who need learning most are too often playing hookey, smoking in the stairwells, or mugging teacher on her way home from work.

There is no question that people of color have exercised wide influence on the course of American and world history, and this influence has been reported in general history books. But the place to teach Negro history as such is in the home or in Negro church and other community groups. The taxpayer should not have to support it, expecially since any resemblance between the Negro mythology that will be taught and the actual facts will be coincidental. For the whole purpose behind teaching Negro "history" is to make the Negro look good.

But what if, by some pedagogic fluke, this black culture and history is actually taught with some degree of objectivity? In that unlikely situation our young knowledge-seekers are in for some disillusionment. In the first place, they would soon learn there has been no white conspiracy to keep the known facts from them. Indeed, Europeans and Arabs have written more than 90 per cent of the black histories during the past three millenia. This is because—it may dawn on some alert students—black Africa did not list among its accomplishments a written language. Teachers will not stress this rather basic point, because it does not say much for the "glories" of black African "civilizations."

The students might also learn the harsh fact that Africa has been a slave reservoir since history began, with sales as far east as China; and that the Arabs, whom they have latterly come to laud, carried on a rigorous slave trade from East Africa and north to the Mediterranean for about a thousand years before the Europeans entered it.

They would further learn that their ancestors—who never discovered the wheel or how to build a road, a stone city or a durable bridge—became rich selling black prisoners and relatives to the Arabs, Persians and Indians, and then after the 15th Century to Portuguese, Spaniards, English, Dutch, French, and Scandinavians.

Every wealthy black family along Africa's west coast, for example, grew rich during the period of the Atlantic slave trade, and deplored the abolition more than anybody.

The great slaver of Central Africa in the late 19th Century was Tippu Tib, a black man of Zanzibar, and once governor of King Leopold's Congo Free State. The grateful Arab elite of Zanzibar raised a statue to him for the profits he brought them by denuding the back country with his gangs of ruthless raiders who marched out every human being, male and female, that could not elude him.

The great African dictators and conquerors were almost without exception bloodthirsty demons on the order of Genghis Khan and Timuerlane, leaving hecatombs of black victims in the wake of their feathered regiments, almost depopulating vast areas of Africa. The longest period of peace the African people have enjoyed was during the century just ended when Europeans enforced it.

Perhaps the most childish demand has been for the teaching of African languages in American schools. Such as Amharic and Swahili, a waste of time and money. Not one Negro in a thousand will ever go to East Africa, and the literature in either language would scarcely fill a telephone booth. Neither has any relationship to English.

Amharic is Semitic while Swahili is an Arabo-African jargon invented by the Arab slave traders who infested the coastal regions. Were they to insist on Haussa, there might be some slight justification since more millions speak it than either Amharic or Swahili. The average black student needs English far more than any African tongue.

While there are at least 700 Bantu and other languages and dialects spoken in Africa today, it is significant that the official language of all the newly emergent countries below the Sahara is either French, Spanish, Portuguese or English. With Negroes on relief here getting paid more in a month than most black Africans earn in a year, it is unlikely there will be many going over there.

For the last century American families have had access to mountains of material on their past; not just books by a succession of dedicated researchers, but the Negro newspapers since 1827, the Journal of Negro History since 1915, the Negro History Bulletin since the mid-20s, and the half-century-old Association for the Study of Negro Life and History with chapters in every large city. It was their duty to teach their children about their background, and not palm this duty off on the public treasury.

With a few bright exceptions, most of the black chronicle has been sad because these people began low on the totem pole and have not yet worked themselves very high. Thus there is little for the young to boast about or use to inflate their egos, encouraging new fantasies and dreams. Perhaps the less said, the better.